Language and Mind

Third Edition

Noam Chomsky

Massachusetts Institute of Technology

CAMBRIDGE
UNIVERSITY PRESS

CAMBRIDGE
UNIVERSITY PRESS

University Printing House, Cambridge CB2 8BS, United Kingdom

Cambridge University Press is part of the University of Cambridge.

It furthers the University's mission by disseminating knowledge in the pursuit of
education, learning and research at the highest international levels of excellence.

www.cambridge.org
Information on this title: www.cambridge.org/9780521674935

© Noam Chomsky 2006

First published 2006
8th printing 2015

Printed in the United Kingdom by Clays, St Ives plc

A catalogue record for this publication is available from the British Library

ISBN-13 978-0-521-85819-9 Hardback
ISBN-13 978-0-521-67493-5 Paperback

Language and Mind

This is the long-awaited third edition of Chomsky's outstanding collection of essays on language and mind. The first six chapters, originally published in the 1960s, made a groundbreaking contribution to linguistic theory. This new edition complements them with an additional chapter and a new preface, bringing Chomsky's influential approach into the twenty-first century. Chapters 1–6 present Chomsky's early work on the nature and acquisition of language as a genetically endowed, biological system (Universal Grammar), through the rules and principles of which we acquire an internalized knowledge (I-language). Over the past fifty years, this framework has sparked an explosion of inquiry into a wide range of languages, and has yielded some major theoretical questions. The final chapter revisits the key issues, reviewing the "biolinguistic" approach that has guided Chomsky's work from its origins to the present day, and raising some novel and exciting challenges for the study of language and mind.

NOAM CHOMSKY is Professor of Linguistics at Massachusetts Institute of Technology. His many books include *New Horizons in the Study of Language and Mind* (Cambridge University Press, 2000) and *On Nature and Language* (Cambridge University Press, 2002).

Contents

Preface to the third edition

The first six chapters that follow are from the late 1960s, mostly based on talks for general university audiences, hence relatively informal. The final chapter is from 2004, based on a talk for a general audience. This recent essay reviews the "biolinguistic approach" that has guided this work from its origins half a century ago, some of the important developments of recent decades, and how the general approach looks today – to me at least.

The dominant approach to questions of language and mind in the 1950s was that of the behavioral sciences. As the term indicates, the object of inquiry was taken to be behavior, or, for linguistics, the products of behavior: perhaps a corpus obtained from informants by the elicitation techniques taught in field methods courses. Linguistic theory consisted of procedures of analysis, primarily segmentation and classification, designed to organize a body of linguistic material, guided by limited assumptions about structural properties and their arrangement. The prominent linguist Martin Joos hardly exaggerated in a 1955 exposition when he identified the "decisive direction" of contemporary structural linguistics as the decision that language can be "described without any preexistent scheme of what a language must be."[1] Prevailing approaches in the behavioral sciences generally were not very different. Of course, no one accepted the incoherent notion of a "blank slate." But it was common to suppose that beyond some initial delimitation of properties detected in the environment (a "quality space," in the framework of the highly influential philosopher W. V. O. Quine), general learning mechanisms of some kind should suffice to account for what organisms, including humans, know and do. Genetic endowment in these domains would not be expected to reach much beyond something like that.

The emerging biolinguistic approach adopted a different stance. It took the object of inquiry to be, not behavior and its products, but the internal cognitive

---

[1] Chapter 3, note 12. Joos was referring explicitly to the "Boasian tradition" of American structuralism, and had only a few – rather disparaging – remarks about European structuralism. But the observations carry over without too much change.

systems that enter into action and interpretation, and, beyond that, the basis in our fixed biological nature for the growth and development of these internal systems. From this point of view, the central topic of concern is what Juan Huarte, in the sixteenth century, regarded as the essential property of human intelligence: the capacity of the human mind to "engender within itself, by its own power, the principles on which knowledge rests,"[2] ideas that were developed in important ways in the philosophical–scientific traditions of later years. For language, "the principles on which knowledge rests" are those of the internalized language (*I-language*) that the person has acquired. Having acquired these principles, Jones has a wide range of knowledge, for example that *glink* but not *glnik* is a possible lexical item of English; that *John is too angry to talk to (Mary)* means that John is to be talked to (if *Mary* is missing) but John is to do the talking (if *Mary* is present); that *him* can be used to refer to John in the sentence *I wonder who John expects to see him*, but not if *I wonder who* is omitted; that if John painted the house brown then he put the paint on the exterior surface though he could paint the house brown on the inside; that when John climbed the mountain he went up although he can climb down the mountain; that books are in some sense simultaneously abstract and concrete as in *John memorized and then burned the book*; and so on over an unbounded range. "The power to engender" the I-language principles on which such particular cases of knowledge rest is understood to be the component of the genetic endowment that accounts for their growth and development.

Linguistics, so conceived, seeks to discover true theories of particular I-languages (*grammars*), and, at a deeper level, the theory of the genetic basis for language acquisition (*universal grammar, UG*, adapting a traditional term to a new usage). Other cognitive systems, it was assumed, should be conceived along similar lines, each with its own principles, and powers of engendering them.

Within this framework, cognitive systems are understood to be, in effect, organs of the body, primarily the brain, to be investigated in much the manner of other subcomponents with distinctive properties that interact in the life of the organism: the systems of vision, motor planning, circulation of the blood, etc. Along with their role in behavior, the "cognitive organs" enter into activities traditionally regarded as mental: thought, planning, interpretation, evaluation, and so on. The term "mental" here is informal and descriptive, pretty much on a par with such loose descriptive terms as "chemical," "electrical," "optical," and others that are used to focus attention on particular aspects of the world that seem to have an integrated character and to be worth abstracting for special investigation, but without any illusion that they carve nature at the joints. Behavior and its products – such as texts – provide data that may be useful as

---

[2] Chapter 1, pp. 8–9.

evidence to determine the nature and origins of cognitive systems, but have no privileged status for such inquiries, just as in the case of other organs of the body.

The general shift of perspective is sometimes called the "cognitive revolution" of the 1950s. However, for reasons discussed in the early essays that follow, I think it might more properly be considered a renewal and further development of the cognitive revolution of the seventeenth century. From the 1950s, many traditional questions were revived – regrettably, without acquaintance with the tradition, which had been largely forgotten or misrepresented. Also revived was the view that had been crystallizing through the eighteenth century that properties "termed mental" are the result of "such an organical structure as that of the brain" (chemist–philosopher Joseph Priestley). This development of "Locke's suggestion," as it is called in the scholarly literature, was a natural, virtually inevitable, concomitant of the Newtonian revolution, which effectively dismantled the only significant notion of "body" or "physical." The basic conclusion was well understood by the nineteenth-century. Darwin asked rhetorically why "thought, being a secretion of the brain," should be considered "more wonderful than gravity, a property of matter." In his classic nineteenth-century history of materialism, Friedrich Lange observes that scientists have "accustomed ourselves to the abstract notion of forces, or rather to a notion hovering in a mystic obscurity between abstraction and concrete comprehension," a "turning-point" in the history of materialism that removes the surviving remnants of the doctrine far from the ideas and concerns of the "genuine Materialists" of the seventeenth century, and deprives them of significance. They need be of no special concern in the study of aspects of the world "termed mental."

It is perhaps worth noting that this traditional understanding is still regarded as highly contentious, and repetition of it, almost in virtually the same words, is regularly proposed as a "bold hypothesis" or "radical new idea" in the study of the domains "termed mental."[3]

Another significant feature of the original cognitive revolution was the recognition that properties of the world termed mental may involve unbounded capacities of a limited finite organ, the "infinite use of finite means," in Wilhelm von Humboldt's phrase. The doctrine was at the heart of the Cartesian concept of mind. It provided the basic criterion to deal with the problem of "other minds" – to determine whether some creature has a mind like ours. Descartes and his followers focused on use of language as the clearest illustration. In a rather similar vein, Hume later recognized that our moral judgments are unbounded in scope, and must be founded on general principles that are part of our nature – genetically determined, in modern terms. That observation poses

[3] For examples and discussion, see my *New Horizons in the Study of Language and Mind* (Cambridge, 2000).

Huarte's problem in a different domain, and is, by now, the topic of intriguing empirical research and conceptual analysis.

By the mid twentieth century, it had become possible to face such problems as these in a more substantive way than in earlier periods. There was, by then, a clear general understanding of finite generative systems with unbounded scope, which could be readily adapted to the reframing and investigation of traditional questions that had necessarily been left obscure. Another influential factor in the renewal of the cognitive revolution was the work of ethologists and comparative psychologists, then just coming to be more readily accessible, with its concern for "the innate working hypotheses present in subhuman organisms," and the "human a priori," which should have much the same character.[4] That framework too could be adapted to the study of human cognitive organs and their genetically determined nature, which constructs experience – the organism's *Umwelt*, in ethological terminology – and guides the general path of development, just as in all other aspects of growth of organisms.

Meanwhile, efforts to sharpen and refine procedural approaches ran into serious difficulties, revealing what appear to be intrinsic inadequacies. A basic problem is that even the most simple elements of discourse are not detectable by procedures of segmentation and classification. They do not have the required "beads on a string" property for such procedures to operate, and often cannot be located in some identifiable part of the physical event that corresponds to the mind-internal expression in which these elements function. It became increasingly clear that even the simplest units – morphemes, elementary lexical items, for that matter even phonological segments – can be identified only by their role in generative procedures that form linguistic expressions. These expressions, in turn, can be regarded as "instructions" to other systems of the mind/body that are used for mental operations, as well as for production of utterances and interpretation of external signals. More generally, study of the postulated mechanisms of learning and control of behavior in the behavioral sciences revealed fundamental inadequacies, and even at the core of the disciplines serious doubts were arising as to whether the entire enterprise was viable, apart from its utility for design of experiments that might be useful for some other purpose.

For the study of language, a natural conclusion seemed to be that the I-language attained has roughly the character of a scientific theory: an integrated system of rules and principles from which the expressions of the language can be derived, each of them a collection of instructions for thought and action. The child must somehow select the I-language from the flux of experience. The problem appeared to be similar to what Charles Sanders Peirce had called *abduction*, in considering the problem of scientific discovery.[5] And as in the

---

[4] Konrad Lorenz; chapter 3, pp. 83–84, below.
[5] See chapter 3, pp. 79–81, below.

case of the sciences, the task is impossible without what Peirce called a "limit on admissible hypotheses" that permits only certain theories to be entertained, but not infinitely many others compatible with relevant data. In the language case, it appeared that the genetic endowment of the language faculty must impose a format for rule systems that is sufficiently restrictive so that candidate I-languages are "scattered," and only a small number can even be considered in the course of language acquisition. In later work in the cognitive sciences, such approaches are often called "theory theory" conceptions.[6] Like abduction, and for that matter every aspect of growth and development, language acquisition faces a problem of *poverty of stimulus*. The general observation is transparent, so much so that outside of the cognitive sciences the ubiquitous phenomenon is not even dignified with a name: no one speaks of the problem of poverty of stimulus for an embryo that has somehow to become a worm or a cat, given the nutritional environment, or in any aspect of post-natal development, say undergoing puberty.

In the essays reprinted below from the 1960s, the nature and acquisition of language presented and discussed adopts the general framework just outlined. "The most challenging theoretical problem in linguistics" was therefore taken to be "that of discovering the principles of universal grammar," which "determine the choice of hypotheses" – that is, restrict the accessible I-languages. It was also recognized, however, that for language, as for other biological organisms, a still more challenging problem lies on the horizon: to discover "the laws that determine possible successful mutation and the nature of complex organisms," quite apart from the particular cognitive organs or other organic systems under investigation.[7] As the same point was made a few years earlier: "there is surely no reason today for taking seriously a position that attributes a complex human achievement entirely to months (or at most years) of experience [as in the behavioral sciences], rather than to millions of years of evolution [as in the study of the specific biological endowment, UG in the language case], or to principles of neural organization that may be more deeply grounded in physical law"[8] – a "third factor" in growth and development, organ- and possibly organism-independent. Investigation of the third factor seemed too remote from inquiry to merit much attention, and was therefore barely mentioned, though, in fact, even some of the earliest work – for example, on elimination of redundancy in rule systems – was implicitly guided by such concerns.

In the years that followed, the topics under investigation were substantially extended, not only in language-related areas but in the cognitive sciences generally. By the early 1980s, a substantial shift of perspective within linguistics

---

[6] Advocates of these approaches disagree, but mistakenly, I believe. See L. Antony and N. Hornstein, *Chomsky and his Critics* (Blackwell, 2003), chapter 10, and reply.

[7] Pp. 47, 85f., below.

[8] Chomsky, *Aspects of the Theory of Syntax* (Cambridge, Mass: MIT Press, 1965), p. 59.

reframed the basic questions considerably, abandoning entirely the format conception of linguistic theory in favor of an approach that sought to limit attainable I-languages to a finite set, aside from lexical choices (these too highly restricted). This *Principles and Parameters* approach may or may not turn out to be justified; one can never know. But as a research program, it has been highly successful, yielding an explosion of empirical inquiry into a very wide range of typologically varied languages, posing new theoretical questions that could scarcely have been formulated before, often providing at least partial answers as well, while also revitalizing related areas of language acquisition and processing. Another consequence is that it removed some basic conceptual barriers to the serious inquiry into the deeper "third factor" issues. These topics are reviewed in the lecture that closes this collection. They raise possibilities that, in my personal view at least, suggest novel and exciting challenges for the study of language in particular and problems of mind more generally.

Preface to the second edition

The six chapters that follow fall into two groups. The first three constitute the monograph *Language and Mind*, published in 1968. As the preface to *Language and Mind*, reprinted below, explains, the three essays on linguistic contributions to the study of mind (past, present, and future) are based on the Beckman lectures, delivered before a university-wide audience at the University of California, Berkeley, in January 1967. These essays constitute a unit distinct from the three chapters that follow them.

Chapter 4, "Form and meaning in natural languages," is the approximate text of a rather informal lecture given in January 1969 at Gustavus Adolphus College in Minnesota to an audience consisting largely of high school and college students and teachers. It reviews some of the basic notions presented in *Language and Mind* and other works, and in addition presents some later work on semantic interpretation of syntactic structures. This material, I believe, reveals some of the limitations and inadequacies of earlier theory and suggests a direction in which this theory should be revised. More technical investigations of this and related matters appear in forthcoming monographs of mine, *Semantics in Generative Grammar* and *Conditions on Rules*, to be published by Mouton and Co., The Hague, in 1972.

Chapter 5 is a considerably more technical study, exploring in some detail material that is presupposed or only informally developed in *Language and Mind*. The intended audience in this case consisted primarily of psychologists and psycholinguists. This chapter, which originally appeared as an appendix to Eric Lenneberg's *Biological Foundations of Language*, is an attempt to give a concise and systematic presentation of the theory of transformational-generative grammar and to explore its potential significance for human psychology. The monographs just cited carry the technical investigations further, in part, in directions that are briefly indicated in this chapter, which was actually written in 1965 and is therefore the earliest of the essays collected here.

Chapter 6 was directed to a rather different audience, namely, professional philosophers. This was a contribution to a symposium on linguistics and philosophy held at New York University in April 1968. The purpose of this lecture was to explore the points of contact between contemporary linguistics and philosophy – in particular, epistemology and philosophy of mind. The suggestion has been made that current work in linguistics has interesting insights to offer into the nature of human knowledge, the basis for its acquisition, and the ways it characteristically is used. In part, this essay is concerned with the debate that has arisen over these issues; in part, with the issues themselves.

There is a certain degree of redundancy in these essays. Chapters 4, 5, and 6 are each more or less self-contained. Each presupposes very little, and therefore some of the expository sections overlap, and overlap further with the chapters that constitute *Language and Mind.* I hope that the somewhat varying formulations of basic points may prove helpful. In fact, even the simplest and most basic points discussed in these essays have been widely misconstrued. For example, there has been a tendency in popular discussion to confuse "deep structure" with "generative grammar" or with "universal grammar." And a number of professional linguists have repeatedly confused what I refer to here as "the creative aspect of language use" with the recursive property of generative grammars, a very different matter. In the hope that such questions as these will be clarified, I have not eliminated redundancies in collecting these essays.

Chapters 4–6 extend and enlarge upon the ideas and material discussed in the Beckman lectures. All of these essays are concerned primarily with the area of intersection of linguistics, philosophy, and psychology. Their primary purpose is to show how the rather technical study of language structure can contribute to an understanding of human intelligence. I believe, and try to show in these essays, that the study of language structure reveals properties of mind that underlie the exercise of human mental capacities in normal activities, such as the use of language in the ordinary free and creative fashion.

At the cost of a final redundancy, I would like to underscore here the observations in the preface to *Language and Mind* concerning the so-called "behavioral sciences." Currently there is a good deal of discussion – and not infrequently, rather extravagant claims – concerning the implications of the behavioral sciences for human affairs. It is important to bear in mind that there are few nontrivial empirical hypotheses relating to the question of how humans behave and why they act as they do under ordinary circumstances. The reader who undertakes the useful exercise of searching the literature will discover, I believe, not only that there is little significant scientific knowledge in this domain, but further that the behavioral sciences have commonly insisted upon certain arbitrary methodological restrictions that make it virtually impossible for scientific knowledge of a nontrivial character to be attained.

We can begin to see how human knowledge and systems of belief might be acquired, in certain areas. The case of language is particularly interesting because language plays an essential role in thinking and human interaction, and because in this case we can begin to describe the system of knowledge that is attained and to formulate some plausible hypotheses about the intrinsic human capacities that make this achievement possible. These glimmerings of understanding are interesting in themselves and suggestive as well for other studies. We can be reasonably certain that the investigation of direct relations between experience and action, between stimuli and responses, will in general be a vain pursuit. In all but the most elementary cases, what a person does depends in large measure on what he knows, believes, and anticipates. A study of human behavior that is not based on at least a tentative formulation of relevant systems of knowledge and belief is predestined to triviality and irrelevance. The study of human learning can begin, in a serious way, only when such a tentative formulation of systems of knowledge and belief is presented. We can then ask by what means these systems are acquired, given the data of experience. Similarly, the study of human behavior can hardly be undertaken in a serious way unless we are in a position to ask how what a person does is related to what he knows, believes, and expects. Only when we have formulated some tentative hypotheses as to what is learned can we undertake a serious study of human learning; only when we have formulated some tentative hypotheses as to what has been learned – what is known and believed – can we turn in a serious way to the investigation of behavior. In the case of language, we can present some tentative but rather detailed and complex formulations of what is known, what has been learned by the normal speaker-hearer. For this reason, the study of language seems to me of particular interest for the study of human learning and behavior.

But it must be emphasized that language may be a rather special case. Knowledge of language is normally attained through brief exposure, and the character of the acquired knowledge may be largely predetermined. One would expect that human language should directly reflect the characteristics of human intellectual capacities, that language should be a direct "mirror of mind" in ways in which other systems of knowledge and belief cannot. Furthermore, even if we were able to account for the acquisition of language along the lines discussed in these essays, we would still be left with the problem of accounting for the normal use of the acquired knowledge. But this problem is, at the moment, quite intractable. It lies beyond the scope of scientific inquiry. Of course, it would be entirely irrational to argue that certain phenomena and certain problems do not exist, merely because they lie beyond the scope of scientific inquiry – at present, and perhaps intrinsically because of the scope of human intelligence, which after all is itself structured and bounded in ways that are unknown in any detail. Given the primitive character of the study of man and society and its general lack of intellectual substance, we can only speculate about the essential and basic factors that enter into human behavior, and it would be quite irresponsible to claim otherwise. Speculation about these matters is quite legitimate, even essential. It should be guided, where this is possible, by such limited and fragmentary knowledge as exists. But speculation should be clearly labeled as such and clearly distinguished from the achievements of scientific inquiry. This is a matter of considerable importance in a society that tends to trust in professional expertise and to rely on professional judgments. The scientist, in particular, has a responsibility to the public in this regard.

Massachusetts Institute of Technology   N. C.

Preface to the first edition

The three chapters of this book are somewhat elaborated versions of three lectures, the Beckman lectures, that I delivered at the University of California, at Berkeley, in January 1967. The first is an attempt to evaluate past contributions to the study of mind that have been based on research and speculation regarding the nature of language. The second is devoted to contemporary developments in linguistics that have a bearing on the study of mind. The third is a highly speculative discussion of directions that the study of language and mind might take in coming years. The three lectures, then, are concerned with the past, the present, and the future.

Given the state of research into the history of linguistics, even the attempt to evaluate past contributions must be regarded as highly tentative. Modern linguistics shares the delusion – the accurate term, I believe – that the modern "behavioral sciences" have in some essential respect achieved a transition from "speculation" to "science" and that earlier work can be safely consigned to the antiquarians. Obviously any rational person will favor rigorous analysis and careful experiment; but to a considerable degree, I feel, the "behavioral sciences" are merely mimicking the surface features of the natural sciences; much of their scientific character has been achieved by a restriction of subject matter and a concentration on rather peripheral issues. Such narrowing of focus can be justified if it leads to achievements of real intellectual significance, but in this case, I think it would be very difficult to show that the narrowing of scope has led to deep and significant results. Furthermore, there has been a natural but unfortunate tendency to "extrapolate," from the thimbleful of knowledge that has been attained in careful experimental work and rigorous data-processing, to issues of much wider significance and of great social concern. This is a serious matter. The experts have the responsibility of making clear the actual limits of their understanding and of the results they have so far achieved, and a careful analysis of these limits will demonstrate, I believe, that in virtually every domain of the social and behavioral sciences the results achieved to date will not support such "extrapolation." Such analysis will also show, I believe, that the contributions of earlier thought and speculation cannot be safely neglected, that in large measure they provide an indispensable basis for serious work today.

I do not attempt here to justify this point of view in general, but merely assert that it is the point of view underlying the lectures that follow.

In the second lecture I have made no attempt to give a systematic presentation of what has been achieved in linguistic research; rather, I have concentrated on problems that are at the borderline of research and that still resist solution. Much of the material in this lecture is to appear in a chapter entitled "Problems of Explanation in Linguistics" in *Explanations in Psychology*, edited by R. Borger and F. Cioffi (New York: Cambridge University Press, 1967), along with interesting critical comments by Max Black. Lectures 1 and 3 make use of some material from a lecture delivered at the University of Chicago in April 1966 that appears in *Changing Perspectives on Man*, edited by B. Rothblatt (Chicago: University of Chicago Press, 1968). A portion of the first lecture was published in the *Columbia University Forum*, Spring 1968 (Vol. XI, No. 1), and a portion of the third lecture will appear in the Fall 1968 issue (Vol. XI, No. 3).

I would like to express my thanks to members of the faculty and the student body at Berkeley for many useful comments and reactions and, more generally, for the rich and stimulating intellectual climate in which I was privileged to spend several months just prior to these lectures. I am also indebted to John Ross and Morris Halle for helpful comments and suggestions.

1   Linguistic contributions to the study of mind: past

In these lectures, I would like to focus attention on the question, What contribution can the study of language make to our understanding of human nature? In one or another manifestation, this question threads its way through modern Western thought. In an age that was less self-conscious and less compartmentalized than ours, the nature of language, the respects in which language mirrors human mental processes or shapes the flow and character of thought – these were topics for study and speculation by scholars and gifted amateurs with a wide variety of interests, points of view, and intellectual backgrounds. And in the nineteenth and twentieth centuries, as linguistics, philosophy, and psychology have uneasily tried to go their separate ways, the classical problems of language and mind have inevitably reappeared and have served to link these diverging fields and to give direction and significance to their efforts. There have been signs in the past decade that the rather artificial separation of disciplines may be coming to an end. It is no longer a point of honor for each to demonstrate its absolute independence of the others, and new interests have emerged that permit the classical problems to be formulated in novel and occasionally suggestive ways – for example, in terms of the new perspectives provided by cybernetics and the communication sciences, and against the background of developments in comparative and physiological psychology that challenge long-standing convictions and free the scientific imagination from certain shackles that had become so familiar a part of our intellectual environment as to be almost beyond awareness. All of this is highly encouraging. I think there is more of a healthy ferment in cognitive psychology – and in the particular branch of cognitive psychology known as linguistics – than there has been for many years. And one of the most encouraging signs is that skepticism with regard to the orthodoxies of the recent past is coupled with an awareness of the temptations and the dangers of premature orthodoxy, an awareness that, if it can persist, may prevent the rise of new and stultifying dogma.

It is easy to be misled in an assessment of the current scene; nevertheless, it seems to me that the decline of dogmatism and the accompanying search for new approaches to old and often still intractable problems are quite unmistakable, not only in linguistics but in all of the disciplines concerned with the study of mind. I remember quite clearly my own feeling of uneasiness as a student at the fact that, so it seemed, the basic problems of the field were solved, and that what remained was to sharpen and improve techniques of linguistic analysis that were reasonably well understood and to apply them to a wider range of linguistic materials. In the postwar years, this was a dominant attitude in most active centers of research. I recall being told by a distinguished anthropological linguist, in 1953, that he had no intention of working through a vast collection of materials that he had assembled because within a few years it would surely be possible to program a computer to construct a grammar from a large corpus of data by the use of techniques that were already fairly well formalized. At the time, this did not seem an unreasonable attitude, though the prospect was saddening for anyone who felt, or at least hoped, that the resources of human intelligence were somewhat deeper than these procedures and techniques might reveal. Correspondingly, there was a striking decline in studies of linguistic method in the early 1950s as the most active theoretical minds turned to the problem of how an essentially closed body of technique could be applied to some new domain – say, to analysis of connected discourse, or to other cultural phenomena beyond language. I arrived at Harvard as a graduate student shortly after B. F. Skinner had delivered his William James Lectures, later to be published in his book *Verbal Behavior*. Among those active in research in the philosophy or psychology of language, there was then little doubt that although details were missing, and although matters could not really be quite that simple, nevertheless a behavioristic framework of the sort Skinner had outlined would prove quite adequate to accommodate the full range of language use. There was now little reason to question the conviction of Leonard Bloomfield, Bertrand Russell, and positivistic linguists, psychologists, and philosophers in general that the framework of stimulus-response psychology would soon be extended to the point where it would provide a satisfying explanation for the most mysterious of human abilities. The most radical souls felt that perhaps, in order to do full justice to these abilities, one must postulate little s's and r's inside the brain alongside the capital S's and R's that were open to immediate inspection, but this extension was not inconsistent with the general picture.

Critical voices, even those that commanded considerable prestige, were simply unheard. For example, Karl Lashley gave a brilliant critique of the prevailing framework of ideas in 1948, arguing that underlying language use – and all organized behavior – there must be abstract mechanisms of some sort that are not analyzable in terms of association and that could not have been developed by any such simple means. But his arguments and proposals, though sound and perceptive, had absolutely no effect on the development of the field and went by unnoticed even at his own university (Harvard), then the leading center of psycholinguistic research. Ten years later Lashley's contribution began to be appreciated, but only after his insights had been independently achieved in another context.

The technological advances of the 1940s simply reinforced the general euphoria. Computers were on the horizon, and their imminent availability reinforced the belief that it would suffice to gain a theoretical understanding of only the simplest and most superficially obvious of phenomena – everything else would merely prove to be "more of the same," an apparent complexity that would be disentangled by the electronic marvels. The sound spectrograph, developed during the war, offered similar promise for the physical analysis of speech sounds. The interdisciplinary conferences on speech analysis of the early 1950s make interesting reading today. There were few so benighted as to question the possibility, in fact the immediacy, of a final solution to the problem of converting speech into writing by available engineering technique. And just a few years later, it was jubilantly discovered that machine translation and automatic abstracting were also just around the corner. For those who sought a more mathematical formulation of the basic processes, there was the newly developed mathematical theory of communication, which, it was widely believed in the early 1950s, had provided a fundamental concept – the concept of "information" – that would unify the social and behavioral sciences and permit the development of a solid and satisfactory mathematical theory of human behavior on a probabilistic base. At about the same time, the theory of automata developed as an independent study, making use of closely related mathematical notions. And it was linked at once, and quite properly, to earlier explorations of the theory of neural nets. There were those – John von Neumann, for example – who felt that the entire development was dubious and shaky at best, and probably quite misconceived, but such qualms did not go far to dispel the feeling that mathematics, technology, and behavioristic linguistics and psychology were converging on a point of view that was very simple, very clear, and fully adequate to provide a basic understanding of what tradition had left shrouded in mystery.

In the United States at least, there is little trace today of the illusions of the early postwar years. If we consider the current status of structural linguistic methodology, stimulus-response psycholinguistics (whether or not extended to "mediation theory"), or probabilistic or automata-theoretic models for language use, we find that in each case a parallel development has taken place: a careful analysis has shown that insofar as the system of concepts and principles that was advanced can be made precise, it can be demonstrated to be inadequate in a fundamental way. The kinds of structures that are realizable in terms of these theories are simply not those that must be postulated to underlie the use of language, if empirical conditions of adequacy are to be satisfied. What is more, the character of the failure and inadequacy is such as to give little reason to believe that these approaches are on the right track. That is, in each case it has been argued – quite persuasively, in my opinion – that the approach is not only inadequate but misguided in basic and important ways. It has, I believe, become quite clear that if we are ever to understand how language is used or acquired, then we must abstract for separate and independent study a cognitive system, a system of knowledge and belief, that develops in early childhood and that interacts with many other factors to determine the kinds of behavior that we observe; to introduce a technical term, we must isolate and study the system of *linguistic competence* that underlies behavior but that is not realized in any direct or simple way in behavior. And this system of linguistic competence is qualitatively different from anything that can be described in terms of the taxonomic methods of structural linguistics, the concepts of S-R psychology, or the notions developed within the mathematical theory of communication or the theory of simple automata. The theories and models that were developed to describe simple and immediately given phenomena cannot incorporate the real system of linguistic competence; "extrapolation" for simple descriptions cannot approach the reality of linguistic competence; mental structures are not simply "more of the same" but are qualitatively different from the complex networks and structures that can be developed by elaboration of the concepts that seemed so promising to many scientists just a few years ago. What is involved is not a matter of degree of complexity but rather a quality of complexity. Correspondingly, there is no reason to expect that the available technology can provide significant insight or understanding or useful achievements; it has noticeably failed to do so, and, in fact, an appreciable investment of time, energy, and money in the use of computers for linguistic research – appreciable by the standards of a small field like linguistics – has not provided any significant advance in our understanding of the use or nature of language. These judgments are harsh, but I think they are defensible. They are, furthermore, hardly debated by active linguistic or psycholinguistic researchers.

At the same time there have been significant advances, I believe, in our understanding of the nature of linguistic competence and some of the ways in which it is put to use, but these advances, such as they are, have proceeded from assumptions very different from those that were so enthusiastically put forth in the period I have been discussing. What is more, these advances have not narrowed the gap between what is known and what can be seen to lie beyond the scope of present understanding and technique; rather, each advance has made it clear that these intellectual horizons are far more remote than was heretofore imagined. Finally, it has become fairly clear, it seems to me, that the assumptions and approaches that appear to be productive today have a distinctly traditional flavor to them; in general, a much despised tradition has been largely revitalized in recent years and its contributions given some serious and, I believe, well-deserved attention. From the recognition of these facts flows the general and quite healthy attitude of skepticism that I spoke of earlier.

In short, it seems to me quite appropriate, at this moment in the development of linguistics and psychology in general, to turn again to classical questions and to ask what new insights have been achieved that bear on them, and how the classical issues may provide direction for contemporary research and study.

When we turn to the history of study and speculation concerning the nature of mind and, more specifically, the nature of human language, our attention quite naturally comes to focus on the seventeenth century, "the century of genius," in which the foundations of modern science were firmly established and the problems that still confound us were formulated with remarkable clarity and perspicuity. There are many far from superficial respects in which the intellectual climate of today resembles that of seventeenth-century Western Europe. One, particularly crucial in the present context, is the very great interest in the potentialities and capacities of automata, a problem that intrigued the seventeenth-century mind as fully as it does our own. I mentioned above that there is a slowly dawning realization that a significant gap – more accurately, a yawning chasm – separates the system of concepts of which we have a fairly clear grasp, on the one hand, and the nature of human intelligence, on the other. A similar realization lies at the base of Cartesian philosophy. Descartes also arrived, quite early in his investigations, at the conclusion that the study of mind faces us with a problem of quality of complexity, not merely degree of complexity. He felt that he had demonstrated that understanding and will, the two fundamental properties of the human mind, involved capacities and principles that are not realizable by even the most complex of automata.

It is particularly interesting to trace the development of this argument in the works of the minor and now quite forgotten Cartesian philosophers, like Cordemoy, who wrote a fascinating treatise extending Descartes' few remarks about language, or La Forge, who produced a long and detailed *Traité de l'esprit de l'homme* expressing, so he claimed with some reason, what Descartes would likely have said about this subject had he lived to extend his theory of man beyond physiology. One may question the details of this argument, and one can show how it was impeded and distorted by certain remnants of scholastic doctrine – the framework of substance and mode, for example. But the general structure of the argument is not unreasonable; it is, in fact, rather analogous to the argument against the framework of ideas of the early postwar years, which I mentioned at the outset of this lecture. The Cartesians tried to show that when the theory of corporeal body is sharpened and clarified and extended to its limits, it is still incapable of accounting for facts that are obvious to introspection and that are also confirmed by our observation of the actions of other humans. In particular, it cannot account for the normal use of human language, just as it cannot explain the basic properties of thought. Consequently, it becomes necessary to invoke an entirely new principle – in Cartesian terms, to postulate a second substance whose essence is thought, alongside of body, with its essential properties of extension and motion. This new principle has a "creative aspect," which is evidenced most clearly in what we may refer to as "the creative aspect of language use," the distinctively human ability to express new thoughts and to understand entirely new expressions of thought, within the framework of an "instituted language," a language that is a cultural product subject to laws and principles partially unique to it and partially reflections of general properties of mind. These laws and principles, it is maintained, are not formulable in terms of even the most elaborate extension of the concepts proper to the analysis of behavior and interaction of physical bodies, and they are not realizable by even the most complex automaton. In fact, Descartes argued that the only sure indication that another body possesses a human mind, that it is not a mere automaton, is its ability to use language in the normal way; and he argued that this ability cannot be detected in an animal or an automaton which, in other respects, shows signs of apparent intelligence exceeding those of a human, even though such an organism or machine might be as fully endowed as a human with the physiological organs necessary to produce speech.

I will return to this argument and the ways in which it was developed. But I think it is important to stress that, with all its gaps and deficiencies, it is an argument that must be taken seriously. There is nothing at all absurd in the conclusion. It seems to me quite possible that at that particular moment in the development of Western thought there was the possibility for the birth of a science of psychology of a sort that still does not exist, a psychology that begins with the problem of characterizing various systems of human knowledge and belief, the concepts in terms of which they are organized and the principles that underlie them, and that only then turns to the study of how these systems might have developed through some combination of innate structure and organism – environment interaction. Such a psychology would contrast rather sharply with the approach to human intelligence that begins by postulating, on a priori grounds, certain specific mechanisms that, it is claimed, *must* be those underlying the acquisition of all knowledge and belief. The distinction is one to which I will return in a subsequent lecture. For the moment, I want merely to stress the reasonableness of the rejected alternative and, what is more, its consistency with the approach that proved so successful in the seventeenth-century revolution in physics.

There are methodological parallels that have perhaps been inadequately appreciated between the Cartesian postulation of a substance whose essence was thought and the post-Newtonian acceptance of a principle of attraction as an innate property of the ultimate corpuscles of matter, an active principle that governs the motions of bodies. Perhaps the most far-reaching contribution of Cartesian philosophy to modern thought was its rejection of the scholastic notion of substantial forms and real qualities, of all those "little images fluttering through the air" to which Descartes referred with derision. With the exorcism of these occult qualities, the stage was set for the rise of a physics of matter in motion and a psychology that explored the properties of mind. But Newton argued that Descartes' mechanical physics wouldn't work – the second book of the *Principia* is largely devoted to this demonstration – and that it is necessary to postulate a new force to account for the motion of bodies. The postulate of an attractive force acting at a distance was inconsistent with the clear and distinct ideas of common sense and could not be tolerated by an orthodox Cartesian – such a force was merely another occult quality. Newton quite agreed, and he attempted repeatedly to find a mechanical explanation of the cause of gravity. He rejected the view that gravity is "essential and inherent to matter" and maintained that "to tell us that every species of things is endowed with an occult specific property (such as gravity) by which it acts and produces manifest effects, is to tell us nothing." Some historians of science have suggested that Newton hoped, like Descartes, to write a *Principles of Philosophy* but that his failure to explain the cause of gravity on mechanical grounds restricted him to a *Mathematical Principles of Natural Philosophy*. Thus, to the common sense of Newton as well as the Cartesians, physics was still not adequately grounded, because it postulated a mystical force capable of action at a distance. Similarly, Descartes' postulation of mind as an explanatory principle was unacceptable to the empiricist temper. But the astonishing success of mathematical physics carried the day against these common-sense objections, and the prestige of the new physics was so high that the speculative psychology of the Enlightenment took for granted the necessity of working within the Newtonian framework, rather than on the Newtonian analogy – a very different matter. The occult force of gravity was accepted as an obvious element of the physical world, requiring no explanation, and it became inconceivable that one might have to postulate entirely new principles of functioning and organization outside the framework of what soon became the new "common sense." Partly for this reason, the search for an analogous scientific psychology that would explore the principles of mind, whatever they might be, was not undertaken with the thoroughness that was then, as now, quite possible.

I do not want to overlook a fundamental distinction between the postulation of gravity and the postulation of a *res cogitans,* namely the enormous disparity in the power of the explanatory theories that were developed. Nevertheless, I think it is instructive to note that the reasons for the dissatisfaction of Newton, Leibnitz, and the orthodox Cartesians with the new physics are strikingly similar to the grounds on which a dualistic rationalist psychology was soon to be rejected. I think it is correct to say that the study of properties and organization of mind was prematurely abandoned, in part on quite spurious grounds, and also to point out that there is a certain irony in the common view that its abandonment was caused by the gradual spread of a more general "scientific" attitude.

I have tried to call attention to some similarities between the intellectual climate of the seventeenth century and that of today. It is illuminating, I think, to trace in somewhat greater detail the specific course of development of linguistic theory during the modern period, in the context of the study of mind and of behavior in general.[1]

A good place to begin is with the writings of the Spanish physician Juan Huarte, who in the late sixteenth century published a widely translated study on the nature of human intelligence. In the course of his investigations, Huarte came to wonder at the fact that the word for "intelligence," *ingenio*, seems to have the same Latin root as various words meaning "engender" or "generate." This, he argued, gives a clue to the nature of mind. Thus, "One may discern two generative powers in man, one common with the beasts and the plants, and the other participating of spiritual substance. Wit (Ingenio) is a generative power. The understanding is a generative faculty." Huarte's etymology is actually not very good; the insight, however, is quite substantial.

Huarte goes on to distinguish three levels of intelligence. The lowest of these is the "docile wit," which satisfies the maxim that he, along with Leibnitz and many others, wrongly attributes to Aristotle, namely that there is nothing in the mind that is not simply transmitted to it by the senses. The next higher level, normal human intelligence, goes well beyond the empiricist limitation: it is able to "engender within itself, by its own power, the principles on which knowledge rests." Normal human minds are such that "assisted by the subject alone, without the help of anybody, they will produce a thousand conceits they never heard spoke of . . . inventing and saying such things as they never heard from their masters, nor any mouth." Thus, normal human intelligence is capable of acquiring knowledge through its own internal resources, perhaps making use of the data of sense but going on to construct a cognitive system in terms of concepts and principles that are developed on independent grounds; and it is capable of generating new thoughts and of finding appropriate and novel ways of expressing them, in ways that entirely transcend any training or experience.

Huarte postulates a third kind of wit, "by means of which some, without art or study, speak such subtle and surprising things, yet true, that were never before seen, heard, or writ, no, nor ever so much as thought of." The reference here is to true creativity, an exercise of the creative imagination in ways that go beyond normal intelligence and may, he felt, involve "a mixture of madness."

Huarte maintains that the distinction between docile wit, which meets the empiricist maxim, and normal intelligence, with its full generative capacities, is the distinction between beast and man. As a physician, Huarte was much

---

[1] For additional details and discussion, see my *Cartesian Linguistics* (New York: Harper & Row, 1966) and the references cited there.

interested in pathology. In particular, he notes that the most severe disability of wit that can afflict a human is a restriction to the lowest of the three levels, to the docile wit that conforms to empiricist principles. This disability, says Huarte, "resembles that of Eunuchs, incapable of generation." Under these sad circumstances, in which the intelligence can only receive stimuli transmitted by sense and associate them with one another, true education is of course impossible, since the ideas and principles that permit the growth of knowledge and understanding are lacking. In this case, then, "neither the lash of the rod, nor cries, nor method, nor examples, nor time, nor experience, nor anything in nature can sufficiently excite him to bring forth anything."

Huarte's framework is useful for discussing "psychological theory" in the ensuing period. Typical of later thought is his reference to use of language as an index of human intelligence, of what distinguishes man from animals, and, specifically, his emphasis on the creative capacity of normal intelligence. These concerns dominated rationalist psychology and linguistics. With the rise of romanticism, attention shifted to the third type of wit, to true creativity, although the rationalist assumption that normal human intelligence is uniquely free and creative and beyond the bounds of mechanical explanation was not abandoned and played an important role in the psychology of romanticism, and even in its social philosophy.

As I have already mentioned, the rationalist theory of language, which was to prove extremely rich in insight and achievement, developed in part out of a concern with the problem of other minds. A fair amount of effort was devoted to a consideration of the ability of animals to follow spoken commands, to express their emotional states, to communicate with one another, and even apparently to cooperate for a common goal; all of this, it was argued, could be accounted for on "mechanical grounds," as this notion was then understood – that is, through the functioning of physiological mechanisms in terms of which one could formulate the properties of reflexes, conditioning and reinforcement, association, and so on. Animals do not lack appropriate organs of communication, nor are they simply lower along some scale of "general intelligence."

In fact, as Descartes himself quite correctly observed, language is a species-specific human possession, and even at low levels of intelligence, at pathological levels, we find a command of language that is totally unattainable by an ape that may, in other respects, surpass a human imbecile in problem-solving ability and other adaptive behavior. I will return later to the status of this observation, in the light of what is now known about animal communication. There is a basic element lacking in animals, Descartes argued, as it is lacking in even the most complex automaton that develops its "intellectual structures" completely in terms of conditioning and association – namely Huarte's second type of wit, the generative ability that is revealed in the normal human use of language as a free instrument of thought. If by experiment we convince ourselves that another organism gives evidence of the normal, creative use of language, we must suppose that it, like us, has a mind and that what it does lies beyond the bounds of mechanical explanation, outside the framework of the stimulus-response psychology of the time, which in relevant essentials is not significantly different from that of today, though it falls short in sharpness of technique and scope and reliability of information.

It should not be thought, incidentally, that the only Cartesian arguments for the beast-machine hypothesis were those derived from the apparent inability of animals to manifest the creative aspect of language use. There were also many others – for example, the natural fear of population explosion in the domains of the spirit if every gnat had a soul. Or the argument of Cardinal Melchior de Polignac, who argued that the beast-machine hypothesis followed from the assumption of the goodness of God, since, as he pointed out, one can see "how much more humane is the doctrine that animals suffer no pain."[2] Or there is the argument of Louis Racine, son of the dramatist, who was struck by the following insight: "If beasts had souls and were capable of feelings, would they show themselves insensible to the affront and injustice done them by Descartes? Would they not rather have risen up in wrath against the leader and the sect which so degraded them?" One should add, I suppose, that Louis Racine was regarded by his contemporaries as the living proof that a brilliant father could not have a brilliant son. But the fact is that the discussion of the existence of other minds, and, in contrast, the mechanical nature of animals, continually returned to the creative aspect of language use, to the claim that – as formulated by another minor seventeenth-century figure – "if beasts reasoned, they would be capable of true speech with its infinite variety."

It is important to understand just what properties of language were most striking to Descartes and his followers. The discussion of what I have been calling "the creative aspect of language use" turns on three important observations. The first is that the normal use of language is innovative, in the sense that much of what we say in the course of normal language use is entirely new, not a repetition of anything that we have heard before and not even similar in pattern – in any useful sense of the terms "similar" and "pattern" – to sentences or discourse that we have heard in the past. This is a truism, but an important one, often overlooked and not infrequently denied in the behaviorist period of linguistics to which I referred earlier, when it was almost universally claimed that a person's knowledge of language is representable as a stored set of patterns, overlearned through constant repetition and detailed training, with innovation being at most a matter of "analogy." The fact surely is, however, that the number of sentences

---

[2] These examples are taken from the excellent study by Leonora Cohen Rosenfield, *From Beast-Machine to Man-Machine* (New York: Oxford University Press, 1941). The quotes are her paraphrases of the original.

in one's native language that one will immediately understand with no feeling of difficulty or strangeness is astronomical; and that the number of patterns underlying our normal use of language and corresponding to meaningful and easily comprehensible sentences in our language is orders of magnitude greater than the number of seconds in a lifetime. It is in this sense that the normal use of language is innovative.

However, in the Cartesian view even animal behavior is potentially infinite in its variety, in the special sense in which the readings of a speedometer can be said, with an obvious idealization, to be potentially infinite in variety. That is, if animal behavior is controlled by external stimuli or internal states (the latter including those established by conditioning), then as the stimuli vary over an indefinite range, so may the behavior of the animal. But the normal use of language is not only innovative and potentially infinite in scope, but also free from the control of detectable stimuli, either external or internal. It is because of this freedom from stimulus control that language can serve as an instrument of thought and self-expression, as it does not only for the exceptionally gifted and talented, but also, in fact, for every normal human.

Still, the properties of being unbounded and free from stimulus control do not, in themselves, exceed the bounds of mechanical explanation. And Cartesian discussion of the limits of mechanical explanation therefore took note of a third property of the normal use of language, namely its coherence and its "appropriateness to the situation" – which of course is an entirely different matter from control by external stimuli. Just what "appropriateness" and "coherence" may consist in we cannot say in any clear or definite way, but there is no doubt that these are meaningful concepts. We can distinguish normal use of language from the ravings of a maniac or the output of a computer with a random element.

Honesty forces us to admit that we are as far today as Descartes was three centuries ago from understanding just what enables a human to speak in a way that is innovative, free from stimulus control, and also appropriate and coherent. This is a serious problem that the psychologist and biologist must ultimately face and that cannot be talked out of existence by invoking "habit" or "conditioning" or "natural selection."

The Cartesian analysis of the problem of other minds, in terms of the creative aspect of language use and similar indications of the limits of mechanical explanation, was not entirely satisfying to contemporary opinion – Bayle's *Dictionary*, for example, cites the inability to give a satisfactory proof of the existence of other minds as the weakest element in the Cartesian philosophy – and there was a long and intriguing series of discussions and polemics regarding the problems that Descartes raised. From the vantage point of several centuries, we can see that the debate was inconclusive. The properties of human thought and human language emphasized by the Cartesians are real enough; they were then, as they are now, beyond the bounds of any well-understood kind of physical explanation. Neither physics nor biology nor psychology gives us any clue as to how to deal with these matters.

As in the case of other intractable problems, it is tempting to try another approach, one that might show the problem to be misconceived, the result of some conceptual confusion. This is a line of argument that has been followed in contemporary philosophy, but, it seems to me, without success. It is clear that the Cartesians understood, as well as Gilbert Ryle and other contemporary critics understand, the difference between providing criteria for intelligent behavior, on the one hand, and providing an explanation for the possibility of such behavior, on the other; but, as distinct from Ryle, they were interested in the latter problem as well as the former. As scientists, they were not satisfied with the formulation of experimental tests that would show the behavior of another organism to be creative, in the special sense just outlined; they were also troubled, and quite rightly so, by the fact that the abilities indicated by such tests and observational criteria transcended the capacities of corporeal bodies as they understood them, just as they are beyond the scope of physical explanation as we understand it today. There is surely nothing illegitimate in an attempt to go beyond elaboration of observational tests and collection of evidence to the construction of some theoretical explanation for what is observed, and this is just what was at stake in the Cartesian approach to the problem of mind. As La Forge and others insisted, it is necessary to go beyond what one can perceive or "imagine" (in the technical, classical sense of this term) if one hopes to understand the nature of "l'esprit de l'homme," just as Newton did – successfully – in trying to understand the nature of planetary motion. On the other hand, the proposals of the Cartesians were themselves of no real substance; the phenomena in question are not explained satisfactorily by attributing them to an "active principle" called "mind," the properties of which are not developed in any coherent or comprehensive way.

It seems to me that the most hopeful approach today is to describe the phenomena of language and of mental activity as accurately as possible, to try to develop an abstract theoretical apparatus that will as far as possible account for these phenomena and reveal the principles of their organization and functioning, without attempting, for the present, to relate the postulated mental structures and processes to any physiological mechanisms or to interpret mental function in terms of "physical causes." We can only leave open for the future the question of how these abstract structures and processes are realized or accounted for in some concrete terms, conceivably in terms that are not within the range of physical processes as presently understood – a conclusion that, if correct, should surprise no one.

This rationalist philosophy of language merged with various other independent developments in the seventeenth century, leading to the first really significant general theory of linguistic structure, namely the general point of view that came to be known as "philosophical" or "universal" grammar. Unfortunately, philosophical grammar is very poorly known today. There are few technical or scholarly studies, and these few are apologetic and disparaging. References to philosophical grammar in modern treatises on language are so distorted as to be quite worthless. Even a scholar with such high standards as Leonard Bloomfield gives an account of philosophical grammar in his major work, *Language*, that bears almost no resemblance to the original and attributes to this tradition views diametrically opposed to those that were most typical of it. For example, Bloomfield and many others describe philosophical grammar as based on a Latin model, as prescriptive, as showing no interest in the sounds of speech, as given to a confusion of speech with writing. All these charges are false, and it is important to dispel these myths to make possible an objective evaluation of what was actually accomplished.

It is particularly ironic that philosophical grammar should be accused of a Latin bias. In fact, it is significant that the original works – the Port-Royal *Grammar* and *Logic*, in particular – were written in French, the point being that they formed part of the movement to replace Latin by the vernacular. The fact is that Latin was regarded as an artificial and distorted language, one positively injurious to the exercise of the plain thinking and common-sense discourse by which the Cartesians set such store. The practitioners of philosophical grammar used such linguistic materials as were available to them; it is noteworthy that some of the topics that were studied with the greatest care and persistence for well over a century involved points of grammar that do not even have an analogue in Latin. A striking example is the so-called rule of Vaugelas, which involves the relation between indefinite articles and relative clauses in French. For 150 years the rule of Vaugelas was the central issue debated in the controversy over the possibility of developing a "rational grammar," one which would go beyond description to achieve a rational explanation for phenomena.

No doubt it is a complete misunderstanding of the issue of rational explanation that leads to the charge of "prescriptivism" that is leveled, quite erroneously, against philosophical grammar. In fact, there is no issue of prescriptivism. It was well understood and frequently reiterated that the facts of usage are what they are, and that it is not the place of the grammarian to legislate. At stake was an entirely different matter, namely the problem of accounting for the facts of usage on the basis of explanatory hypotheses concerning the nature of language and, ultimately, the nature of human thought. Philosophical grammarians had little interest in the accumulation of data, except insofar as such data could be used as evidence bearing on deeper processes of great generality. The contrast, then, is not between descriptive and prescriptive grammar, but between description and explanation, between grammar as "natural history" and grammar as a kind of "natural philosophy" or, in modern terms, "natural science." A largely irrational objection to explanatory theories as such has made it difficult for

modern linguistics to appreciate what was actually at stake in these developments and has led to a confusion of philosophical grammar with the effort to
teach better manners to a rising middle class.

The whole matter is not without interest. I mentioned earlier that there are
striking similarities between the seventeenth-century climate of opinion and that
of contemporary cognitive psychology and linguistics. One point of similarity
has to do with precisely this matter of explanatory theory. Philosophical grammar, very much like current generative grammar, developed in self-conscious
opposition to a descriptive tradition that interpreted the task of the grammarian
to be merely that of recording and organizing the data of usage – a kind of
natural history. It maintained – quite correctly, I believe – that such a restriction
was debilitating and unnecessary and that, whatever justification it may have,
it has nothing to do with the method of science – which is typically concerned
with data not for itself but as evidence for deeper, hidden organizing principles,
principles that cannot be detected "in the phenomena" nor derived from them by
taxonomic data-processing operations, any more than the principles of celestial
mechanics could have been developed in conformity with such strictures.

Contemporary scholarship is not in a position to give a definitive assessment
of the achievements of philosophical grammar. The ground-work has not been
laid for such an assessment, the original work is all but unknown in itself, and
much of it is almost unobtainable. For example, I have been unable to locate a
single copy, in the United States, of the only critical edition of the Port-Royal
Grammar, produced over a century ago; and although the French original is
now once again available,[3] the one English translation of this important work
is apparently to be found only in the British Museum. It is a pity that this work
should have been so totally disregarded, since what little is known about it is
intriguing and quite illuminating.

This is not the place to attempt a preliminary assessment of this work or
even to sketch its major outlines as they now appear, on the basis of present,
quite inadequate knowledge. However, I do want to mention at least a few of
the persistent themes. It seems that one of the innovations of the Port-Royal
Grammar of 1660 – the work that initiated the tradition of philosophical grammar – was its recognition of the importance of the notion of the phrase as a
grammatical unit. Earlier grammar had been largely a grammar of word classes
and inflections. In the Cartesian theory of Port-Royal, a phrase corresponds to
a complex idea and a sentence is subdivided into consecutive phrases, which
are further subdivided into phrases, and so on, until the level of the word is
reached. In this way we derive what might be called the "surface structure" of
the sentence in question. To use what became a standard example, the sentence
"Invisible God created the visible world" contains the subject "invisible God"

[3] Menston, England: Scolar Press Limited, 1967.

and the predicate "created the visible world," the latter contains the complex idea "the visible world" and the verb "created," and so on. But it is interesting that although the Port-Royal *Grammar* is apparently the first to rely in a fairly systematic way on analysis into surface structure, it also recognized the inadequacy of such analysis. According to the Port-Royal theory, surface structure corresponds only to sound – to the corporeal aspect of language; but when the signal is produced, with its surface structure, there takes place a corresponding mental analysis into what we may call the deep structure, a formal structure that relates directly not to the sound but to the meaning. In the example just given, "Invisible God created the visible world," the deep structure consists of a system of three propositions, "that God is invisible," "that he created the world," "that the world is visible." The propositions that interrelate to form the deep structure are not, of course, asserted when the sentence is used to make a statement; if I say that a wise man is honest, I am not asserting that men are wise or honest, even though in the Port-Royal theory the propositions "a man is wise" and "a man is honest" enter into the deep structure. Rather, these propositions enter into the complex ideas that are present to the mind, though rarely articulated in the signal, when the sentence is uttered.

The deep structure is related to the surface structure by certain mental operations – in modern terminology, by grammatical transformations. Each language can be regarded as a particular relation between sound and meaning. Following the Port-Royal theory to its logical conclusions, then, the grammar of a language must contain a system of rules that characterizes deep and surface structures and the transformational relation between them, and – if it is to accommodate the creative aspect of language use – that does so over an infinite domain of paired deep and surface structures. To use the terminology Wilhelm von Humboldt used in the 1830s, the speaker makes infinite use of finite means. His grammar must, then, contain a finite system of rules that generates infinitely many deep and surface structures, appropriately related. It must also contain rules that relate these abstract structures to certain representations of sound and meaning – representations that, presumably, are constituted of elements that belong to universal phonetics and universal semantics, respectively. In essence, this is the concept of grammatical structure as it is being developed and elaborated today. Its roots are clearly to be found in the classical tradition that I am now discussing, and the basic concepts were explored with some success in this period.

The theory of deep and surface structure seems straightforward enough, at least in rough outline. Nevertheless, it was rather different from anything that preceded it, and, somewhat more surprising, it disappeared almost without a trace as modern linguistics developed in the late nineteenth century. I want to say just a word about the relationship of the theory of deep and surface structure to earlier and later thinking about language.

There is a similarity, which I think can be highly misleading, between the theory of deep and surface structure and a much older tradition. The practitioners of philosophical grammar were very careful to stress this similarity in their detailed development of the theory and had no hesitation in expressing their debt to classical grammar as well as to such major figures of renaissance grammar as the Spanish scholar Sanctius. Sanctius, in particular, had developed a theory of ellipsis that had great influence on philosophical grammar. As I have already remarked, philosophical grammar is poorly understood today. But such antecedents as Sanctius have fallen into total oblivion. Furthermore, as in the case of all such work, there is a problem of determining not only what he said but also, more importantly, what he meant.

There is no doubt that in developing his concept of ellipsis as a fundamental property of language, Sanctius gave many linguistic examples that superficially are closely parallel to those that were used to develop the theory of deep and surface structure, both in classical philosophical grammar and in its far more explicit modern variants. It means, however, that the concept of ellipsis is intended by Sanctius merely as a device for the interpretation of texts. Thus, to determine the true meaning of an actual literary passage one must very often, according to Sanctius, regard it as an elliptical variant of a more elaborate paraphrase. But the Port-Royal theory and its later development, particularly at the hands of the encyclopedist Du Marsais, gave a rather different interpretation to ellipsis. The clear intent of philosophical grammar was to develop a psychological theory, not a technique of textual interpretation. The theory holds that the underlying deep structure, with its abstract organization of linguistic forms, is "present to the mind," as the signal, with its surface structure, is produced or perceived by the bodily organs. And the transformational operations relating deep and surface structure are actual mental operations, performed by the mind when a sentence is produced or understood. The distinction is fundamental. Under the latter interpretation, it follows that there must be, represented in the mind, a fixed system of generative principles that characterize and associate deep and surface structures in some definite way – a grammar, in other words, that is used in some fashion as discourse is produced or interpreted. This grammar represents the underlying linguistic competence to which I referred earlier. The problem of determining the character of such grammars and the principles that govern them is a typical problem of science, perhaps very difficult, but in principle admitting of definite answers that are right or wrong as they do or do not correspond to the mental reality. But the theory of ellipsis as a technique of textual interpretation need not consist of a set of principles represented somehow in the mind as an aspect of normal human competence and intelligence. Rather, it can be in part ad hoc and can involve many cultural and personal factors relevant to the literary work under analysis.

The Port-Royal theory of deep and surface structure belongs to psychology as an attempt to elaborate Huarte's second type of wit, as an exploration of the properties of normal human intelligence. The concept of ellipsis in Sanctius, if I understand it correctly, is one of many techniques, to be applied as conditions warrant and having no necessary mental representation as an aspect of a normal intelligence. Although the linguistic examples used are often similar, the context in which they are introduced and the framework in which they fit are fundamentally different; in particular, they are separated by the Cartesian revolution. I propose this with some diffidence, because of the obscurity of the relevant texts and their intellectual backgrounds, but this interpretation seems to me correct.

The relation of the Port-Royal theory to modern structural and descriptive linguistics is somewhat clearer. The latter restricts itself to the analysis of what I have called surface structure, to formal properties that are explicit in the signal and to phrases and units that can be determined from the signal by techniques of segmentation and classification. This restriction is a perfectly self-conscious one, and it was regarded – I believe quite erroneously – as a great advance. The great Swiss linguist Ferdinand de Saussure, who at the turn of the century laid the groundwork for modern structural linguistics, put forth the view that the only proper methods of linguistic analysis are segmentation and classification. Applying these methods, the linguist determines the patterns into which the units so analyzed fall, where these patterns are either syntagmatic – that is, patterns of literal succession in the stream of speech – or paradigmatic – that is, relations among units that occupy the same position in the stream of speech. He held that when all such analysis is complete, the structure of the language is, of necessity, completely revealed, and the science of linguistics will have realized its task completely. Evidently, such taxonomic analysis leaves no place for deep structure in the sense of philosophical grammar. For example, the system of three propositions underlying the sentence "Invisible God created the visible world" cannot be derived from this sentence by segmentation and classification of segmented units, nor can the transformational operations relating the deep and surface structure, in this case, be expressed in terms of paradigmatic and syntagmatic structures. Modern structural linguistics has been faithful to these limitations, which were held to be necessary limitations.

In fact, Saussure in some respects even went beyond this in departing from the tradition of philosophical grammar. He occasionally expressed the view that processes of sentence formation do not belong to the system of language at all – that the system of language is restricted to such linguistic units as sounds and words and perhaps a few fixed phrases and a small number of very general patterns; the mechanisms of sentence formation are otherwise free from any constraint imposed by linguistic structure as such. Thus, in his terms, sentence formation is not strictly a matter of *langue*, but is rather assigned to what he called *parole*, and thus placed outside the scope of linguistics proper; it is a process of free creation, unconstrained by linguistic rule except insofar as such rules govern the forms of words and the patterns of sounds. Syntax, in this view, is a rather trivial matter. And, in fact, there is very little work in syntax throughout the period of structural linguistics.

In taking this position, Saussure echoed an important critique of Humboldtian linguistic theory by the distinguished American linguist William Dwight Whitney, who evidently greatly influenced Saussure. According to Whitney, Humboldtian linguistic theory, which in many ways extended the Cartesian views that I have been discussing, was fundamentally in error. Rather, a language is simply "made up of a vast number of items, each of which has its own time, occasion, and effect." He maintained that "language in the concrete sense . . . is . . . the sum of words and phrases by which any man expresses his thought"; the task of the linguist, then, is to list these linguistic forms and to study their individual histories. In contrast to philosophical grammar, Whitney argued that there is nothing universal about the form of language and that one can learn nothing about the general properties of human intelligence from the study of the arbitrary agglomeration of forms that constitutes a human language. As he put it, "The infinite diversity of human speech ought alone to be a sufficient bar to the assertion that an understanding of the powers of the soul involves the explanation of speech." Similarly, Delbrück, in the standard work on Indo-European comparative syntax, denounced traditional grammar for having set up ideal sentence types underlying the observed signals, referring to Sanctius as the "major dogmatist in this domain."

With the expression of such sentiments as these, we enter the modern age of the study of language. The death-knell of philosophical grammar was sounded with the remarkable successes of comparative Indo-European studies, which surely rank among the outstanding achievements of nineteenth-century science. The impoverished and thoroughly inadequate conception of language expressed by Whitney and Saussure and numerous others proved to be entirely appropriate to the current stage of linguistic research. As a result, this conception was held to be vindicated, a not unnatural but thoroughly mistaken conviction. Modern structural-descriptive linguistics developed within the same intellectual framework and also made substantial progress, to which I will return directly. In contrast, philosophical grammar did not provide appropriate concepts for the new comparative grammar or for the study of exotic languages unknown to the investigator, and it was, in a sense, exhausted. It had reached the limits of what could be achieved within the framework of the ideas and techniques that were available. There was no clear understanding a century ago as to how one might proceed to construct generative grammars that "make infinite use of finite means" and that express the "organic form" of human language, "that marvellous invention" (in the words of the Port-Royal *Grammar*) "by which we construct from twenty-five or thirty sounds an infinity of expressions, which, having no resemblance in themselves to what takes place in our minds, still enable us to let others know the secret of what we conceive and of all the various mental activities that we carry out."

Thus, the study of language had arrived at a situation in which there was, on the one hand, a set of simple concepts that provided the basis for some startling successes and, on the other, some deep but rather vague ideas that did not seem to lead to any further productive research. The outcome was inevitable and not at all to be deplored. There developed a professionalization of the field, a shift of interest away from the classical problems of general interest to intellectuals like Arnauld and Humboldt, for example, toward a new domain largely defined by the techniques that the profession itself has forged in the solution of certain problems. Such a development is natural and quite proper, but not without its dangers. Without wishing to exalt the cult of gentlemanly amateurism, one must nevertheless recognize that the classical issues have a liveliness and significance that may be lacking in an area of investigation that is determined by the applicability of certain tools and methods, rather than by problems that are of intrinsic interest in themselves.

The moral is not to abandon useful tools; rather, it is, first, that one should maintain enough perspective to be able to detect the arrival of that inevitable day when the research that can be conducted with these tools is no longer important; and, second, that one should value ideas and insights that are to the point, though perhaps premature and vague and not productive of research at a particular stage of technique and understanding. With the benefits of hindsight, I think we can now see clearly that the disparagement and neglect of a rich tradition proved in the long run to be quite harmful to the study of language. Furthermore, this disparagement and neglect were surely unnecessary. Perhaps it would have been psychologically difficult, but there is no reason in principle why the successful exploitation of the structuralist approach in historical and descriptive study could not have been coupled with a clear recognition of its essential limitations and its ultimate inadequacy, in comparison with the tradition it temporarily, and quite justifiably, displaced. Here, I think, lies a lesson that may be valuable for the future study of language and mind.

To conclude, I think there have been two really productive traditions of research that have unquestionable relevance to anyone concerned with the study of language today. One is the tradition of philosophical grammar that flourished from the seventeenth century through romanticism; the second is the tradition that I have rather misleadingly been referring to as "structuralist," which has dominated research for the past century, at least until the early 1950s. I have dwelt on the achievements of the former because of their unfamiliarity as well as their contemporary relevance. Structural linguistics has enormously broadened the scope of information available to us and has extended immeasurably the reliability of such data. It has shown that there are structural relations in language that can be studied abstractly. It has raised the precision of discourse about language to entirely new levels. But I think that its major contribution may prove to be one for which, paradoxically, it has been very severely criticized. I refer to the careful and serious attempt to construct "discovery procedures," those techniques of segmentation and classification to which Saussure referred. This attempt was a failure – I think that is now generally understood. It was a failure because such techniques are at best limited to the phenomena of surface structure and cannot, therefore, reveal the mechanisms that underlie the creative aspect of language use and the expression of semantic content. But what remains of fundamental importance is that this attempt was directed to the basic question in the study of language, which was for the first time formulated in a clear and intelligible way. The problem raised is that of specifying the mechanisms that operate on the data of sense and produce knowledge of language – linguistic competence. It is obvious that such mechanisms exist. Children do learn a first language; the language that they learn is, in the traditional sense, an "instituted language," not an innately specified system. The answer that was proposed in structural linguistic methodology has been shown to be incorrect, but this is of small importance when compared with the fact that the problem itself has now received a clear formulation.

Whitehead once described the mentality of modern science as having been forged through "the union of passionate interest in the detailed facts with equal devotion to abstract generalization." It is roughly accurate to describe modern linguistics as passionately interested in detailed fact, and philosophical grammar as equally devoted to abstract generalization. It seems to me that the time has arrived to unite these two major currents and to develop a synthesis that will draw from their respective achievements. In the next two lectures, I will try to illustrate how the tradition of philosophical grammar can be reconstituted and turned to new and challenging problems and how one can, finally, return in a productive way to the basic questions and concerns that gave rise to this tradition.

2 Linguistic contributions to the study of mind: present

One difficulty in the psychological sciences lies in the familiarity of the phenomena with which they deal. A certain intellectual effort is required to see how such phenomena can pose serious problems or call for intricate explanatory theories. One is inclined to take them for granted as necessary or somehow "natural."

The effects of this familiarity of phenomena have often been discussed. Wolfgang Köhler, for example, has suggested that psychologists do not open up "entirely new territories" in the manner of the natural sciences, "simply because man was acquainted with practically all territories of mental life a long time before the founding of scientific psychology . . . because at the very beginning of their work there were no entirely unknown mental facts left which they could have discovered."[1] The most elementary discoveries of classical physics have a certain shock value – man has no intuition about elliptical orbits or the gravitational constant. But "mental facts" of even a much deeper sort cannot be "discovered" by the psychologist, because they are a matter of intuitive acquaintance and, once pointed out, are obvious.

There is also a more subtle effect. Phenomena can be so familiar that we really do not see them at all, a matter that has been much discussed by literary theorists and philosophers. For example, Viktor Shklovskij in the early 1920s developed the idea that the function of poetic art is that of "making strange" the object depicted. "People living at the seashore grow so accustomed to the murmur of the waves that they never hear it. By the same token, we scarcely ever hear the words which we utter . . . We look at each other, but we do not see each other any more. Our perception of the world has withered away; what has remained is mere recognition." Thus, the goal of the artist is to transfer what is depicted to the "sphere of new perception"; as an example, Shklovskij cites a story by Tolstoy in which social customs and institutions are "made strange" by the device of presenting them from the viewpoint of a narrator who happens to be a horse.[2]

[1] W. Köhler, *Dynamics in Psychology* (New York: Liveright, 1940).
[2] See V. Ehrlich, *Russian Formalism*, 2nd rev. edn. (New York: Humanities, 1965), pp. 176–77.

The observation that "we look at each other, but we do not see each other any more" has perhaps itself achieved the status of "words which we utter but scarcely ever hear." But familiarity, in this case as well, should not obscure the importance of the insight.

Wittgenstein makes a similar observation, pointing out that "the aspects of things that are most important for us are hidden because of their simplicity and familiarity (one is unable to notice something – because it is always before one's eyes)."[3] He sets himself to "supplying . . . remarks on the natural history of human beings: we are not contributing curiosities however, but observations which no one has doubted, but which have escaped remark only because they are always before our eyes."[4]

Less noticed is the fact that we also lose sight of the need for explanation when phenomena are too familiar and "obvious." We tend too easily to assume that explanations must be transparent and close to the surface. The greatest defect of classical philosophy of mind, both rationalist and empiricist, seems to me to be its unquestioned assumption that the properties and content of the mind are accessible to introspection; it is surprising to see how rarely this assumption has been challenged, insofar as the organization and function of the intellectual faculties are concerned, even with the Freudian revolution. Correspondingly, the far-reaching studies of language that were carried out under the influence of Cartesian rationalism suffered from a failure to appreciate either the abstractness of those structures that are "present to the mind" when an utterance is produced or understood, or the length and complexity of the chain of operations that relate the mental structures expressing the semantic content of the utterance to the physical realization.

A similar defect mars the study of language and mind in the modern period. It seems to me that the essential weakness in the structuralist and behaviorist approaches to these topics is the faith in the shallowness of explanations, the belief that the mind must be simpler in its structure than any known physical organ and that the most primitive of assumptions must be adequate to explain whatever phenomena can be observed. Thus, it is taken for granted without argument or evidence (or is presented as true by definition) that a language is a "habit structure" or a network of associative connections, or that knowledge of language is merely a matter of "knowing how," a skill expressible as a system of dispositions to respond. Accordingly, knowledge of language must develop slowly through repetition and training, its apparent complexity resulting from the proliferation of very simple elements rather than from deeper principles of mental organization that may be as inaccessible to introspection

---

[3] Ludwig Wittgenstein, *Philosophical Investigations* (New York: Oxford University Press, 1953), Section 129.

[4] *Ibid.*, Section 415.

as the mechanisms of digestion or coordinated movement. Although there is nothing inherently unreasonable in an attempt to account for knowledge and use of language in these terms, it also has no particular plausibility or a priori justification. There is no reason to react with uneasiness or disbelief if study of the knowledge of language and use of this knowledge should lead in an entirely different direction.

I think that in order to achieve progress in the study of language and human cognitive faculties in general it is necessary first to establish "psychic distance" from the "mental facts" to which Köhler referred, and then to explore the possibilities for developing explanatory theories, whatever they may suggest with regard to the complexity and abstractness of the underlying mechanisms. We must recognize that even the most familiar phenomena require explanation and that we have no privileged access to the underlying mechanisms, no more so than in physiology or physics. Only the most preliminary and tentative hypotheses can be offered concerning the nature of language, its use, and its acquisition. As native speakers, we have a vast amount of data available to us. For just this reason it is easy to fall into the trap of believing that there is nothing to be explained, that whatever organizing principles and underlying mechanisms may exist must be "given" as the data is given. Nothing could be further from the truth, and an attempt to characterize precisely the system of rules we have mastered that enables us to understand new sentences and produce a new sentence on an appropriate occasion will quickly dispel any dogmatism on this matter. The search for explanatory theories must begin with an attempt to determine these systems of rules and to reveal the principles that govern them.

The person who has acquired knowledge of a language has internalized a system of rules that relate sound and meaning in a particular way. The linguist constructing a grammar of a language is in effect proposing a hypothesis concerning this internalized system. The linguist's hypothesis, if presented with sufficient explicitness and precision, will have certain empirical consequences with regard to the form of utterances and their interpretations by the native speaker. Evidently, knowledge of language – the internalized system of rules – is only one of the many factors that determine how an utterance will be used or understood in a particular situation. The linguist who is trying to determine what constitutes knowledge of a language – to construct a correct grammar – is studying one fundamental factor that is involved in performance, but not the only one. This idealization must be kept in mind when one is considering the problem of confirmation of grammars on the basis of empirical evidence. There is no reason why one should not also study the interaction of several factors involved in complex mental acts and underlying actual performance, but such a study is not likely to proceed very far unless the separate factors are themselves fairly well understood.

In a good sense, the grammar proposed by the linguist is an explanatory theory; it suggests an explanation for the fact that (under the idealization mentioned) a speaker of the language in question will perceive, interpret, form, or use an utterance in certain ways and not in other ways. One can also search for explanatory theories of a deeper sort. The native speaker has acquired a grammar on the basis of very restricted and degenerate evidence; the grammar has empirical consequences that extend far beyond the evidence. At one level, the phenomena with which the grammar deals are explained by the rules of the grammar itself and the interaction of these rules. At a deeper level, these same phenomena are explained by the principles that determine the selection of the grammar on the basis of the restricted and degenerate evidence available to the person who has acquired knowledge of the language, who has constructed for himself this particular grammar. The principles that determine the form of grammar and that select a grammar of the appropriate form on the basis of certain data constitute a subject that might, following a traditional usage, be termed "universal grammar." The study of universal grammar, so understood, is a study of the nature of human intellectual capacities. It tries to formulate the necessary and sufficient conditions that a system must meet to qualify as a potential human language, conditions that are not accidentally true of the existing human languages, but that are rather rooted in the human "language capacity," and thus constitute the innate organization that determines what counts as linguistic experience and what knowledge of language arises on the basis of this experience. Universal grammar, then, constitutes an explanatory theory of a much deeper sort than particular grammar, although the particular grammar of a language can also be regarded as an explanatory theory.[5]

In practice, the linguist is always involved in the study of both universal and particular grammar. When he constructs a descriptive, particular grammar in one way rather than another on the basis of what evidence he has available, he is guided, consciously or not, by certain assumptions as to the form of grammar, and these assumptions belong to the theory of universal grammar. Conversely, his formulation of principles of universal grammar must be justified by the study of their consequences when applied in particular grammars. Thus, at several levels the linguist is involved in the construction of explanatory theories, and at each level there is a clear psychological interpretation for his theoretical and descriptive work. At the level of particular grammar, he is attempting to characterize knowledge of a language, a certain cognitive system that has been developed – unconsciously, of course – by the normal speaker–hearer. At the level of universal grammar, he is trying to establish certain general properties

---

[5] To bring out this difference in depth of explanation, I have suggested in my *Current Issues in Linguistic Theory* (New York: Humanities, 1965) that the term "level of descriptive adequacy" might be used for the study of the relation between grammars and data and the term "level of explanatory adequacy" for the relation between a theory of universal grammar and these data.

of human intelligence. Linguistics, so characterized, is simply the subfield of psychology that deals with these aspects of mind.

I will try to give some indication of the kind of work now in progress that aims, on the one hand, to determine the systems of rules that constitute knowledge of a language, and on the other, to reveal the principles that govern these systems. Obviously, any conclusions that can be reached today regarding particular or universal grammar must be quite tentative and restricted in their coverage. And in a brief sketch such as this only the roughest outlines can be indicated. To try to give something of the flavor of what is being done today I will concentrate on problems that are current in that they can be formulated with some clarity and studied, though they still resist solution.

As I indicated in the first lecture, I believe that the most appropriate general framework for the study of problems of language and mind is the system of ideas developed as part of the rationalist psychology of the seventeenth and eighteenth centuries, elaborated in important respects by the romantics and then largely forgotten as attention shifted to other matters. According to this traditional conception, a system of propositions expressing the meaning of a sentence is produced in the mind as the sentence is realized as a physical signal, the two being related by certain formal operations that, in current terminology, we may call *grammatical transformations*. Continuing with current terminology, we can thus distinguish the *surface structure* of the sentence, the organization into categories and phrases that is directly associated with the physical signal, from the underlying *deep structure*, also a system of categories and phrases, but with a more abstract character. Thus, the surface structure of the sentence "A wise man is honest" might analyze it into the subject "a wise man" and the predicate "is honest." The deep structure, however, will be rather different. It will, in particular, extract from the complex idea that constitutes the subject of the surface structure an underlying proposition with the subject "man" and the predicate "be wise." In fact, the deep structure, in the traditional view, is a system of two propositions, neither of which is asserted, but which interrelate in such a way as to express the meaning of the sentence "A wise man is honest." We might represent the deep structure in this sample case by formula 1, and the surface structure by formula 2, where paired brackets are labeled to show the category of phrase that they bound. (Many details are omitted.)

1
$$_{S}\left[_{NP}\left[_{S}\text{a man}\left[_{NP}\text{[man]}_{NP}\,_{VP}\text{[is wise]}_{VP}\right]_{S}\right]_{NP}\,_{VP}\text{[is honest]}_{VP}\right]_{S}$$

2
$$_{S}\left[_{NP}\text{[a wise man]}_{NP}\,_{VP}\text{[is honest]}_{VP}\right]_{S}$$

An alternative and equivalent notation, widely used, expresses the labeled bracketing of 1 and 2 in tree form, as 1′ and 2′ respectively:

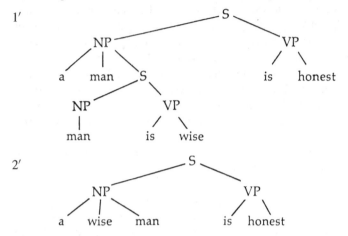

If we understand the relation "subject-of" to hold between a phrase of the category noun phrase (NP) and the sentence (S) that directly dominates it, and the relation "predicate-of" to hold between a phrase of the category verb phrase (VP) and the sentence that directly dominates it, then structures 1 and 2 (equivalently, 1′ and 2′) specify the grammatical functions of subject and predicate in the intended way. The grammatical functions of the deep structure (1) play a central role in determining the meaning of the sentence. The phrase structure indicated in 2, on the other hand, is closely related to its phonetic shape – specifically, it determines the intonation contour of the utterance represented.

Knowledge of a language involves the ability to assign deep and surface structures to an infinite range of sentences, to relate these structures appropriately, and to assign a semantic interpretation and a phonetic interpretation to the paired deep and surface structures. This outline of the nature of grammar seems to be quite accurate as a first approximation to the characterization of "knowledge of a language."

How are the deep and surface structures related? Clearly, in the simple example given, we can form the surface structure from the deep structure by performing such operations as the following:

3   a. assign the marker *wh-* to the most deeply embedded NP, "man"
     b. replace the NP so marked by "who"
     c. delete "who is"
     d. invert "man" and "wise."

Applying just operations a and b, we derive the structure underlying the sentence "a man who is wise is honest," which is one possible realization of the underlying structure (1). If, furthermore, we apply the operation c (deriving "a man wise is honest"), we must, in English, also apply the subsidiary operation d, deriving the surface structure (2), which can then be phonetically interpreted.

If this approach is correct in general, then a person who knows a specific language has control of a grammar that *generates* (that is, characterizes) the infinite set of potential deep structures, maps them onto associated surface structures, and determines the semantic and phonetic interpretations of these abstract objects.[6] From the information now available, it seems accurate to propose that the surface structure determines the phonetic interpretation completely and that the deep structure expresses those grammatical functions that play a role in determining the semantic interpretation, although certain aspects of the surface structure may also participate in determining the meaning of the sentence in ways that I will not discuss here. A grammar of this sort will therefore define a certain infinite correlation of sound and meaning. It constitutes a first step toward explaining how a person can understand an arbitrary sentence of his language.

Even this artificially simple example serves to illustrate some properties of grammars that appear to be general. An infinite class of deep structures much like 1 can be generated by very simple rules that express a few rudimentary grammatical functions, if we assign to these rules a recursive property – in particular, one that allows them to embed structures of the form [s . . .]s within other structures. Grammatical transformations will then iterate to form, ultimately, a surface structure that may be quite remote from the underlying deep structure. The deep structure may be highly abstract; it may have no close point-by-point correlation to the phonetic realization. Knowledge of a language – "linguistic competence," in the technical sense of this term discussed briefly in the first lecture – involves a mastery of these grammatical processes.

With just this much of a framework, we can begin to formulate some of the problems that call for analysis and explanation. One major problem is posed by the fact that the surface structure generally gives very little indication in itself of the meaning of the sentence. There are, for example, numerous sentences

---

[6] For a detailed development of this point of view, see J. Katz and P. Postal, *An Integrated Theory of Linguistic Descriptions* (Cambridge, Mass.: MIT Press, 1964) and my *Aspects of the Theory of Syntax* (Cambridge, Mass.: MIT Press, 1965). See also Peter S. Rosenbaum, *The Grammar of English Predicate Complement Constructions* (Cambridge, Mass.: MIT Press, 1967). These contain references to earlier work that they extend and modify. There has been a great deal of work in the past few years extending and modifying this general approach still further and exploring alternatives. At present the field is in considerable ferment, and it will probably be some time before the dust begins to settle and a number of outstanding issues are even tentatively resolved. Current work is too extensive for detailed reference to be called for in a sketch such as this. Some idea of its scope and general directions can be obtained from collections such as R. Jacobs and P. S. Rosenbaum, eds., *Readings in English Transformational Grammar* (Waltham, Mass.: Ginn and Company, 1970).

that are ambiguous in some way that is not indicated by the surface structure.
Consider sentence 4:

4   I disapprove of John's drinking.

This sentence can refer either to the fact of John's drinking or to its character.
The ambiguity is resolved, in different ways, in sentences 5 and 6:

5   I disapprove of John's drinking the beer.

6   I disapprove of John's excessive drinking.

It is clear that grammatical processes are involved. Notice that we cannot simultaneously extend 4 in both of the ways illustrated in 5 and 6; that would give
us 7:

7   *I disapprove of John's excessive drinking the beer.[7]

Our internalized grammar assigns two different abstract structures to 4, one
of which is related to the structure that underlies 5, the other to the structure
that underlies 6. Bu it is at the level of deep structure that the distinction is
represented; it is obliterated by the transformations that map the deep structures
onto the surface form associated with 4.

The processes that are involved in examples 4, 5, and 6 are quite common
in English. Thus, the sentence "I disapprove of John's cooking" may imply
either that I think his wife should cook or that I think he uses too much garlic,
for example. Again, the ambiguity is resolved if we extend the sentence in the
manner indicated in 5 and 6.

The fact that 7 is deviant requires explanation. The explanation in this case
would be provided, at the level of particular grammar, by formulation of the
grammatical rules that assign alternative deep structures and that in each case
permit one but not the other of the extensions to 5 or 6. We would then explain
the deviance of 7 and the ambiguity of 4 by attributing this system of rules to
the person who knows the language, as one aspect of his knowledge. We might,
of course, try to move to a deeper level of explanation, asking how it is that
the person has internalized these rules instead of others that would determine a
different sound–meaning correlation and a different class of generated surface
structures (including, perhaps, 7). This is a problem of universal grammar, in
the sense described earlier. Using the terminology of note 5, the discussion at
the level of particular grammar would be one of descriptive adequacy, and at the
level of universal grammar it would be one of explanatory adequacy.

Notice that the internalized rules of English grammar have still further consequences in a case like the one just discussed. There are transformations of great
generality that permit or require the deletion of repeated elements, in whole

---

[7] I use the asterisk in the conventional way, to indicate a sentence that deviates in some respect
from grammatical rule.

or in part, under well-defined conditions. Applied to structure 8, these rules derive 9.[8]

8   I don't like John's cooking any more than Bill's cooking.

9   I don't like John's cooking any more than Bill's.

Sentence 9 is ambiguous. It can mean either that I don't like the fact that John cooks any more than I like the fact that Bill cooks, or that I don't like the quality of John's cooking any more than I like the quality of Bill's cooking.[9] However, it cannot mean that I don't like the quality of John's cooking any more than I like the fact that Bill cooks, or conversely, with "fact" and "quality" interchanged. That is, in the underlying structure (8) we must understand the ambiguous phrases "John's cooking" and "Bill's cooking" in the same way if we are to be able to delete "cooking." It seems reasonable to assume that what is involved is some general condition on the applicability of deletion operations such as the one that gives 9 from 8, a rather abstract condition that takes into account not only the structure to which the operation applies but also the history of derivation of this structure.

Other examples can be found where a similar principle seems to be at work. Thus, consider sentence 10, which is presumably derived from either 11 or 12 and is therefore ambiguous:[10]

10   I know a taller man than Bill.

11   I know a taller man than Bill does.

12   I know a taller man than Bill is.

---

[8] Henceforth I shall generally delete brackets in giving a deep, surface, or intermediate structure, where this will not lead to confusion. One should think of 8 and 9 as each having a full labeled bracketing associated with it. Notice that 8 is not, of course, a deep structure, but rather the result of applying transformations to a more primitive abstract object.

[9] There may also be other interpretations, based on other ambiguities in the structure "John's cooking" – specifically, the cannibalistic interpretation and the interpretation of "cooking" as "that which is cooked."

[10] I should emphasize that when I speak of a sentence as derived by transformation from another sentence, I am speaking loosely and inaccurately. What I should say is that the structure associated with the first sentence is derived from the structure underlying the second. Thus, in the case now being discussed, it is the surface structure of 10 that is derived, on one analysis, from the abstract structure which, were it to undergo a different transformational development, would be converted into the surface structure of 11. That sentences are not derived from other sentences but rather from the structures underlying them has been explicitly assumed since the earliest work in transformational generative grammar about fifteen years ago, but informal statements such as those in the text here have misled many readers and have led to a good deal of confusion in the literature. Adding to the confusion, perhaps, is the fact that a very different theory of transformational relations developed by Zellig Harris, Henry Hiz, and others, does in fact regard the transformational operations as applied to sentences. See, for example, Z. S. Harris, "Co-occurrence and Transformation in Linguistic Structure," in *Language*, Vol. 33, No. 3, 1957, pp. 283-340, and many later publications. For me, and most other speakers, sentence 12 is deviant. Nevertheless, the association structure that underlies 10 under one analysis must be postulated, perhaps deriving from the structure associated with "I know a man who is taller than Bill is."

It seems clear that the ambiguity of 10 is not represented in the surface structure; the deletion of "does" in 11 leaves exactly the same structure as the deletion of "is" in 12. But now consider sentence 13.

13   I know a taller man than Bill, and so does John.

This sentence, like 9, is two-ways ambiguous rather than four-ways ambiguous. It can have the meaning of either 14 or 15, but not 16 or 17:[11]

14   I know a taller man than Bill does and John knows a taller man than Bill does.

15   I know a taller man than Bill is and John knows a taller man than Bill is.

16   I know a taller man than Bill is and John knows a taller man than Bill does.

17   I know a taller man than Bill does and John knows a taller man than Bill is.

But now a problem arises, as we can see by considering more carefully the derivation of 13. Let us refer to the deletion operation that gives 10 from 11 as T_1, and to the deletion operation that gives 10 from 12 as T_2. If we apply T_1 to each of the conjuncts of 14, we derive 18:

18   I know a taller man than Bill and John knows a taller man than Bill.

Application of T_2 to each of the conjuncts of 15 will also yield 18. But application of T_1 to one conjunct and T_2 to the other conjunct in 16 will also give 18, as will the same procedure (in the opposite order) when applied to the two conjuncts of 17. Thus, 18 can be derived by application of T_1 and T_2 to any of the four underlying forms, 14, 15, 16, or 17. The structure of 18 itself does not indicate which of these is the underlying form; the distinction has been eliminated by the deletion operations T_1 and T_2. But now consider the operation T_3, which derives "I saw Bill and so did John" from "I saw Bill and John saw Bill." Applying T_3 to 18, we derive 13. However, we have noted that 13 can

---

[11] It also cannot have the meaning "I know a taller man than Bill and John likes ice cream." Hence, if deep structure determines meaning (insofar as grammatical relations are involved), it must be that something like 14 or 15 is the immediately underlying structure for 13. It is a general property of deletion operations that some sort of recoverability is involved, a nontrivial matter with interesting empirical consequences. For some discussion, see my *Current Issues*, Section 2.2, and *Aspects*, Section 4.2.2. The problem posed by such examples as 9 and 13 was pointed out to me by John Ross. The first reference to the possibility that history of derivation may play a role in determining applicability of transformations appears in R. B. Lees, *The Grammar of English Nominalizations* (New York: Humanities, 1960), p. 76, in connection with his discussion – also the first – of the problem of identity of constituent structure as a factor in determining applicability of transformations.

have the interpretation of 14 or 15, but not of 16 or 17. Thus we can see that T_3 can apply to 18 only if either 14 or 15, but not 16 or 17, was the structure underlying 18 in the given derivations of 18. However, this information is not represented in 18 itself, as we have just observed. Therefore, to apply T_3 to 18 we must know something about the history of derivation of 18 – we must have information that would not be contained in the labeled bracketing of 18 itself. What we must know, in fact, is that the two conjuncts of 18 derive from underlying structures in which the same element was deleted.[12] It appears, once again, that some general condition on applicability of deletion transformations must be involved, a principle that somehow brings into consideration the history of derivation of deleted strings, perhaps certain properties of the deep structure from which they ultimately derive.

To see how complex the problem is, consider such sentences as "John's intelligence, which is his most remarkable quality, exceeds his prudence" or "The book, which weighs five pounds, was written by John." Presumably, the relative pronoun in the embedded appositive clause replaces a deleted noun phrase, and the condition on deletion that we are discussing implies that this noun phrase should be identical to the antecedent noun phrase "John's intelligence" or "the book" in the underlying structure of the appositive clause. In each case, however, it can be argued that there is a difference between the antecedent and the noun phrase of the appositive clause. Thus, in the first case, we are referring to the degree of John's intelligence in the main clause but to the quality of his intelligence in the embedded clause; and in the second case we are referring to the book as an abstract object in the main clause but as a concrete physical object in the embedded clause; one might expect these differences to be represented in deep structure, thus contradicting the principle to which we seem to be driven by the earlier examples. I will not go on with this discussion here, but the reader will discover, if he pursues the matter, that the problem is compounded when a richer class of cases is considered.

In fact, the correct principle is unknown in such cases as these, although some of the conditions it must meet are clear. The problem posed by these examples is a quite typical one. Attention to linguistic fact reveals certain properties of sentences, relating to their sound, their meaning, their deviance, and so on. Evidently no explanation for these facts will be forthcoming so long as we restrict ourselves to vague talk about "habits" and "skills" and "dispositions to respond," or about the formation of sentences "by analogy." We do not have the "habit" of understanding sentences 4, 9, and 13 in a certain way: it is unlikely that the reader has ever encountered sentences closely resembling these, but he understands them in a highly specific way nevertheless. To refer to

---

[12] If 18 itself is only two-ways ambiguous, a problem in fact arises at an even earlier point. The unnaturalness of 18 makes it difficult to determine this with any confidence.

the processes involved as "analogy" is simply to give a name to what remains a mystery. To explain such phenomena we must discover the rules that relate sound and meaning in the language in question – the grammar that has been internalized by the person who knows the language – and the general principles that determine the organization and function of these rules.

The misleading and inadequate character of surface structure becomes evident as soon as even the most simple patterns are studied. Consider, for example, sentence 19 – again, an artificially simple example:

19   John was persuaded to leave.

The deep structure underlying this sentence must indicate that the subject–predicate relation holds in an underlying proposition of the form of 20 (assuming grammatical functions to be represented in the same manner suggested earlier), and that the verb–object relation holds in an underlying proposition of the form of 21:

20     $\left[_S\left[_{NP}{}^{John}\right]_{NP}\left[_{VP}{}^{leave}\right]_{VP}\right]_S$

21     $\left[_S\left[_{NP}\cdots\right]_{NP}\left[_{VP}{}^{persuade}\left[_{NP}{}^{John}\right]_{NP}\right]_{VP}\right]_S$

Thus, "John" is understood to be the subject of "leave" and the object of "persuade" in 19, and these facts are properly expressed in the deep structure underlying 19 if this deep structure embodies the propositions informally represented as 20 and 21. Although the deep structure must be constituted of such propositions, if the approach loosely outlined earlier is correct, there is no trace of them in the surface structure of the utterance. The various transformations that produce 19 have thoroughly obliterated the system of grammatical relations and functions that determine the meaning of the sentence.

The point becomes still more obvious if we take note of the variety of sentences that seem superficially to resemble 19, but that differ widely in the ways they are understood and the formal operations that apply to them. Suppose that "persuaded" in 19 is replaced by one of the following words:[13]

22   expected, hired, tired, pleased, happy, lucky, eager, certain, easy

With "expected" replacing "persuaded," the sentence can mean roughly that the fact of John's leaving was expected; but it is impossible to speak of the fact of John's leaving being persuaded. With "hired," the sentence has an entirely different meaning, roughly that the purpose of hiring John was so that he would leave – an interpretation that becomes more natural if we replace "leave" by a phrase like "fix the roof." When "tired" is substituted, we derive a nonsentence;

---

[13] See R. B. Lees, "A Multiply Ambiguous Adjectival Construction in English," in *Language*, Vol. 36, No. 2, 1960, pp. 207-21, for a discussion of such structures.

it becomes a sentence if "too tired" replaces "persuaded," the sentence now implying that John didn't leave. The word "pleased" is still different. In this case we can have "too pleased," implying that John didn't leave, but we can also extend the sentence to "John was too pleased to leave to suit me," which is impossible in the earlier cases. "Happy" is rather like "pleased," though one might argue that the verb–object relation holds between "please" and "John." The sentence "John was lucky to leave" is interpreted in still another way. It means, roughly, that John was lucky in that he left, an interpretation that is impossible in the earlier cases; furthermore, we can construct such sentences as "John was a lucky fellow to leave (so early)," but none of the earlier examples can replace "lucky" in such sentences. "John was eager to leave" differs from the earlier cases in that it is formally associated with such expressions as "John was eager for Bill to leave" and "John's eagerness (for Bill) to leave." "John was certain to leave" can be paraphrased as "it was certain that John would leave"; of the other examples, only "expected" is subject to this interpretation, but "expected" obviously differs from "certain" in numerous other respects – for example, it appears in a sentence such as "They expected John to leave." The word "easy" is of course entirely different; in this and only this case the verb–object relation holds between "leave" and "John."

It is clear, in short, that the surface structure is often misleading and uninformative and that our knowledge of language involves properties of a much more abstract nature, not indicated directly in the surface structure. Furthermore, even such artificially simple examples as these show how hopeless it would be to try to account for linguistic competence in terms of "habits," "dispositions," "knowing how," and other concepts associated with the study of behavior, as this study has been circumscribed, quite without warrant, in recent years.

Even at the level of sound structure, there is evidence that abstract representations are formed and manipulated in the mental operations involved in language use. We have a more detailed understanding of the nature of linguistic representation and the intricate conditions on rule application in this domain than in any other. The work of the past few years on sound structure seems to me to provide substantial evidence in support of the view that the form of particular grammars is determined, in highly significant ways, by a restrictive schematism that specifies the choice of relevant phonetic properties, the kinds of rules that can relate surface structure to phonetic representation, and the conditions on organization and application of these rules. It thus relates closely to the general topics discussed in the first lecture, topics that I will take up again below in considering the question of how this restrictive, universal schematism comes to be used in language acquisition. Furthermore, these investigations of sound structure, insofar as they support the conclusion that abstract phonological structures are manipulated by tightly organized and intricate systems of rules, are relevant to the very interesting problem of developing empirically adequate models of performance. They suggest that all current approaches to problems of perception and organization of behavior suffer from a failure to attribute sufficient depth and complexity to the mental processes that must be represented in any model that attempts to come to grips with the empirical phenomena. Space does not permit a detailed development of these topics, either with respect to the matter of phonological structure or with respect to its potential significance for cognitive psychology.[14] However, one simple illustrative example, which is quite typical, may give some idea of the nature of the evidence that is available and the conclusions to which it points.

Recall that the syntactic rules of the language generate an infinite set of surface structures, each of which is a labeled bracketing of a string of minimal elements, such as 2, in which we may take the minimal elements to be the items *a*, *wise*, *man*, *is*, honest. Each of these items can itself be represented as a string of segments, for example *man* as the string of segments /m/, /æ/, /n/. Each of these segments may be regarded in turn as a set of specified features; thus, /m/ stands for the feature complex [+ consonantal], [− vocalic], [+ nasal], and so on. The segmental constitution of an item will be given by a lexical entry − a characterization of the inherent phonetic, semantic, and syntactic properties of the items in question. The lexicon of the language is the set of such lexical entries, with, perhaps, additional structure that need not concern us here. We are concerned now only with the phonetic properties of the lexical entry.

The lexical entry of an item must specify just those properties that are idiosyncratic, that are not determined by linguistic rule. For example, the lexical entry for *man* must indicate that its second segment is a low front vowel, but the degree of tenseness, diphthongization, nasalization, and so on, of this vowel need not be indicated in the lexical entry, since these are a matter of general rule, in part particular to various English dialects, in part common to all English dialects, in part a matter of universal phonology. Similarly, the lexical entry for *man* must indicate that it has an irregular plural, with the vowel shifting from low to mid. The segments of the lexical entry are abstract in the sense that the phonological rules of the language will frequently modify and elaborate them in a variety of ways; hence there need not be, in general, a simple point-by-point correspondence between the lexical entry and the actual phonetic representation. In discussing examples, I will use phonetic symbols in the usual way, each being regarded as a complex of a certain set of features. I will use the symbol / / to

---

[14] For discussion of these topics, see my article "Some General Properties of Phonological Rules," in *Language*, Vol. 47, No. 1, 1967. For a much fuller and more detailed discussion of phonological theory and its application to English, with examples drawn from many languages and some discussion of the history of the English sound system as well, see N. Chomsky and M. Halle, *The Sound Pattern of English* (New York: Harper & Row, 1968). The example in the text is discussed in detail, in the context of a more general framework of rules and principles, in Chapter 4, Section 4, of *The Sound Pattern of English*. See P. Postal, *Aspects of Phonological Theory* (New York: Harper & Row, 1968), for a general development of many related topics, along with a critical analysis of alternative approaches to the study of sound structure.

enclose lexical representations, and the symbol [ ] to enclose all representations derived from lexical representations by application of phonological rules, including, in particular, the final phonetic representation derived by application of the full set of phonological rules.

Consider first such words as *sign-signify*, *paradigm-paradigmatic*, and so on. For reasons that will become clearer as we proceed, it is the derived form, in this case, that is most closely related to the underlying abstract lexical representation. Suppose, then, that we tentatively assign to the stem in these forms the lexical representation /sign/ and /pærædigm/ where the symbols have their conventional phonetic interpretation. Thus, the underlying element /sign/ is realized as phonetic [sign] before -*ify*. However, it is realized as phonetic [sayn] in isolation. A similar observation holds of *paradigm*.

The forms of *sign* and *paradigm* in isolation are determined by certain phonological rules that, operating jointly, have the effect of converting the representation /ig/ to [ay] when followed by a word-final nasal. A careful analysis of English phonology shows that this process can be broken into a sequence of steps, including the following (the second and third of which, in fact, require further analysis).

23   a. velar becomes continuant before word-final nasal
        b. vowel + velar continuant becomes tense vowel
        c. /ī/ becomes [ay] (where /ī/ is the tense segment corresponding to [i])

Applying these rules to underlying /sign/ in isolation, we derive first [siɣn] (where [ɣ] is the velar continuant) by 23a; then [sīn] by 23b; and finally [sayn] by 24c.

Rules 23a and 23b are of little interest, but 23c is a part of a very general system of rules of "vowel shift" that is quite central to English phonology. There are, for example, strong reasons for supposing that the stem underlying the forms *divine-divinity* is /divīn/, where the segment /ī/ is weakened to [i] before -*ity* and becomes [ay] by rule 23c in isolation. Similarly, *reptile* derives from underlying /reptīl/, which becomes [reptayl] by 23c in isolation and [reptil] before -*ian*, with the same shortening of vowel that takes place in *divinity*; and so on, in many other cases.

Consider next such words as *ignite-ignition*, *expedite-expeditious*, and *contrite-contrition*. Just as *reptile* and *divine* derive, by vowel shift, from /reptīl/ and /divīn/, so we can derive the first member of each of these pairs from /ignīt/, /expedīt/, and /contrīt/, respectively. The rule that applies to give the phonetic realization is 23c, a special case of the general process of vowel shift. Evidently, the second member of each pair is derived by such processes as 24 and 25:

24   Vowels become nontense before -*ion*, -*ious*, -*ian*, -*ity*, and so on.

25   The segment /t/ followed by a high front vowel is realized as [š].

The first of these rules is the one that gives [divin] from /divīn/ in *divinity* and [reptil] from /reptīl/ in *reptilian*. Similarly, it gives [ignit] from /ignīt/ in *ignition*, [expedit] from /expedīt/ in *expeditious*, and [contrit] from /contīt/ in *contrition*. There is an obvious underlying generalization, namely that a vowel becomes nontense before an unstressed vowel that is not in a word-final syllable; when properly formulated, this rule, along with vowel shift and a few others, constitutes the central portion of the English phonological system.

The second rule, 25, applies to the element /ti/ in /ignition/, /expeditious/, and /contrition/, replacing it by [š] and giving, finally, the phonetic realizations [ignišən], [ekspədišəs], [kəntrišən], after the application of the rule that reduces unstressed vowels to [ə]. In short, the segments realized as [ayt] in *ignite*, *expedite*, and *contrite* are realized as [iš] in *ignition, expeditious*, and *contrition*.

But now consider the words *right-righteous*, phonetically [rayt]-[rayčəs]. The latter form appears to deviate from the regular pattern in two respects, namely in vowel quality (we would expect [i] rather than [ay], by rule 24), and in the final consonant of the stem (we would expect [š] rather than [č], by rule 25). If *right* were subject to the same processes as *expedite*, we would have [rišəs] rather than [rayčəs] as the phonetic realization, analogous to [ekspədišəs]. What is the explanation for this double deviation?

Notice first that rule 25 is not quite exact; there are, in fact, other cases in which /ti/ is realized as [č] rather than as [š], for example *question* [kwesčən], contrasted with *direction* [dərekšən]. A more accurate formulation of 25 would be 26:

26   /t/ followed by a high front vowel is realized as [č] after a continuant and as [š] elsewhere.

Returning to the form *right*, we see that the final consonant would be correctly determined as [č] rather than [š] if in the underlying representation there were a continuant preceding it – that is, if the underlying representation were /riφt/, where φ is some continuant. The continuant φ must, furthermore, be distinct from any of the continuants that actually appear phonetically in this position, namely the dental, labial, or palatal continuants in the unitalicized portion of *wrist, rift*, or *wished*. We may assume, then, that φ is the velar continuant /x/, which does not, of course, appear phonetically in English. The underlying form, then, would be /rixt/.

Consider now the derivation of *right*. By rule 23b, the representation /rixt/ becomes [rīt]. By rule 23c, the representation / rīt / becomes [rayt], which is the phonetic realization of *right*.

Consider next the derivation of *righteous*. Assuming that it has the same affix as *expeditious* and *repetitious*, we can represent it lexically as /rixtious/ (I do not concern myself here with the proper representation for *-ous*). Let us suppose that the ordering of the rules so far discussed is the following: 23a, 24, 26, 23b, 23c, an ordering consistent with other relevant facts of English, given certain simplifications for convenience of exposition. Rule 23a is inapplicable and rule 24 is vacuous, when applied to the underlying form /rixtious/. Turning to rule 26, we see that it gives the form [rixčous]. Rule 23b now applies, giving [rīčous], and rule 23c gives [rayčous], which becomes [rayčəs] by reduction of unstressed vowels. Thus by rules 26 and 23, which are independently motivated, the underlying representation /rixt/ will be realized phonetically as [rayt] in isolation and as [rayč] in *righteous*, exactly as required.

These facts strongly suggest that the underlying phonological representation must be /rixt/ (in accord with the orthography and, of course, the history). A sequence of rules that must be in the grammar for other reasons gives the alternation *right-righteous*. Therefore, this alternation is not at all exceptional, but rather perfectly regular. Of course, the underlying representation is quite abstract; it is connected with the superficial phonetic shape of the signal only by a sequence of interpretive rules.

Putting the matter differently, suppose that a person knows English but does not happen to have the vocabulary item *righteous*. Hearing this form for the first time, he must assimilate it to the system he has learned. If he were presented with the derived form [rišəs], he would, of course, take the underlying representation to be exactly like that of *expedite*, *contrite*, and so on. But hearing [rayčəs], he knows that this representation is impossible; although the consonantal distinction [š]-[č] might easily be missed under ordinary conditions of language use, the vocalic distinction [i]-[ay] would surely be obvious. Knowing the rules of English and hearing the vocalic element [ay] instead of [i], he knows that either the form is a unique exception or it contains a sequence /i/ followed by velar and is subject to rule 26. The velar must be a continuant,[15] that is, /x/. But given that the velar is a continuant, it follows, if the form is regular (the null hypothesis, always), that the consonant must be [č], not [š], by rule 26. Thus, the hearer should perceive [rayčəs] rather than [rayšəs], even if the information as to the medial consonant is lacking in the received signal. Furthermore, the pressure to preserve regularity of alternations should act to block the superficial analogy to *expedite-expeditious* and *ignite-ignition*, and to preserve [č] as the phonetic realization of underlying /t/, as long as [ay] appears in place of expected [i], exactly as we observe to have occurred.

I do not mean this as a literal step-by-step account of how the form is learned, of course, but rather as a possible explanation of why the form resists a superficial (and in fact incorrect) analogy and preserves its status. We can explain the

---

[15]   If it were a noncontinuant, it would have to be unvoiced, that is, /k/, since there are no voiced–voiceless consonant clusters in final position, by general rule. But it cannot be /k/, since /k/ remains in this position (for example, "direct," "evict," and so on).

perception and preservation in the grammar of the [č]-[š] contrast in *righteous-expeditious* on the basis of the perceived distinction between [ay] and [i] and the knowledge of a certain system of rules. The explanation rests on the assumption that the underlying representations are quite abstract, and the evidence cited suggests that this assumption is, in fact, correct.

A single example can hardly carry much conviction. A careful investigation of sound structure, however, shows that there are a number of examples of this sort, and that, in general, highly abstract underlying structures are related to phonetic representations by a long sequence of rules, just as on the syntactic level abstract deep structures are in general related to surface structures by a long sequence of grammatical transformations. Assuming the existence of abstract mental representations and interpretive operations of this sort, we can find a surprising degree of organization underlying what appears superficially to be a chaotic arrangement of data, and in certain cases we can also explain why linguistic expressions are heard, used, and understood in certain ways. One cannot hope to determine either the underlying abstract forms or the processes that relate them to signals by introspection; there is, furthermore, no reason why one should find this consequence in any way surprising.

The explanation sketched above is at the level of particular rather than universal grammar, as this distinction was formulated earlier. That is, we have accounted for a certain phenomenon on the basis of the assumption that certain rules appear in the internalized grammar, noting that these rules are, for the most part, independently motivated. Of course, considerations of universal grammar enter into this explanation insofar as they affect the choice of grammar on the basis of data. This interpenetration is unavoidable, as noted earlier. There are cases, however, where explicit principles of universal grammar enter more directly and clearly into a pattern of explanation. Thus, investigation of sound systems reveals certain very general principles of organization, some quite remarkable, governing phonological rules (see references in note 14). For example, it has been observed that certain phonological rules operate in a cycle, in a manner determined by the surface structure. Recall that the surface structure can be represented as a labeled bracketing of the utterance, such as 2. In English, the very intricate phonological rules that determine stress contours and vowel reduction apply to phrases bounded by paired brackets, in the surface structure, applying first to a minimal phrase of this sort, then to the next larger phrase, and so on, until the maximal domain of phonological processes is reached (in simple cases, the sentence itself). Thus, in the case of 2 the rules apply to the individual words (which, in a full description, would be assigned to categories and therefore bracketed), then to the phrases *a wise man* and *is honest*, and finally to the whole sentence. A few simple rules will give quite varied results, as the surface structures that determine their cyclic application vary.

Some simple effects of the principle of cyclic application are illustrated by such forms as those of 27:

27   a. *relaxation, emendation, elasticity, connectivity*
       b. *illustration, demonstration, devastation, anecdotal*

The unitalicized vowels are reduced to [ə] in 27b, but they retain their original quality in 27a. In some cases, we can determine the original quality of the reduced vowels of 27b from other derived forms (for example, *illustrative, demonstrative*). The examples of 27a differ from those of 27b morphologically in that the former are derived from underlying forms (namely, *relax, emend, elastic, connective*) that contain primary stress on the unitalicized vowel when these underlying forms appear in isolation; those of 27b do not have this property. It is not difficult to show that vowel reduction in English, the replacement of a vowel by [ə], is contingent upon lack of stress. We can therefore account for the distinction between 27a and 27b by assuming the cyclic principle just formulated. In the case of 27a, on the first, innermost cycle, stress will be assigned by general rules to the unitalicized vowels. On the next cycle, stress is shifted,[16] but the abstract stress assigned on the first cycle is sufficient to protect the vowel from reduction. In the examples of 27b, earlier cycles never assign an abstract stress to the unitalicized vowel, which thus reduces. Observe that it is an *abstract* stress that protects the vowel from reduction. The actual, phonetic stress on the unitalicized nonreduced vowels is very weak; it would be stress 4, in the usual convention. In general, vowels with this weak a phonetic stress reduce, but in this case the abstract stress assigned in the earlier cycle prevents reduction. Thus, it is the abstract underlying representation that determines the phonetic form, a primary role being played by the abstract stress that is virtually eliminated in the phonetic form.

In this case, we can provide an explanation for a certain aspect of perception and articulation in terms of a very general abstract principle, namely the principle of cyclic application of rules (see page 38). It is difficult to imagine how the language learner might derive this principle by "induction" from the data presented to him. In fact, many of the effects of this principle relate to perception and have little or no analogue in the physical signal itself, under normal conditions of language use, so that the phenomena on which the induction would have been based cannot be part of the experience of one who is not already making use of the principle. In fact, there is no procedure of induction or association that offers any hope of leading from such data as is available to a principle of this sort (unless, begging the question, we introduce the principle of cyclic application into the "inductive procedure" in some manner). Therefore, the conclusion

---

[16] In "connectivity," it is on the third cycle that the stress is shifted. The second cycle merely reassigns stress to the same syllable that is stressed on the first cycle.

seems warranted that the principle of cyclic application of phonological rules is an innate organizing principle of universal grammar that is used in determining the character of linguistic experience and in constructing a grammar that constitutes the acquired knowledge of language. At the same time, this principle of universal grammar offers an explanation for such phenomena as were noted in 27.

There is some evidence that a similar principle of cyclic application applies also on the syntactic level. John Ross has presented an ingenious analysis of some aspects of English pronominalization illustrating this.[17] Let us assume that pronominalization involves a process of "deletion" analogous to those processes discussed earlier in connection with examples 8– 18. This process, to first approximation, replaces one of two identical noun phrases by an appropriate pronoun. Thus, the underlying structure 28 will be converted into 29, by pronominalization.

28   John learned that John had won.

29   John learned that he had won.

Abstracting away from properties of 28 that are not essential to this discussion, we can present it in the form 30, where x and y are the identical noun phrases and y is the one pronominalized, and where the brackets bound sentential expressions.

30     $[\ldots x \ldots [\ldots y \ldots]]$

Notice that we cannot form 31 from 28 by pronominalization:[18]

31   He learned that John had won.

That is, we cannot have pronominalization in the case that would be represented as 32, using the conventions of 30:

32     $[\ldots y \ldots [\ldots x \ldots]]$

Consider next the sentences of 33:

33   a. That John won the race surprised him.
          $[[\ldots x \ldots] \ldots y \ldots]$

       b. John's winning the race surprised him.
          $[[\ldots x \ldots] \ldots y \ldots]$

[17] J. Ross, "On the Cyclic Nature of English Pronominalization," in *To Honor Roman Jakobson* (New York: Humanities, 1967).
[18] Of course, 31 is a sentence, but "he" in the sentence does not refer to John as it does in 29. Thus, 31 is not formed by pronominalization if the two occurrences of "John" are intended to be different in reference. We exclude this case from discussion here. For some remarks bearing on this problem, see my *Aspects*, pp. 144–47.

    c. That he won the race surprised John.

$$[[\ldots y \ldots] \ldots x \ldots]$$

    d. His winning the race surprised John.

$$[[\ldots y \ldots] \ldots x \ldots]$$

Continuing with the same conventions, the forms are represented underneath, in each case. Summarizing, we see that of the possible types 30, 32, 33a, b and 33c, d, all permit pronominalization except 32. These remarks belong to the particular grammar of English.

Notice that alongside 33d we also have sentence 34:

34   Winning the race surprised John.

Given the framework we have been assuming throughout, 34 must be derived from the structure "John's winning the race surprised John." Hence, in this case pronominalization can be a full deletion.

Consider now sentences 35 and 36:

35   Our learning that John had won the race surprised him.

36   Learning that John had won the race surprised him.

Sentence 35 can be understood with "him" referring to John, but 36 cannot. Thus, 35 can be derived by pronominalization from 37, but 36 is not derived from 28:

37    $\Big[$ [Our learning [that John had won the race]] surprised John. $\Big]$

38    $\Big[$ [John's learning [that John had won the race]] surprised John. $\Big]$

What might be the explanation for this phenomenon? As Ross observes, it can be explained in terms of the particular grammar of English if we assume, in addition, that certain transformations apply in a cycle, first to innermost phrases, then to larger phrases, and so on – that is, if we assume that these transformations apply to the deep structure by a process analogous to the process by which phonological rules apply to the surface structure.[19] Making this assumption, let

---

[19] That transformational rules may be supposed to function in this way, itself a nontrivial fact if true, is suggested in my *Aspects*, Chapter 3. Ross's observation suggests that this principle of application is not only possible but also necessary. Other interesting arguments to this effect are presented in R. Jacobs and P. S. Rosenbaum, eds., *Readings in English Transformational Grammar*, Chapter 28. The matter is far from settled. In general, understanding of syntactic structure is much more limited than that of phonological structure, descriptions are much more rudimentary, and, correspondingly, principles of universal syntax are much less firmly established than principles of universal phonology, though the latter, needless to say, must also be regarded as tentative. In part, this may be due to the inherent complexity of the subject matter.

us consider the underlying structure 38. On the innermost cycle, pronominal-ization does not apply at all, since there is no second noun phrase identical to "John" in the most deeply embedded proposition. On the second cycle, we consider the phrase "[John's learning [that John had won the race]]." This can be regarded as a structure of the form 30, giving 39 by pronominalization; it cannot be regarded as of the form 32, giving 40 by pronominalization, because the particular grammar of English does not permit pronominalization in the case of 32, as we have noted:

39   John's learning [that he had won the race]

40   his learning [that John had won the race]

But 40 would have to be the form underlying 36. Hence, 36 cannot be derived by pronominalization from 38, although 35 can be derived from 37.

In this case, then, a principle of universal grammar combines with an independently established rule of particular English grammar to yield a certain rather surprising empirical consequence, namely that 35 and 36 must differ in the referential interpretation of the pronoun "him." Once again, as in the formally somewhat analogous case of vowel reduction discussed earlier in connection with examples 27a and 27b, it is quite impossible to provide an explanation in terms of "habits" and "dispositions" and "analogy." Rather, it seems that certain abstract and in part universal principles governing human mental faculties must be postulated to explain the phenomena in question. If the principle of cyclic application is indeed a regulative principle determining the form of knowl-edge of language for humans, a person who has learned the particular rules governing pronominalization in English would know, intuitively and without instruction or additional evidence, that 35 and 36 differ in the respect just noted.

The most challenging theoretical problem in linguistics is that of discovering the principles of universal grammar that interweave with the rules of particular grammars to provide explanations for phenomena that appear arbitrary and chaotic. Probably the most persuasive examples at this time (and also the most important ones, in that the principles involved are highly abstract and their operations quite intricate) are in the domain of phonology, but these are too complex to present within the scope of this lecture.[20] Another syntactic example

In part, it results from the fact that universal phonetics, which provides a kind of "empirical control" for phonological theory, is much more firmly grounded than universal semantics, which should, in principle, provide a partially analogous control for syntactic theory. In modern linguistics, phonetics (and, in part, phonology) has been studied in considerable depth and with much success, but the same cannot be said as yet for semantics, despite much interesting work.

[20] See references in note 14. The issue is discussed in a general way in my "Explanatory Models in Linguistics," in E. Nagel, P. Suppes, and A. Tarski, eds., *Logic, Methodology, and Philosophy of Science* (Stanford, Calif.: Stanford University Press, 1962); in my *Current Issues*, Section 2; in my *Aspects*, Chapter 1; and in other publications referred to in these references.

that illustrates the general problem in a fairly simple way is provided by the rules for formation of *wh*-questions in English.[21]

Consider such sentences as the following:

41   a. Who expected Bill to meet Tom?
      b. Who(m) did John expect to meet Tom?
      c. Who(m) did John expect Bill to meet?
      d. What (books) did you order John to ask Bill to persuade his friends to stop reading?

As examples a, b, and c show, a noun phrase in any of the three italicized positions in a sentence such as *"John* expected *Bill* to meet *Tom"* can be questioned. The process is essentially this:

42   a. *wh-placement:* assign the marker *wh-* to a noun phrase.
      b. *wh-inversion:* place the marked noun phrase at the beginning of the sentence.
      c. *auxiliary attraction:* move a part of the verbal auxiliary or the copula to the second position in the sentence.
      d. *phonological interpretation:* replace the marked noun phrase by an appropriate interrogative form.[22]

All four of these processes apply nonvacuously in the case of 41b and 41c. Sentence 41b, for example, is formed by applying *wh-placement* to the noun phrase "someone" in "John expected someone to meet Tom." Application of the process of *wh-inversion* (42b) gives "*wh*-someone John expected to meet Tom." The process of *auxiliary attraction* (42c) gives "*wh*-someone did John expect to meet Tom." Finally, the process of *phonological interpretation* (42d) gives 41b. Sentence 41d illustrates the fact that these processes can extract a noun phrase that is deeply embedded in a sentence – without limit, in fact.

Of the processes listed in 42, all but auxiliary attraction apply as well in the formation of relative clauses, giving such phrases as "the man who(m) John expected to meet Tom," and so on.

---

[21] This matter is discussed in my *Current Issues.* There are several versions of this monograph. The first, presented at the International Congress of Linguistics, 1962, appears in the *Proceedings of the Congress* with the title of the session at which it was presented, "Logical Basis of Linguistic Theory," ed. H. Lunt (New York: Humanities, 1964); a second appears in J. Fodor and J. J. Katz, eds., *Structure of Language: Readings in the Philosophy of Language* (Englewood Cliffs, N.J.: Prentice-Hall, 1964); the third, as a separate monograph (New York: Humanities, 1965). These versions differ in the treatment of the examples discussed here; none of the treatments is satisfactory, and the general problem remains open. New and interesting ideas on this matter are presented in J. Ross, "Constraints on Variables in Syntax," MIT doctoral thesis (unpublished). I follow here the general lines of the earliest of the three versions of *Current Issues,* which, in retrospect, seems to me to offer the most promising approach of the three.

[22] Actually, it seems that only indefinite singular noun phrases can be questioned (that is, "someone," "something," and so on), a fact that relates to the matter of recoverability of deletion mentioned in note 11. See my *Current Issues* for some discussion.

Notice, however, that there are certain restrictions on the formation of questions and relatives in this manner. Consider, for example, the sentences of 43:

43   a. For him to understand *this lecture* is difficult.
        b. It is difficult for him to understand *this lecture*.
        c. He read the book that interested *the boy*.
        d. He believed the claim that John tricked *the boy*.
        e. He believed the claim that John made about *the boy*.
        f. They intercepted John's message to *the boy*.

Suppose that we try applying the processes of interrogative and relative formation to the italicized noun phrases in 43. We should derive the following interrogatives and relatives from 43a–43f, respectively:

44   aI. *What is for him to understand difficult?
        aR. *a lecture that for him to understand is difficult
        bI. What is it difficult for him to understand?
        bR. a lecture that it is difficult for him to understand
        cI. *Who did he read the book that interested?
        cR. *the boy who he read the book that interested
        dI. *Who did he believe the claim that John tricked?
        dR. *the boy who he believed the claim that John tricked
        eI. *Who did he believe the claim that John made about?
        eR. *the boy who he believed the claim that John made about
        fI. *Who did they intercept John's message to?
        fR. *the boy who they intercepted John's message to

Of these, only bI and bR are fully acceptable, and cases a, c, d, and e are quite impossible, although it would be quite clear what they meant, were they grammatically permissible. It is not at all obvious how the speaker of English knows this to be so. Thus, sentences 43a and 43b are synonymous, yet only 43b is subject to the processes in question. And although these processes do not apply to 43d and 43f, they can be applied, with much more acceptable results, to the very similar sentences 45a and 45b:

45   a. He believed that John tricked *the boy*. (Who did he believe that
           John tricked? – the boy who he believed that John tricked)
        b. They intercepted a message to *the boy*. (Who did they intercept a
           message to? – the boy who they intercepted a message to)

In some unknown way, the speaker of English devises the principles of 42 on the basis of data available to him; still more mysterious, however, is the fact that he knows under what formal conditions these principles are applicable. It can hardly be seriously maintained that every normal speaker of English has had his behavior "shaped" in the indicated ways by appropriate reinforcement. The sentences of 43, 44, and 45 are as "unfamiliar" as the vast majority of those that we encounter in daily life, yet we know intuitively, without instruction or awareness, how they are to be treated by the system of grammatical rules that we have mastered.

It seems, once again, that there is a general principle that accounts for many such facts. Notice that in 43a the italicized noun phrase is contained within another noun phrase, namely "for him to understand this lecture," which is the subject of the sentence. In 43b, however, a rule of *extraposition* has placed the phrase "for him to understand this lecture" outside of the subject noun phrase, and in the resulting structure this phrase is not a noun phrase at all, so that the italicized phrase in 43b is no longer contained within a noun phrase. Suppose we were to impose on grammatical transformations the condition that no noun phrase can be extracted from within another noun phrase – more generally, that if a transformation applies to a structure of the form

$$[S \ldots [A \ldots] A \ldots] S$$

for any category A, then it must be so interpreted as to apply to the *maximal* phrase of the type A.[23] Then the processes of 42 would be blocked, as required, in cases 43a, c, d , e, and f, but not in 43b. We will return shortly to 45.

There are other examples that support a principle of this sort, which we will refer to as the *A-over-A* principle. Consider the sentences of 46:

46   a. John kept the car in *the garage.*
       b. Mary saw the man walking toward *the railroad station.*

Each of these is ambiguous. Thus, 46a can mean that the car in the garage was kept by John, or that the car was kept in the garage by John. In the first case, the italicized phrase is part of a noun phrase, "the car in the garage"; in the latter case it is not. Similarly, 46b can mean that the man walking toward the railroad station was seen by Mary, or that the man was seen walking toward the railroad station by Mary (or, irrelevantly to this discussion, that Mary, while walking toward the railroad station, saw the man). Again, in the first case, the italicized phrase is part of a noun phrase, "the man walking toward the railroad station"; in the latter case, it is not. But now consider the two interrogatives of 47:

47   a. What (garage) did John keep the car in?
       b. What did Mary see the man walking toward?

---

[23] We might extend this principle to the effect that this transformation must also apply to the *minimal* phrase of the type S (sentence). Thus, the sentence

$$\left[{}_S \text{ John was convinced that } [{}_S \text{ Bill would leave before dark}]{}_S \right]{}_S$$

can be transformed to "John was convinced that before dark Bill would leave" but not to "before dark John was convinced that Bill would leave," which must have a different source. Like the original principle, this extension is not without its problems, but it has a certain amount of support nevertheless.

Each of these is unambiguous and can have only the interpretation of the underlying sentence in which the italicized phrase is not part of another noun phrase. The same is true of the relatives formed from 46, and these facts too would be explained by the A-over-A principle. There are many similar examples.

A slightly more subtle case that might, perhaps, be explained along the same lines is provided by such sentences as 48 and 49:

48   John has the best proof of that theorem.

49   What theorem does John have the best proof of?

In its most natural interpretation, sentence 48 describes a situation in which a number of people have proofs of that theorem, and John's is the best. The sense thus suggests that "best" modifies the nominal phrase "proof of that theorem," which contains another nominal phrase, "that theorem."[24] The A-over-A principle would therefore imply that the phrase "that theorem" not be subject to the processes of 42. Hence, 49 would not be derived by these processes from 48. And, in fact, sentence 49 has an interpretation rather different from that of 48. Sentence 49 is appropriate to a situation in which John has proofs of a number of theorems, and the questioner is asking which of these proofs is the best. The underlying structure, whatever it may be, would associate "best" with "proof," not with "proof of that theorem," so that "that theorem" is not embedded within a phrase of the same type and is therefore subject to questioning (and, similarly, to relativization).

The general principle just proposed has a certain explanatory force, as such examples illustrate. If postulated as a principle of universal grammar, it can explain why the particular rules of English operate to generate certain sentences while rejecting others, and to assign sound–meaning relations in ways that appear, superficially, to violate regular analogies. Putting the matter in different terms, if we assume that the A-over-A principle is a part of the innate schematism that determines the form of knowledge of language, we can account for certain aspects of the knowledge of English possessed by speakers who obviously have not been trained and who have not even been presented with data bearing on the phenomena in question in any relevant way, so far as can be ascertained.

Further analysis of data of English reveals, not unexpectedly, that this account is oversimplified and runs up against many difficulties. Consider, for example, sentences 50 and 51:

---

[24] Space does not permit a discussion of the distinction implied here in the loose terminology, "noun phrase"–"nominal phrase," but this is not crucial to the point at issue. See my "Remarks on Nominalization," in R. Jacobs and P. S. Rosenbaum, eds., *Readings in English Transformational Grammar.* There are other interpretations of 49 (for example, with contrastive stress on "John"), and there are many open problems relating to such structures as these.

50   John thought (that) Bill had read *the book.*

51   John wondered why Bill had read *the book.*

In the case of 50, the italicized phrase is subject to interrogation and relativization, but not in the case of 51. It is unclear whether the phrases "that Bill had
read the book" and "why Bill had read the book" are noun phrases. Suppose
that they are not. Then sentence 50 is handled in accordance with the A-over-A
principle, but not 51. To explain the blocking of the processes of 42 in the case
of 51, we would have to assign the phrase "why Bill had read the book" to the
same category as "the book." In fact, there is a natural suggestion along these
lines. Sentence 51 is typical in that the phrase from which the noun phrase is to
be extracted is itself a *wh-* phrase, rather than a *that-* phrase. Suppose that the
process of *wh-* placement (42a) assigns the element *wh-* not only to "the book"
in 51 but also to the proposition containing it. Thus, both "*wh-* the book" and
"why Bill had read the book" belong to the category *wh-*, which would now be
regarded as a syntactic feature of a sort discussed in my *Aspects of the Theory of
Syntax*, Chapter 2 (see note 6). Under these assumptions, the A-over-A principle
will serve to explain the difference between 50 and 51.

Suppose that the phrases in question are noun phrases. Now it is 50, not 51,
that poses the problem. Assuming that our analysis is correct so far, there must
be some rule that assigns to the proposition "that Bill had read the book" a
property of "transparency" that permits noun phrases to be extracted from it
even though it is a noun phrase. There are, in fact, other examples that suggest
the necessity for such a rule, presumably a rule of the particular grammar of
English. Thus, consider sentences 52, 53, and 54:

52   Who would you approve of my seeing?

53   What would you approve of John's drinking?

54   *What would you approve of John's excessive drinking of?

Sentences 52 and 53 are formed by applying the processes of interrogation
to a noun phrase contained in the larger phrases "my seeing –," "John's
drinking –." Hence, these larger noun phrases are transparent to the extraction operation. However, as 54 indicates, the italicized noun phrase in 55 is not
transparent to this operation:

55   You would approve of John's excessive drinking of the beer.

These examples are typical of many that suggest what the rule might be that
assigns transparency. Earlier we discussed sentence 56 (sentence 4), pointing
out that it is ambiguous:

56   I disapprove of John's drinking.

Under one interpretation, the phrase "John's drinking" has the internal structure of a noun phrase. Thus, the rule that inserts adjectives (**3d**) between a determiner and a noun applies, giving "John's excessive drinking"; and, in fact, other determiners may replace "John's" – "the," "that," "much of that," and so on. Under this interpretation, the phrase "John's drinking" behaves exactly like "John's refusal to leave," "John's rejection of the offer," and so on. Under the other interpretation, "John's drinking (the beer)" does not have the internal structure of a noun phrase and is handled analogously to "John's having read the book," "John's refusing to leave," "John's rejecting the offer," and so on, none of which permits adjective insertion or replacement of "John's" by other determiners. Suppose that we postulate a rule of English grammar that assigns transparency, in the sense just defined, to noun phrases that are also propositions lacking the internal structure of noun phrases. Thus, the phrases "that Bill had read the book" in 50, "my seeing –" in the structure underlying 52, and "John's drinking –" in the structure underlying 53 would be assigned transparency; more precisely, the dominant noun phrase in these examples would not serve to block extraction by the A-over-A principle. In sentence 51, extraction would still be blocked by the category *wh-*, along the lines indicated earlier. And sentence 54 is ruled out because the relevant noun phrase of the underlying structure, "John's excessive drinking of –," does have the internal structure of a noun phrase, as just noted, and therefore is not subject to the special rule of English grammar that assigns transparency to the category NP when this category dominates a proposition that lacks the internal structure of an NP.

There are a few other cases that suggest the need for rules of particular grammar assigning transparency in this sense. Consider sentences 57 and 58:

57   a. They intercepted John's message to *the boy*. (Sentence 43f)
      b. He saw John's picture of *Bill*.
      c. He saw the picture of *Bill*.

58   a. They intercepted a message to *the boy*. (Sentence 45b)
      b. He saw a picture of *Bill*.
      c. He has a belief in *justice*.
      d. He has faith in *Bill's integrity*.

The italicized noun phrases in 57 are not subject to the processes of interrogation and relativization, in accordance with the A-over-A principle, as we have already noted. In the case of 58, interrogation and relativization seem much more natural in these positions, at least in informal spoken English. Thus, the noun phrases containing the italicized phrases must be assigned transparency. It seems that what is involved is indefiniteness of the dominating noun phrase; if so, then for certain dialects there is a rule assigning transparency to a noun phrase of the form

59   [NP indefinite . . . NP]NP

There remain a number of very serious problems that seem to resist solution by such extensions and modifications of the A-over-A principle. Notice that this principle is formulated in a way that is not really well supported by the examples so far given. If the A-over-A principle were true in general, we would expect to find cases in which a phrase of category A cannot be extracted from a larger phrase of category A, for various choices of A. In fact, the examples given so far involve only A = noun phrase (or, perhaps, A = [+ *wh*-], as in the discussion of 51). Hence, an alternative formulation of the principle consistent with the facts just noted would assign nontransparency as an ad hoc property of certain types of noun phrases (and perhaps other constructions), rather than as a property of a category A dominating another category of the type A. Given just the facts so far presented, it would be proper to postulate the A-over-A principle instead of this alternative precisely because the A-over-A principle has a certain naturalness, whereas the alternative is entirely ad hoc, a listing of nontransparent structures. But there is crucial evidence, pointed out by John Ross (see reference in note 21), suggesting that the A-over-A principle is not correct. Ross points out that in the constructions from which noun phrases cannot be extracted, adjectives also cannot be extracted. Thus, consider the contexts "I believe that John saw –," "I believe the claim that John saw –," and "I wonder whether John saw –." From the first of these, but not the second or third, we can extract a noun phrase in interrogation or relativization, a fact that we have been attempting to account for by modifications of the A-over-A principle. But the same is true of extraction of adjectives. Thus we can form "handsome though I believe that John is," but not *"handsome though I believe the claim that John is," *"handsome though I wonder whether John is," etc. Whether one can extend the approach just discussed to account for this problem in some natural way, I do not know; at the moment, I see no approach that does not involve a perfectly ad hoc step. Perhaps this indicates that the approach through the A-over-A principle is incorrect, leaving us for the moment with only a collection of constructions in which extraction is, for some reason, impossible to accomplish.

Whatever the answer will prove to be, the complex of problems just discussed is a typical and important illustration of the kind of topic that is at the border of research today, in the sense mentioned at the outset of this lecture: that is, certain problems can be formulated clearly within a framework of ideas that is reasonably clear and well understood; certain partial solutions can be advanced; and a range of examples can be discovered where these solutions fail, leaving open for the time being the question whether what is needed is further elaboration and sharpening or a radically different approach.

I have so far discussed several kinds of conditions that transformations must meet: conditions of deletion, of the sort brought out by examples 8–18; the principle of cyclic application, illustrated by the discussion of examples 28–40 (with the phonological analogue discussed in connection with 27); and the

A-over-A principle that was proposed as the basis for an explanation of such phenomena as are illustrated by examples 44–58. In each case, there is some reason to believe that the principle is appropriate, though there is no lack of evidence showing that the principle is inadequately formulated or, perhaps, misconceived. As a final illustration of this state of affairs, typical of the borderline of research that exists in linguistics as in any other field, consider a problem first discussed by Peter Rosenbaum (see reference in note 6). Consider the sentences of 60:

60   a. John agreed to go.
        b. John persuaded Bill to leave.
        c. Finding Tom there caused Bill to wonder about John.

In interpreting these sentences, we supply a "missing subject" for the verbs "go," "leave," and "find," respectively. In 60a, we understand the subject of "go" to be "John"; in 60b, we understand the subject of "leave" to be "Bill"; in 60c, we understand the subject of "find" and the subject of "wonder" to be "Bill." In terms of the framework presupposed so far, it would be natural (though perhaps not necessary, as we will see below) to regard this missing subject as the actual subject in the deep structure, eliminated by a deletion operation. Thus, the underlying deep structures might be something like 61:

61   a. John agreed [John go]
        b. John persuaded Bill [Bill leave]
        c. [Bill find Tom there] caused Bill to wonder about John

On the other hand, the facts indicate clearly that the sentences of 60 cannot derive from, say, 62:

62   a. John agreed [someone go]
        b. John persuaded Bill [John leave]
        c. [John find Tom there] caused Bill to wonder about John

It would be difficult to argue that in such cases there is an intrinsic semantic consideration ruling against such structures as 62. For example, one might interpret 62a as meaning that John agreed that someone should go; 62b as meaning that John persuaded Bill that he (John) would (should) leave; 62c as meaning that John's finding Tom there caused Bill to wonder about John. There must be some general syntactic principle that rules against 62 as possible sources for 60 and that causes us to interpret 60 as based rather on 61. Rosenbaum suggests that what is involved is a certain condition on deletion operations, an "erasure principle" that prescribes roughly that the subject of an embedded proposition is deleted by the nearest noun phrase outside of this proposition, "nearness" being measured in terms of the number of branches in a representation such as

1′ or 2′.[25] As he shows, a great many examples of varied sorts can be explained on this general assumption, which, like the others that I have been reviewing, involves a condition on transformations that would constitute part of universal grammar.

Here too, however, certain problems arise. Consider, for example, the following cases:[26]

63   John promised Bill to leave.

64   a. John gave me the impression of working on that problem.
            b. John gave me the suggestion of working on that problem.

65   a. John asked me what to wear.
            b. John told me what to wear.

66   John asked Bill for permission to leave.

67   a. John begged Bill to permit him to stay.
            b. John begged Bill to be permitted to stay.
            c. John begged Bill to be shown the new book.

68   John made an offer to Bill (received advice from Bill, received an invitation from Bill) to stay.

69   John helped Bill write the book.

Sentence 63 violates the principle, since it is John, not Bill, who is to leave. In 64a, "John" is understood to be the subject of "work," whereas in the apparently analogous sentence 64b the subject is understood to be "I." In the case of 65a, it is "John" that is the understood subject of "wear"; in 65b, it is "I." In the case of 66, "John" is the understood subject of "leave" and "Bill" of "permit," underlying "permission," presumably; in the case of 67a, "Bill" is the understood surface subject of the embedded proposition, but in 67b and 67c it is "John," although "Bill" is the "nearest" noun phrase in all three cases, in Rosenbaum's sense. In 68, it is "John" that is understood as the subject of "stay," in apparent contradiction to the principle, though much depends on unresolved questions as to how these sentences are to be analyzed. The case of 69 is obscure in other ways. The erasure principle would suggest that "Bill" is the subject of "write," although of course the sentence does not imply that Bill wrote the book – rather John and Bill did, together. But there is a difficulty in pursuing this interpretation. Thus, from 69 we can conclude that John helped

---

[25] In yet-unpublished work, David Perlmutter has presented a strong argument that what is involved is not a condition on transformations but rather a condition on well-formed deep structures. The distinction is not crucial for what follows but would become important at a less superficial level of discussion.

[26] Examples 63 and 67 are discussed by Rosenbaum; 64 was pointed out by Maurice Gross; 65 was pointed out in a different connection by Zeno Vendler, "Nominalizations," in *Transformations and Discourse Analysis Papers*, No. 55 (Philadelphia: University of Pennsylvania, 1964), p. 67.

write the book, but from the apparently analogous sentence "John helped the cat have kittens," we cannot deduce that "John helped have kittens," which is deviant, a fact that suggests that somehow there must be a grammatical relation between "John" and "write" in 69. To put it differently, the problem is how to account for "John helped write the book" as analogous to 60a, since obviously the analogue to 61a won't do as a source.

Without pursuing the matter any further, we can see that although the erasure principle has much to recommend it and is probably somehow involved in the correct solution to this network of problems, there is much evidence still to be accounted for. As in the other cases mentioned, there are a variety of problems relating to the conditions that determine applicability of transformations, problems that still resist any near-definitive solution, though some interesting and illuminating proposals can be made that seem to go part of the way toward a general solution.

In discussing the nature of grammatical operations, I have restricted myself to syntactic and phonological examples, avoiding questions of semantic interpretation. If a grammar is to characterize the full linguistic competence of the speaker–hearer, it must comprise rules of semantic interpretation as well, but little is known of any depth regarding this aspect of grammar. In the references cited earlier (see note 6), it is proposed that a grammar consists of a syntactic component that specifies an infinite set of paired deep and surface structures and expresses the transformational relationship between these paired elements, a phonological component that assigns a phonetic representation to the surface structure, and a semantic component that assigns a semantic representation to the deep structure. As noted earlier (p. 27; see also pp. 94–97), I think there is strong evidence that aspects of the surface structure are also relevant to semantic interpretation.[27] However this may be, there can be little doubt that a full grammar must contain fairly intricate rules of semantic interpretation, keyed, at least in part, to fairly specific properties of the lexical items and formal structures of the language in question. To mention just one example, consider sentence 70:

70   John has lived in Princeton.

From the assumption that this sentence has been properly used to make a statement, we can conclude that John is a person (one would not say that his dog has lived in Princeton); that Princeton is a place meeting certain physical and

---

[27] For some remarks concerning this problem, see my "Surface Structure and Semantic Interpretation," in R. Jakobson, ed., *Studies in General and Oriental Linguistics* (Tokyo: TEC Corporation for Language and Educational Research, 1970). Literature on semantic interpretation of syntactic structures is expanding fairly rapidly. For recent discussion, see J. J. Katz, *The Philosophy of Language* (New York: Harper & Row, 1966); U. Weinreich, "Explorations in Semantic Theory," in T. A. Sebeok, ed., *Current Trends in Linguistics*, Vol. III (New York: Humanities, 1966); J. J. Katz, "Recent Issues in Semantic Theory," in *Foundations of Language*, Vol. 3, No. 2, May 1967, pp. 124–94; and many other papers.

sociological conditions (given that "Princeton" is a proper noun); that John is now alive (I can say that I have lived in Princeton, but I cannot now say "Einstein has lived in Princeton" – rather, "Einstein lived in Princeton"); and so on. The semantic interpretation of 70 must be such as to account for these facts.

In part, such questions as these might be subsumed under a still-to-be-developed universal semantics, in which concepts and their relations are analyzed in a very general way; to take a classical example, it might be argued that the relation of meaning between "John is proud of what Bill did" and "John has some responsibility for Bill's actions" should be explained in terms of the universal concepts of pride and responsibility, just as on the level of sound structure one might appeal to a principle of universal phonetics to account for the fact that when a velar consonant becomes palatal it ordinarily becomes strident (see references in note 14, for discussion). The proposal looks less attractive when applied to the case of 70, for example, with respect to the fact that proper use of 70 implies that John is now alive. When we try to pursue such questions, we soon become lost in a tangle of confused issues and murky problems, and it is difficult to propose answers that carry any conviction. For this reason, I am unable to discuss conditions on rules of semantic interpretation that might be analogous to the conditions on syntactic and phonological rules mentioned earlier.

Observe that I might well have been mistaken in the preceding remarks in assuming that the topics discussed belong to syntax rather than to the semantic component of a grammar, or to some domain in which semantic and syntactic rules interpenetrate. The issues are too clouded for us to be able to say that this is an empirical question, as matters now stand; but when they are sharpened, we may find that an empirical question can be posed. Consider, for example, the discussion of the erasure principle in syntax. Joseph Emonds has suggested (in unpublished work) that it is incorrect to assume, as I did, that the sentences of 60 are interpreted through reference to the underlying structures of 61. Rather, he argues that what I took to be the embedded proposition has no subject at all in the underlying form generated by the syntactic component, and a general rule of semantic interpretation takes the place of Rosenbaum's erasure principle. Whether this is correct I do not know, but it is certainly a possibility. We can expect, as research continues into problems of grammar, that the boundaries that seem clear today may shift in unpredictable ways, or that some new basis for the organization of grammar may replace the framework that now seems appropriate.

The conditions on grammatical rules that I have been discussing are complex and only partially understood. It should be emphasized, however, that even some of the simplest and clearest conditions of the form of grammar are in no sense necessary properties of a system that fulfills the functions of human language. Correspondingly, the fact that they hold true of human languages in general and play a role in the acquired linguistic competence of the speaker–hearer cannot be lightly dismissed. Consider, for example, the simple fact that grammatical transformations are invariably *structure-dependent* in the sense that they apply to a string of words[28] by virtue of the organization of these words into phrases. It is easy to imagine *structure-independent* operations that apply to a string of elements quite independently of its abstract structure as a system of phrases. For example, the rule that forms the interrogatives of 71 from the corresponding declaratives of 72 (see note 10) is a structure-dependent rule interchanging a noun phrase with the first element of the auxiliary.

71   a. Will the members of the audience who enjoyed the play stand?
      b. Has Mary lived in Princeton?
      c. Will the subjects who will act as controls be paid?

72   a. The members of the audience who enjoyed the play will stand.
      b. Mary has lived in Princeton.
      c. The subjects who will act as controls will be paid.

In contrast, consider the operation that inverts the first and last words of a sentence, or that arranges the words of a sentence in increasing length in terms of phonetic segments ("alphabetizing" in some specified way for items of the same length), or that moves the left-most occurrence of the word "will" to the extreme left – call these O_1, O_2, and O_3, respectively. Applying O_1 to 72a, we derive 73a; applying O_2 to 72b, we derive 73b; applying O_3 to 72c, we derive 73c:

73   a. stand the members of the audience who enjoyed the play will
      b. in has lived Mary Princeton
      c. will the subjects who act as controls will be paid

The operations O_1, O_2, and O_3 are structure-independent. Innumerable other operations of this sort can be specified.

There is no a priori reason why human language should make use exclusively of structure-dependent operations, such as English interrogation, instead of structure-independent operations, such as O_1, O_2, and O_3. One can hardly argue that the latter are more "complex" in some absolute sense; nor can they be shown to be more productive of ambiguity or more harmful to communicative efficiency. Yet no human language contains structure-independent operations among (or replacing) the structure-dependent grammatical transformations. The language-learner knows that the operation that gives 71 is a possible candidate for a grammar, whereas O_1, O_2, and O_3, and any operations like them, need not be considered as tentative hypotheses.

---

[28] More properly, to a string of minimal linguistic units that may or may not be words.

If we establish the proper "psychic distance" from such elementary and commonplace phenomena as these, we will see that they really pose some nontrivial problems for human psychology. We can speculate about the reason for the reliance on structure-dependent operations,[29] but we must recognize that any such speculation must involve assumptions regarding human cognitive capacities that are by no means obvious or necessary. And it is difficult to avoid the conclusion that whatever its function may be, the reliance on structure-dependent operations must be predetermined for the language-learner by a restrictive initial schematism of some sort that directs his attempts to acquire linguistic competence. Similar conclusions seem to me warranted, a fortiori, in the case of the deeper and more intricate principles discussed earlier, whatever their exact form may turn out to be.

To summarize: along the lines that have been outlined here, we might develop on the one hand a system of general principles of universal grammar,[30] and on the other, particular grammars that are formed and interpreted in accordance with these principles. The interplay of universal principles and particular rules leads to empirical consequences such as those we have illustrated; at various levels of depth, these rules and principles provide explanations for facts about linguistic competence – the knowledge of language possessed by each normal speaker – and about some of the ways in which this knowledge is put to use in the performance of the speaker or hearer.

The principles of universal grammar provide a highly restrictive schema to which any human language must conform, as well as specific conditions determining how the grammar of any such language can be used. It is easy to imagine alternatives to the conditions that have been formulated (or those that are often tacitly assumed). These conditions have in the past generally escaped notice, and we know very little about them today. If we manage to establish the appropriate "psychic distance" from the relevant phenomena and succeed in "making them strange" to ourselves, we see at once that they pose very serious problems that cannot be talked or defined out of existence. Careful consideration of such problems as those sketched here indicates that to account for the normal

---

[29] See G. A. Miller and N. Chomsky, "Finitary Models of Language Users, Part II," in R. D. Luce, R. Bush, and E. Galanter, eds., *Handbook of Mathematical Psychology*, Vol. II (New York: Wiley, 1963), for some proposals regarding this matter.

[30] Notice that we are interpreting "universal grammar" as a system of conditions on grammars. It may involve a skeletal substructure of rules that any human language must contain, but it also incorporates conditions that must be met by such grammars and principles that determine how they are interpreted. This formulation is something of a departure from a traditional view that took universal grammar to be simply a substructure of each particular grammar, a system of rules at the very core of each grammar. This traditional view has also received expression in recent work. It seems to me to have little merit. As far as information is available, there are heavy constraints on the form and interpretation of grammar at all levels, from the deep structures of syntax, through the transformational component, to the rules that interpret syntactic structures semantically and phonetically.

use of language we must attribute to the speaker–hearer an intricate system of rules that involve mental operations of a very abstract nature, applying to representations that are quite remote from the physical signal. We observe, furthermore, that knowledge of language is acquired on the basis of degenerate and restricted data and that it is to a large extent independent of intelligence and of wide variations in individual experience.

If a scientist were faced with the problem of determining the nature of a device of unknown properties that operates on data of the sort available to a child and gives as "output" (that is, as a "final state of the device," in this case) a particular grammar of the sort that it seems necessary to attribute to the person who knows the language, he would naturally search for inherent principles of organization that determine the form of the output on the basis of the limited data available. There is no reason to adopt a more prejudiced or dogmatic view when the device of unknown properties is the human mind; specifically, there is no reason to suppose, in advance of any argument, that the general empiricist assumptions that have dominated speculation about these matters have any particular privileged claim. No one has succeeded in showing why the highly specific empiricist assumptions about how knowledge is acquired should be taken seriously. They appear to offer no way to describe or account for the most characteristic and normal constructions of human intelligence, such as linguistic competence. On the other hand, certain highly specific assumptions about particular and universal grammar give some hope of accounting for the phenomena that we face when we consider knowledge and use of language. Speculating about the future, it seems not unlikely that continued research along the lines indicated here will bring to light a highly restrictive schematism that determines both the content of experience and the nature of the knowledge that arises from it, thus vindicating and elaborating some traditional thinking about problems of language and mind. It is to this matter, among others, that I shall turn in the final lecture.

3 Linguistic contributions to the study of mind: future

In discussing the past, I referred to two major traditions that have enriched the study of language in their separate and very different ways; and in my last lecture, I tried to give some indication of the topics that seem on the immediate horizon today, as a kind of synthesis of philosophical grammar and structural linguistics begins to take shape. Each of the major traditions of study and speculation that I have been using as a point of reference was associated with a certain characteristic approach to the problems of mind; we might say, without distortion, that each evolved as a specific branch of the psychology of its time, to which it made a distinctive contribution.

It may seem a bit paradoxical to speak of structural linguistics in this way, given its militant anti-psychologism. But the paradox is lessened when we take note of the fact that this militant anti-psychologism is no less true of much of contemporary psychology itself, particularly of those branches that until a few years ago monopolized the study of use and acquisition of language. We live, after all, in the age of "behavioral science," not of "the science of mind." I do not want to read too much into a terminological innovation, but I think that there is some significance in the ease and willingness with which modern thinking about man and society accepts the designation "behavioral science." No sane person has ever doubted that behavior provides much of the evidence for this study – all of the evidence, if we interpret "behavior" in a sufficiently loose sense. But the term "behavioral science" suggests a not-so-subtle shift of emphasis toward the evidence itself and away from the deeper underlying principles and abstract mental structures that might be illuminated by the evidence of behavior. It is as if natural science were to be designated "the science of meter readings." What, in fact, would we expect of natural science in a culture that was satisfied to accept this designation for its activities?

Behavioral science has been much preoccupied with data and organization of data, and it has even seen itself as a kind of technology of control of behavior. Anti-mentalism in linguistics and in philosophy of language conforms to this shift of orientation. As I mentioned in my first lecture, I think that one major indirect contribution of modern structural linguistics results from its success in making explicit the assumptions of an anti-mentalistic, thoroughly operational

57

and behaviorist approach to the phenomena of language. By extending this approach to its natural limits, it laid the groundwork for a fairly conclusive demonstration of the inadequacy of any such approach to the problems of mind.

More generally, I think that the long-range significance of the study of language lies in the fact that in this study it is possible to give a relatively sharp and clear formulation of some of the central questions of psychology and to bring a mass of evidence to bear on them. What is more, the study of language is, for the moment, unique in the combination it affords of richness of data and susceptibility to sharp formulation of basic issues.

It would, of course, be silly to try to predict the future of research, and it will be understood that I do not intend the subtitle of this lecture to be taken very seriously. Nevertheless, it is fair to suppose that the major contribution of the study of language will lie in the understanding it can provide as to the character of mental processes and the structures they form and manipulate. Therefore, instead of speculating on the likely course of research into the problems that are coming into focus today,[1] I will concentrate here on some of the issues that arise when we try to develop the study of linguistic structure as a chapter of human psychology.

It is quite natural to expect that a concern for language will remain central to the study of human nature, as it has been in the past. Anyone concerned with the study of human nature and human capacities must somehow come to grips with the fact that all normal humans acquire language, whereas acquisition of even its barest rudiments is quite beyond the capacities of an otherwise intelligent ape – a fact that was emphasized, quite correctly, in Cartesian philosophy.[2] It is widely thought that the extensive modern studies of animal communication challenge this classical view; and it is almost universally taken

[1] A number of such problems might be enumerated – for example, the problem of how the intrinsic content of phonetic features determines the functioning of phonological rules, the role of universal formal conditions in restricting the choice of grammars and the empirical interpretation of such grammars, the relations of syntactic and semantic structure, the nature of universal semantics, performance models that incorporate generative grammars, and so on.

[2] Modern attempts to train apes in behavior that the investigators regard as language-like confirm this incapacity, though it may be that the failures are to be attributed to the technique of operant conditioning and therefore show little about the animal's actual abilities. See, for example, the report by C. B. Ferster, "Arithmetic Behavior in Chimpanzees," in *Scientific American*, May 1964, pp. 98–106. Ferster attempted to teach chimpanzees to match the binary numbers 001, . . . , 111 to sets of one to seven objects. He reports that hundreds of thousands of trials were required for 95 percent accuracy to be achieved, even in this trivial task. Of course, even at this stage the apes had not learned the principle of binary arithmetic; they would not, for example, be able to match a four-digit binary number correctly, and, presumably, they would have done just as badly in the experiment had it involved an arbitrary association of the binary numbers to sets rather than the association determined by the principle of the binary notation. Ferster overlooks this crucial point and therefore concludes, mistakenly, that he has taught the rudiments of symbolic behavior. The confusion is compounded by his definition of language as "a set of symbolic stimuli that control behavior" and by his strange belief that the "effectiveness" of language arises from the fact that utterances "control almost identical performances in speaker and listener."

for granted that there exists a problem of explaining the "evolution" of human language from systems of animal communication. However, a careful look at recent studies of animal communication seems to me to provide little support for these assumptions. Rather, these studies simply bring out even more clearly the extent to which human language appears to be a unique phenomenon, without significant analogue in the animal world. If this is so, it is quite senseless to raise the problem of explaining the evolution of human language from more primitive systems of communication that appear at lower levels of intellectual capacity. The issue is important, and I would like to dwell on it for a moment.

The assumption that human language evolved from more primitive systems is developed in an interesting way by Karl Popper in his recently published Arthur Compton Lecture, "Clouds and Clocks." He tries to show how problems of freedom of will and Cartesian dualism can be solved by the analysis of this "evolution." I am not concerned now with the philosophical conclusions that he draws from this analysis, but with the basic assumption that there is an evolutionary development of language from simpler systems of the sort that one discovers in other organisms. Popper argues that the evolution of language passed through several stages, in particular a "lower stage" in which vocal gestures are used for expression of emotional state, for example, and a "higher stage" in which articulated sound is used for expression of thought – in Popper's terms, for description and critical argument. His discussion of stages of evolution of language suggests a kind of continuity, but in fact he establishes no relation between the lower and higher stages and does not suggest a mechanism whereby transition can take place from one stage to the next. In short, he gives no argument to show that the stages belong to a single evolutionary process. In fact, it is difficult to see what links these stages at all (except for the metaphorical use of the term "language"). There is no reason to suppose that the "gaps" are bridgeable. There is no more of a basis for assuming an evolutionary development of "higher" from "lower" stages, in this case, than there is for assuming an evolutionary development from breathing to walking; the stages have no significant analogy, it appears, and seem to involve entirely different processes and principles.

A more explicit discussion of the relation between human language and animal communication systems appears in a recent discussion by the comparative ethologist W. H. Thorpe.[3] He points out that mammals other than man appear to lack the human ability to imitate sounds, and that one might therefore have expected birds (many of which have this ability to a remarkable extent) to

---

[3] W. H. Thorpe, "Animal Vocalization and Communication," in F. L. Darley, ed., *Brain Mechanisms Underlying Speech and Language* (New York: Grune and Stratton, 1967), pp. 2–10 and the discussions on pp. 19 and 84–85.

be "the group which ought to have been able to evolve language in the true sense, and not the mammals." Thorpe does not suggest that human language "evolved" in any strict sense from simpler systems, but he does argue that the characteristic properties of human language can be found in animal communication systems, although "we cannot at the moment say definitely that they are all present in one particular animal." The characteristics shared by human and animal language are the properties of being "purposive," "syntactic," and "propositional." Language is purposive "in that there is nearly always in human speech a definite intention of getting something over to somebody else, altering his behavior, his thoughts, or his general attitude toward a situation." Human language is "syntactic" in that an utterance is a performance with an internal organization, with structure and coherence. It is "propositional" in that it transmits information. In this sense, then, both human language and animal communication are purposive, syntactic, and propositional.

All this may be true, but it establishes very little, since when we move to the level of abstraction at which human language and animal communication fall together, almost all other behavior is included as well. Consider walking: clearly, walking is purposive behavior, in the most general sense of "purposive." Walking is also "syntactic" in the sense just defined, as, in fact, Karl Lashley pointed out a long time ago in his important discussion of serial order in behavior, to which I referred in the first lecture.[4] Furthermore, it can certainly be informative; for example, I can signal my interest in reaching a certain goal by the speed or intensity with which I walk.

It is, incidentally, precisely in this manner that the examples of animal communication that Thorpe presents are "propositional." He cites as an example the song of the European robin, in which the rate of alternation of high and low pitch signals the intention of the bird to defend its territory; the higher the rate of alternation, the greater the intention to defend the territory. The example is interesting, but it seems to me to show very clearly the hopelessness of the attempt to relate human language to animal communication. Every animal communication system that is known (if we disregard some science fiction about dolphins) uses one of two basic principles: either it consists of a fixed, finite number of signals, each associated with a specific range of behavior or emotional state, as is illustrated in the extensive primate studies that have been carried out by Japanese scientists for the past several years; or it makes use of a fixed, finite number of linguistic dimensions, each of which is associated with a particular nonlinguistic dimension in such a way that selection of a point along the linguistic dimension determines and signals a certain point along the associated nonlinguistic dimension. The latter is the principle realized in Thorpe's

[4] K. S. Lashley, "The Problem of Serial Order in Behavior," in L. A. Jeffress, ed., *Cerebral Mechanisms in Behavior* (New York: Wiley, 1951), pp. 112–36.

bird-song example. Rate of alternation of high and low pitch is a linguistic dimension correlated with the nonlinguistic dimension of intention to defend a territory. The bird signals its intention to defend a territory by selecting a correlated point along the linguistic dimension of pitch alternation – I use the word "select" loosely, of course. The linguistic dimension is abstract, but the principle is clear. A communication system of the second type has an indefinitely large range of potential signals, as does human language. The mechanism and principle, however, are entirely different from those employed by human language to express indefinitely many new thoughts, intentions, feelings, and so on. It is not correct to speak of a "deficiency" of the animal system, in terms of range of potential signals; rather the opposite, since the animal system admits in principle of continuous variation along the linguistic dimension (insofar as it makes sense to speak of "continuity" in such a case), whereas human language is discrete. Hence, the issue is not one of "more" or "less," but rather of an entirely different principle of organization. When I make some arbitrary statement in a human language – say, that "the rise of supranational corporations poses new dangers for human freedom" – I am not selecting a point along some linguistic dimension that signals a corresponding point along an associated nonlinguistic dimension, nor am I selecting a signal from a finite behavioral repertoire, innate or learned.

Furthermore, it is wrong to think of human use of language as characteristically informative, in fact or in intention. Human language can be used to inform or mislead, to clarify one's own thoughts or to display one's cleverness, or simply for play. If I speak with no concern for modifying your behavior or thoughts, I am not using language any less than if I say exactly the same things *with* such intention. If we hope to understand human language and the psychological capacities on which it rests, we must first ask what it is, not how or for what purposes it is used. When we ask what human language is, we find no striking similarity to animal communication systems. There is nothing useful to be said about behavior or thought at the level of abstraction at which animal and human communication fall together. The examples of animal communication that have been examined to date do share many of the properties of human gestural systems, and it might be reasonable to explore the possibility of direct connection in this case. But human language, it appears, is based on entirely different principles. This, I think, is an important point, often overlooked by those who approach human language as a natural, biological phenomenon; in particular, it seems rather pointless, for these reasons, to speculate about the evolution of human language from simpler systems – perhaps as absurd as it would be to speculate about the "evolution" of atoms from clouds of elementary particles.

As far as we know, possession of human language is associated with a specific type of mental organization, not simply a higher degree of intelligence.

There seems to be no substance to the view that human language is simply a more complex instance of something to be found elsewhere in the animal world. This poses a problem for the biologist, since, if true, it is an example of true "emergence" – the appearance of a qualitatively different phenomenon at a specific stage of complexity of organization. Recognition of this fact, though formulated in entirely different terms, is what motivated much of the classical study of language by those whose primary concern was the nature of mind. And it seems to me that today there is no better or more promising way to explore the essential and distinctive properties of human intelligence than through the detailed investigation of the structure of this unique human possession. A reasonable guess, then, is that if empirically adequate generative grammars can be constructed and the universal principles that govern their structure and organization determined, then this will be an important contribution to human psychology, in ways to which I will turn directly, in detail.

In the course of these lectures I have mentioned some of the classical ideas regarding language structure and contemporary efforts to deepen and extend them. It seems clear that we must regard linguistic competence – knowledge of a language – as an abstract system underlying behavior, a system constituted by rules that interact to determine the form and intrinsic meaning of a potentially infinite number of sentences. Such a system – a generative grammar – provides an explication of the Humboldtian idea of "form of language," which in an obscure but suggestive remark in his great posthumous work, *Über die Verschiedenheit des Menschlichen Sprachbaues*, Humboldt defines as "that constant and unvarying system of processes underlying the mental act of raising articulated structurally organized signals to an expression of thought." Such a grammar defines a language in the Humboldtian sense, namely as "a recursively generated system, where the laws of generation are fixed and invariant, but the scope and the specific manner in which they are applied remain entirely unspecified."

In each such grammar there are particular, idiosyncratic elements, selection of which determines one specific human language; and there are general universal elements, conditions on the form and organization of any human language, that form the subject matter for the study of "universal grammar." Among the principles of universal grammar are those I discussed in the preceding lecture – for example, the principles that distinguish deep and surface structure and that constrain the class of transformational operations that relate them. Notice, incidentally, that the existence of definite principles of universal grammar makes possible the rise of the new field of mathematical linguistics, a field that submits to abstract study the class of generative systems meeting the conditions set forth in universal grammar. This inquiry aims to elaborate the formal properties of any possible human language. The field is in its infancy; it is only in the last decade that the possibility of such an enterprise has been envisioned. It has some promising initial results, and it suggests one possible direction for future research that might prove to be of great importance. Thus, mathematical linguistics seems for the moment to be in a uniquely favorable position, among mathematical approaches in the social and psychological sciences, to develop not simply as a theory of data, but as the study of highly abstract principles and structures that determine the character of human mental processes. In this case, the mental processes in question are those involved in the organization of one specific domain of human knowledge, namely knowledge of language.

The theory of generative grammar, both particular and universal, points to a conceptual lacuna in psychological theory that I believe is worth mentioning. Psychology conceived as "behavioral science" has been concerned with behavior and acquisition or control of behavior. It has no concept corresponding to "competence," in the sense in which competence is characterized by a generative grammar. The theory of learning has limited itself to a narrow and surely inadequate concept of what is learned – namely a system of stimulus-response connections, a network of associations, a repertoire of behavioral items, a habit hierarchy, or a system of dispositions to respond in a particular way under specifiable stimulus conditions.[5] Insofar as behavioral psychology has been applied to education or therapy, it has correspondingly limited itself to this concept of "what is learned." But a generative grammar cannot be characterized in these terms. What is necessary, in addition to the concept of behavior and learning, is a concept of what is learned – a notion of competence – that lies beyond the conceptual limits of behaviorist psychological theory. Like much of modern linguistics and modern philosophy of language, behaviorist psychology has quite consciously accepted methodological restrictions that do not permit the study of systems of the necessary complexity and abstractness.[6] One important future

[5] This limitation is revealed, for example, in such statements as this from W. M. Wiest, in "Recent Criticisms of Behaviorism and Learning," in *Psychological Bulletin*, Vol. 67, No. 3, 1967, pp. 214–25: "An empirical demonstration . . . that a child has learned the rules of grammar would be his exhibiting the verbal performance called 'uttering the rules of grammar.' That this performance is not usually acquired without special training is attested to by many grammar school teachers. One may even speak quite grammatically without having literally learned the rules of grammar." Wiest's inability to conceive of another sense in which the child may be said to have learned the rules of grammar testifies to the conceptual gap we are discussing. Since he refuses to consider the question of *what* is learned, and to clarify this notion before asking *how* it is learned, he can only conceive of "grammar" as the "behavioral regularities in the understanding and production of speech" – a characterization that is perfectly empty, as it stands, there being no "behavioral regularities" associated with (let alone "in") the understanding and production of speech. One cannot quarrel with the desire of some investigators to study "the acquisition and maintenance of *actual occurrences of verbal behavior*" (*ibid.*). It remains to be demonstrated that this study has something to do with the study of language. As of now, I see no indication that this claim can be substantiated.

[6] See my paper, "Some Empirical Assumptions in Modern Philosophy of Language," in S. Morgenbesser, P. Suppes, and M. White, eds., *Essays in Honor of Ernest Nagel* (New York: St. Martin's, 1969), for a discussion of the work of Quine and Wittgenstein from this point of view.

contribution of the study of language to general psychology may be to focus attention on this conceptual gap and to demonstrate how it may be filled by the elaboration of a system of underlying competence in one domain of human intelligence.

There is an obvious sense in which any aspect of psychology is based ultimately on the observation of behavior. But it is not at all obvious that the study of learning should proceed directly to the investigation of factors that control behavior or of conditions under which a "behavioral repertoire" is established. It is first necessary to determine the significant characteristics of this behavioral repertoire, the principles on which it is organized. A meaningful study of learning can proceed only after this preliminary task has been carried out and has led to a reasonably well-confirmed theory of underlying competence – in the case of language, to the formulation of the generative grammar that underlies the observed use of language. Such a study will concern itself with the relation between the data available to the organism and the competence that it acquires; only to the extent that the abstraction to competence has been successful – in the case of language, to the extent that the postulated grammar is "descriptively adequate" in the sense described in Lecture 2 – can the investigation of learning hope to achieve meaningful results. If, in some domain, the organization of the behavioral repertoire is quite trivial and elementary, then there will be little harm in avoiding the intermediate stage of theory construction, in which we attempt to characterize accurately the competence that is acquired. But one cannot count on this being the case, and in the study of language it surely is not the case. With a richer and more adequate characterization of "what is learned" – of the underlying competence that constitutes the "final state" of the organism being studied – it may be possible to approach the task of constructing a theory of learning that will be much less restricted in scope than modern behavioral psychology has proved to be. Surely it is pointless to accept methodological strictures that preclude such an approach to problems of learning.

Are there other areas of human competence where one might hope to develop a fruitful theory, analogous to generative grammar? Although this is a very important question, there is very little that can be said about it today. One might, for example, consider the problem of how a person comes to acquire a certain concept of three-dimensional space, or an implicit "theory of human action," in similar terms. Such a study would begin with the attempt to characterize the implicit theory that underlies actual performance and would then turn to the question of how this theory develops under the given conditions of time and access to data – that is, in what way the resulting system of beliefs is determined by the interplay of available data, "heuristic procedures," and the innate schematism that restricts and conditions the form of the acquired system. At the moment, this is nothing more than a sketch of a program of research.

There have been some attempts to study the structure of other, language-like systems – the study of kinship systems and folk taxonomies comes to mind, for example. But so far, at least, nothing has been discovered that is even roughly comparable to language in these domains. No one, to my knowledge, has devoted more thought to this problem than Lévi-Strauss. For example, his recent book on the categories of primitive mentality[7] is a serious and thoughtful attempt to come to grips with this problem. Nevertheless, I do not see what conclusions can be reached from a study of his materials beyond the fact that the savage mind attempts to impose some organization on the physical world – that humans classify, if they perform any mental acts at all. Specifically, Lévi-Strauss's well-known critique of totemism seems to reduce to little more than this conclusion.

Lévi-Strauss models his investigations quite consciously on structural linguistics, particularly on the work of Troubetzkoy and Jakobson. He repeatedly and quite correctly emphasizes that one cannot simply apply procedures analogous to those of phonemic analysis to subsystems of society and culture. Rather, he is concerned with structures "where they may be found . . . in the kinship system, political ideology, mythology, ritual, art," and so on,[8] and he wishes to examine the formal properties of these structures in their own terms. But several reservations are necessary when structural linguistics is used as a model in this way. For one thing, the structure of a phonological system is of very little interest as a formal object; there is nothing of significance to be said, from a formal point of view, about a set of forty-odd elements cross-classified in terms of eight or ten features. The significance of structuralist phonology, as developed by Troubetzkoy, Jakobson, and others, lies not in the formal properties of phonemic systems but in the fact that a fairly small number of features that can be specified in absolute, language-independent terms appear to provide the basis for the organization of all phonological systems. The achievement of structuralist phonology was to show that the phonological rules of a great variety of languages apply to classes of elements that can be simply characterized in terms of these features; that historical change affects such classes in a uniform way; and that the organization of features plays a basic role in the use and acquisition of language. This was a discovery of the greatest importance, and it provides the groundwork for much of contemporary linguistics. But if we abstract away from the specific universal set of features and the rule systems in which they function, little of any significance remains.

Furthermore, to a greater and greater extent, current work in phonology is demonstrating that the real richness of phonological systems lies not in the structural patterns of phonemes but rather in the intricate systems of rules by

[7] C. Lévi-Strauss, *The Savage Mind* (Chicago: University of Chicago Press, 1967).
[8] C. Lévi-Strauss, *Structural Anthropology* (New York: Basic Books, 1963), p. 85.

which these patterns are formed, modified, and elaborated.[9] The structural patterns that arise at various stages of derivation are a kind of epiphenomenon. The system of phonological rules makes use of the universal features in a fundamental way,[10] but it is the properties of the systems of rules, it seems to me, that really shed light on the specific nature of the organization of language. For example, there appear to be very general conditions, such as the principle of cyclic ordering (discussed in the preceding lecture) and others that are still more abstract, that govern the application of these rules, and there are many interesting and unsolved questions as to how the choice of rules is determined by intrinsic, universal relations among features. Furthermore, the idea of a mathematical investigation of language structures, to which Lévi-Strauss occasionally alludes, becomes meaningful only when one considers systems of rules with infinite generative capacity. There is nothing to be said about the abstract structure of the various patterns that appear at various stages of derivation. If this is correct, then one cannot expect structuralist phonology, in itself, to provide a useful model for investigation of other cultural and social systems.

In general, the problem of extending concepts of linguistic structure to other cognitive systems seems to me, for the moment, in not too promising a state, although it is no doubt too early for pessimism.

Before turning to the general implications of the study of linguistic competence and, more specifically, to the conclusions of universal grammar, it is well to make sure of the status of these conclusions in the light of current knowledge of the possible diversity of language. In my first lecture, I quoted the remarks of William Dwight Whitney about what he referred to as "the infinite diversity of human speech," the boundless variety that, he maintained, undermines the claims of philosophical grammar to psychological relevance.

Philosophical grammarians had typically maintained that languages vary little in their deep structures, though there may be wide variability in surface manifestations. Thus there is, in this view, an underlying structure of grammatical relations and categories, and certain aspects of human thought and mentality are essentially invariant across languages, although languages may differ as to whether they express the grammatical relations formally by inflection or word order, for example. Furthermore, an investigation of their work indicates that the underlying recursive principles that generate deep structure were assumed to be restricted in certain ways – for example, by the condition that new structures are formed only by the insertion of new "propositional content," new structures that themselves correspond to actual simple sentences, in fixed positions in already

---

[9] See discussion in the preceding lecture and the references cited there.
[10] The study of universal features is itself in considerable flux. See N. Chomsky and M. Halle, *The Sound Pattern of English* (New York: Harper & Row, 1968), Chapter 7, for recent discussion.

formed structures. Similarly, the grammatical transformations that form surface structures through reordering, ellipsis, and other formal operations must themselves meet certain fixed general conditions, such as those discussed in the preceding lecture. In short, the theories of philosophical grammar, and the more recent elaborations of these theories, make the assumption that languages will differ very little, despite considerable diversity in superficial realization, when we discover their deeper structures and unearth their fundamental mechanisms and principles.

It is interesting to observe that this assumption persisted even through the period of German romanticism, which was, of course, much preoccupied with the diversity of cultures and with the many rich possibilities for human intellectual development. Thus, Wilhelm von Humboldt, who is now best remembered for his ideas concerning the variety of languages and the association of diverse language structures with divergent "world-views," nevertheless held firmly that underlying any human language we will find a system that is universal, that simply expresses man's unique intellectual attributes. For this reason, it was possible for him to maintain the rationalist view that language is not really learned – certainly not taught – but rather develops "from within," in an essentially predetermined way, when the appropriate environmental conditions exist. One cannot really teach a first language, he argued, but can only "provide the thread along which it will develop of its own accord," by processes more like maturation than learning. This Platonistic element in Humboldt's thought is a pervasive one; for Humboldt, it was as natural to propose an essentially Platonistic theory of "learning" as it was for Rousseau to found his critique of repressive social institutions on a conception of human freedom that derives from strictly Cartesian assumptions regarding the limitations of mechanical explanation. And in general it seems appropriate to construe both the psychology and the linguistics of the romantic period as in large part a natural outgrowth of rationalist conceptions.[11]

The issue raised by Whitney against Humboldt and philosophical grammar in general is of great significance with respect to the implications of linguistics for general human psychology. Evidently, these implications can be truly far-reaching only if the rationalist view is essentially correct, in which case the structure of language can truly serve as a "mirror of mind," in both its particular and its universal aspects. It is widely believed that modern anthropology has established the falsity of the assumptions of the rationalist universal grammarians by demonstrating through empirical study that languages may, in fact, exhibit the widest diversity. Whitney's claims regarding the diversity of languages are reiterated throughout the modern period; Martin Joos, for example,

---

[11] For some discussion of these matters, see my *Cartesian Linguistics* (New York: Harper & Row, 1966).

is simply expressing the conventional wisdom when he takes the basic conclusion of modern anthropological linguistics to be that "languages can differ
without limit as to either extent or direction."[12]

The belief that anthropological linguistics has demolished the assumptions
of universal grammar seems to me to be quite false in two important respects.
First, it misinterprets the views of classical rationalist grammar, which held that
languages are similar only at the deeper level, the level at which grammatical
relations are expressed and at which the processes that provide for the creative
aspect of language use are to be found. Second, this belief seriously misinterprets the findings of anthropological linguistics, which has, in fact, restricted
itself almost completely to fairly superficial aspects of language structure.

To say this is not to criticize anthropological linguistics, a field that is faced
with compelling problems of its own – in particular, the problem of obtaining at least some record of the rapidly vanishing languages of the primitive
world. Nevertheless, it is important to bear in mind this fundamental limitation on its achievements in considering the light it can shed on the theses of
universal grammar. Anthropological studies (like structural linguistic studies
in general) do not attempt to reveal the underlying core of generative processes
in language – that is, the processes that determine the deeper levels of structure and that constitute the systematic means for creating ever novel sentence
types. Therefore, they obviously cannot have any real bearing on the classical
assumption that these underlying generative processes vary only slightly from
language to language. In fact, what evidence is now available suggests that if
universal grammar has serious defects, as indeed it does from a modern point
of view, then these defects lie in the failure to recognize the abstract nature of
linguistic structure and to impose sufficiently strong and restrictive conditions
on the form of any human language. And a characteristic feature of current
work in linguistics is its concern for linguistic universals of a sort that can only
be detected through a detailed investigation of particular languages, universals
governing properties of language that are simply not accessible to investigation within the restricted framework that has been adopted, often for very good
reasons, within anthropological linguistics.

I think that if we contemplate the classical problem of psychology, that of
accounting for human knowledge, we cannot avoid being struck by the enormous disparity between knowledge and experience – in the case of language,
between the generative grammar that expresses the linguistic competence of the

---

[12] M. Joos, ed., *Readings in Linguistics*, 4th edn. (Chicago: University of Chicago Press, 1966),
p. 228. This is put forth as the "Boas Tradition." American linguistics, Joos maintains, "got its
decisive direction when it was decided that an indigenous language could be described without
any preexistent scheme of what a language must be . . ." (p. 1). Of course this could not literally
be true – the procedures of analysis themselves express a hypothesis concerning the possible
diversity of language. But there is, nevertheless, much justice in Joos's characterization.

native speaker and the meager and degenerate data on the basis of which he has constructed this grammar for himself. In principle the theory of learning should deal with this problem; but in fact it bypasses the problem, because of the conceptual gap that I mentioned earlier. The problem cannot even be formulated in any sensible way until we develop the concept of competence, alongside the concepts of learning and behavior, and apply this concept in some domain. The fact is that this concept has so far been extensively developed and applied only in the study of human language. It is only in this domain that we have at least the first steps toward an account of competence, namely the fragmentary generative grammars that have been constructed for particular languages. As the study of language progresses, we can expect with some confidence that these grammars will be extended in scope and depth, although it will hardly come as a surprise if the first proposals are found to be mistaken in fundamental ways.

Insofar as we have a tentative first approximation to a generative grammar for some language, we can for the first time formulate in a useful way the problem of origin of knowledge. In other words, we can ask the question, What initial structure must be attributed to the mind that enables it to construct such a grammar from the data of sense? Some of the empirical conditions that must be met by any such assumption about innate structure are moderately clear. Thus, it appears to be a species-specific capacity that is essentially independent of intelligence, and we can make a fairly good estimate of the amount of data that is necessary for the task to be successfully accomplished. We know that the grammars that are in fact constructed vary only slightly among speakers of the same language, despite wide variations not only in intelligence but also in the conditions under which language is acquired. As participants in a certain culture, we are naturally aware of the great differences in ability to use language, in knowledge of vocabulary, and so on that result from differences in native ability and from differences in conditions of acquisition; we naturally pay much less attention to the similarities and to common knowledge, which we take for granted. But if we manage to establish the requisite psychic distance, if we actually compare the generative grammars that must be postulated for different speakers of the same language, we find that the similarities that we take for granted are quite marked and that the divergences are few and marginal. What is more, it seems that dialects that are superficially quite remote, even barely intelligible on first contact, share a vast central core of common rules and processes and differ very slightly in underlying structures, which seem to remain invariant through long historical eras. Furthermore, we discover a substantial system of principles that do not vary among languages that are, as far as we know, entirely unrelated.

The central problems in this domain are empirical ones that are, in principle at least, quite straightforward, difficult as they may be to solve in a satisfactory way. We must postulate an innate structure that is rich enough to account for the disparity between experience and knowledge, one that can account for the construction of the empirically justified generative grammars within the given limitations of time and access to data. At the same time, this postulated innate mental structure must not be so rich and restrictive as to exclude certain known languages. There is, in other words, an upper bound and a lower bound on the degree and exact character of the complexity that can be postulated as innate mental structure. The factual situation is obscure enough to leave room for much difference of opinion over the true nature of this innate mental structure that makes acquisition of language possible. However, there seems to me to be no doubt that this is an empirical issue, one that can be resolved by proceeding along the lines that I have just roughly outlined.

My own estimate of the situation is that the real problem for tomorrow is that of discovering an assumption regarding innate structure that is sufficiently rich, not that of finding one that is simple or elementary enough to be "plausible." There is, as far as I can see, no reasonable notion of "plausibility," no a priori insight into what innate structures are permissible, that can guide the search for a "sufficiently elementary assumption." It would be mere dogmatism to maintain without argument or evidence that the mind is simpler in its innate structure than other biological systems, just as it would be mere dogmatism to insist that the mind's organization must necessarily follow certain set principles, determined in advance of investigation and maintained in defiance of any empirical findings. I think that the study of problems of mind has been very definitely hampered by a kind of apriorism with which these problems are generally approached. In particular, the empiricist assumptions that have dominated the study of acquisition of knowledge for many years seem to me to have been adopted quite without warrant and to have no special status among the many possibilities that one might imagine as to how the mind functions.

In this connection, it is illuminating to follow the debate that has arisen since the views I have just sketched were advanced a few years ago as a program of research – I should say, since this position was resurrected, because to a significant extent it is the traditional rationalist approach, now amplified and sharpened and made far more explicit in terms of the tentative conclusions that have been reached in the recent study of linguistic competence. Two outstanding American philosophers, Nelson Goodman and Hilary Putnam, have made recent contributions to this discussion – both misconceived, in my opinion, but instructive in the misconceptions that they reveal.[13]

---

[13] N. Goodman, "The Epistemological Argument," and H. Putnam, "The Innateness Hypothesis and Explanatory Models in Linguistics." Together with a paper of mine, these were presented at the Innate Ideas Symposium of the American Philosophical Association and the Boston Colloquium for the Philosophy of Science in December 1966. The three essays appear in *Synthèse*, Vol. 17, No. 1, 1967, pp. 2–28, and in R. S. Cohen and W. M. Wartofsky, eds., *Boston Studies in the Philosophy of Science*, Vol. III (New York: Humanities, 1968),

Goodman's treatment of the question suffers first from an historical misunderstanding and second from a failure to formulate correctly the exact nature of the problem of acquisition of knowledge. His historical misunderstanding has to do with the issue between Locke and whomever Locke thought he was criticizing in his discussion of innate ideas. According to Goodman, "Locke made . . . acutely clear" that the doctrine of innate ideas is "false or meaningless." In fact, however, Locke's critique had little relevance to any familiar doctrine of the seventeenth century. The arguments that Locke gave were considered and dealt with in quite a satisfactory way in the earliest seventeenth-century discussions of innate ideas, for example those of Lord Herbert and Descartes, both of whom took for granted that the system of innate ideas and principles would not function unless appropriate stimulation took place. For this reason, Locke's arguments, none of which took cognizance of this condition, are without force;[14] for some reason, he avoided the issues that had been discussed in the preceding half-century. Furthermore, as Leibnitz observed, Locke's willingness to make use of a principle of "reflection" makes it almost impossible to distinguish his approach from that of the rationalists, except for his failure to take even those steps suggested by his predecessors toward specifying the character of this principle.

But, historical issues aside, I think that Goodman misconstrues the substantive problem as well. He argues that first-language learning poses no real problem, because prior to first-language learning the child has already acquired the rudiments of a symbolic system in his ordinary dealings with the environment. Hence, first-language learning is analogous to second-language learning in that the fundamental step has already been taken, and details can be elaborated within an already existing framework. This argument might have some force if it were possible to show that the specific properties of grammar – say, the distinction of deep and surface structure, the specific properties of grammatical transformations, the principles of rule ordering, and so on – were present in some form in these already acquired prelinguistic "symbolic systems." But since there is not the slightest reason to believe that this is so, the argument

---

pp. 81–107. A more extensive discussion of the papers of Putnam and Goodman, along with a number of others, appears in my contribution to the symposium "Linguistics and Philosophy," New York University, April 1968, in S. Hook, ed., *Philosophy and Language* (New York: New York University Press, 1969). The essay is reprinted in this volume.

[14] This observation is a commonplace. See, for example, the commentary by A. C. Fraser in his edition of Locke's *Essay Concerning Human Understanding*, 1894 (reprinted by Dover, 1959), notes 1 and 2, Chapter 1 (p. 38 of the Dover edition). As Fraser notes, Descartes' position is one "which Locke's argument always fails to reach . . . Locke assails [the hypothesis of innate ideas] . . . in its crudest form, in which it is countenanced by no eminent advocate." Goodman is free to use the term "innate idea" in conformity with Locke's misinterpretation of the doctrine if he wishes, but not to charge "sophistry," as he does, when others examine and develop rationalist doctrine in the form in which it was actually presented.

collapses. It is based on an equivocation similar to that discussed earlier in connection with the argument that language evolved from animal communication. In that case, as we observed, the argument turned on a metaphorical use of the term "language." In Goodman's case, the argument is based entirely on a vague use of the term "symbolic system," and it collapses as soon as we attempt to give this term a precise meaning. If it were possible to show that these prelinguistic symbolic systems share certain significant properties with natural language, we could then argue that these properties of natural language are acquired by analogy. Of course, we would then face the problem of explaining how the prelinguistic symbolic systems developed these properties. But since no one has succeeded in showing that the fundamental properties of natural language – those discussed in Lecture 2, for example – appear in prelinguistic symbolic systems or any others, the latter problem does not arise.

According to Goodman, the reason why the problem of second-language learning is different from that of first-language learning is that "once one language is available," it "can be used for giving explanation and instruction." He then goes on to argue that "acquisition of an initial language is acquisition of a secondary symbolic system" and is quite on a par with normal second-language acquisition. The primary symbolic systems to which he refers are "rudimentary prelinguistic symbolic systems in which gestures and sensory and perceptual occurrences of all sorts function as signs." But evidently these prelinguistic symbolic systems cannot be "used for giving explanation and instruction" in the way a first language can be used in second-language instruction. Therefore, even on his own grounds, Goodman's argument is incoherent.

Goodman maintains that "the claim we are discussing cannot be experimentally tested even when we have an acknowledged example of a 'bad' language" and that "the claim has not even been formulated to the extent of citation of a single general property of 'bad' languages." The first of these conclusions is correct, in his sense of "experimental test," namely a test in which we "take an infant at birth, isolate it from all the influences of our language-bound culture, and attempt to inculcate it with one of the 'bad' artificial languages." Obviously this is not feasible. But there is no reason why we should be dismayed by the impossibility of carrying out such a test as this. There are many other ways – for example, those discussed in Lecture 2 and the references cited there – in which evidence can be obtained concerning the properties of grammars and conclusions regarding the general properties of such grammars can be put to empirical test. Any such conclusion immediately specifies, correctly or incorrectly, certain properties of "bad" languages. Since there are dozens of papers and books that attempt to formulate such properties, his second claim, that not "a single general property of 'bad' languages" has been formulated, is rather surprising. One might try to show that these attempts are misguided or questionable, but one can hardly maintain seriously that they do not exist. Any formulation of a principle of universal grammar makes a strong empirical claim, which can be falsified by finding counter-instances in some human language, along the lines of the discussion in Lecture 2. In linguistics, as in any other field, it is only in such indirect ways as this that one can hope to find evidence bearing on nontrivial hypotheses. Direct experimental tests of the sort that Goodman mentions are rarely possible, a matter that may be unfortunate but is nevertheless characteristic of most research.

At one point Goodman remarks, correctly, that even though "for certain remarkable facts I have no alternative explanation . . . that alone does not dictate acceptance of whatever theory may be offered; for the theory might be worse than none. Inability to explain a fact does not condemn me to accept an intrinsically repugnant and incomprehensible theory." But now consider the theory of innate ideas that Goodman regards as "intrinsically repugnant and incomprehensible." Notice, first, that the theory is obviously not "incomprehensible," on his terms. Thus he appears to be willing, in this article, to accept the view that in some sense the mature mind contains ideas; it is obviously not "incomprehensible," then, that some of these ideas are "implanted in the mind as original equipment," to use his phraseology. And if we turn to the actual doctrine as developed in rationalist philosophy, rather than Locke's caricature, the theory becomes even more obviously comprehensible. There is nothing incomprehensible in the view that stimulation provides the occasion for the mind to apply certain innate interpretive principles, certain concepts that proceed from "the power of understanding" itself, from the faculty of thinking rather than from external objects directly. To take an example from Descartes (*Reply to Objections*, V):

> When first in infancy we see a triangular figure depicted on paper, this figure cannot show us how a real triangle ought to be conceived, in the way in which geometricians consider it, because the true triangle is contained in this figure, just as the statue of Mercury is contained in a rough block of wood. But because we already possess within us the idea of a true triangle, and it can be more easily conceived by our mind than the more complex figure of the triangle drawn on paper, we, therefore, when we see the composite figure, apprehend not it itself, but rather the authentic triangle.[15]

In this sense the idea of a triangle is innate. Surely the notion is comprehensible; there would be no difficulty, for example, in programing a computer to react to stimuli along these lines (though this would not satisfy Descartes, for other reasons). Similarly, there is no difficulty in principle in programing a computer with a schematism that sharply restricts the form of a generative grammar, with an evaluation procedure for grammars of the given form, with a

---

[15] E. S. Haldane and G. R. T. Ross, eds., *Descartes' Philosophical Works*, 1911 (reprinted by Dover, 1955). The citation, and the preceding remarks, appear in my contribution to the Innate Ideas Symposium of December 1966 (see note 13).

technique for determining whether given data are compatible with a grammar of the given form, with a fixed substructure of entities (such as distinctive features), rules, and principles, and so on – in short, with a universal grammar of the sort that has been proposed in recent years. For reasons that I have already mentioned, I believe that these proposals can be properly regarded as a further development of classical rationalist doctrine, as an elaboration of some of its main ideas regarding language and mind. Of course, such a theory will be "repugnant" to one who accepts empiricist doctrine and regards it as immune to question or challenge. It seems to me that this is the heart of the matter.

Putnam's paper (see note 13) deals more directly with the points at issue, but it seems to me that his arguments are also inconclusive, because of certain incorrect assumptions that he makes about the nature of the acquired grammars. Putnam assumes that on the level of phonetics the only property proposed in universal grammar is that a language has "a short list of phonemes." This, he argues, is not a similarity among languages that requires elaborate explanatory hypotheses. The conclusion is correct; the assumption is quite wrong. In fact, as I have now pointed out several times, very strong empirical hypotheses have been proposed regarding the specific choice of universal features, conditions on the form and organization of phonological rules, conditions on rule application, and so on. If these proposals are correct or near correct, then "similarities among languages" at the level of sound structure are indeed remarkable and cannot be accounted for simply by assumptions about memory capacity, as Putnam suggests.

Above the level of sound structure, Putnam assumes that the only significant properties of language are that they have proper names, that the grammar contains a phrase structure component, and that there are rules "abbreviating" sentences generated by the phrase structure component. He argues that the nature of the phrase structure component is determined by the existence of proper names; that the existence of a phrase structure component is explained by the fact that "all the natural measures of complexity of an algorithm – size of the machine table, length of computations, time, and space required for the computation – lead to the . . . result"; that phrase structure systems provide the "algorithms which are 'simplest' for virtually any computing system," hence also "for naturally evolved 'computing systems'"; and that there is nothing surprising in the fact that languages contain rules of abbreviation.

Each of the three conclusions involves a false assumption. From the fact that a phrase structure system contains proper names one can conclude almost nothing about its other categories. In fact, there is much dispute at the moment about the general properties of the underlying phrase structure system for natural languages; the dispute is not in the least resolved by the existence of proper names.

As to the second point, it is simply untrue that all measures of complexity and speed of computation lead to phrase structure rules as the "simplest possible algorithm." The only existing results that are even indirectly relevant show that context-free phrase structure grammars (a reasonable model for rules generating deep structures, when we exclude the lexical items and the distributional conditions they meet) receive an automata-theoretic interpretation as nondeterministic pushdown storage automata, but the latter is hardly a "natural" notion from the point of view of "simplicity of algorithms" and so forth. In fact, it can be argued that the somewhat similar but not formally related concept of real-time deterministic automation is far more "natural" in terms of time and space conditions on computation.[16]

However, it is pointless to pursue this topic, because what is at stake is not the "simplicity" of phrase structure grammars but rather of transformational grammars with a phrase structure component that plays a role in generating deep structures. And there is absolutely no mathematical concept of "ease of computation" or "simplicity of algorithm" that even vaguely suggests that such systems may have some advantage over the kinds of automata that have been seriously investigated from this point of view – for example, finite state automata, linear bounded automata, and so on. The basic concept of "structure-dependent operation" has never even been considered in a strictly mathematical concept. The source of this confusion is a misconception on Putnam's part as to the nature of grammatical transformations. They are not rules that "abbreviate" sentences; rather, they are operations that form surface structures from underlying deep structures, in such ways as are illustrated in the preceding lecture and the references there cited.[17] Hence, to show that transformational grammars are the "simplest possible," one would have to demonstrate that the "optimal" computing system would take a string of symbols as input and determine its surface structure, its underlying deep structure, and the sequence of transformational operations that relates them. Nothing of the sort has been shown; in fact, the question has never even been raised.

Putnam argues that even if significant uniformities among languages were to be discovered, there would be a simpler explanation than the hypothesis of an innate universal grammar, namely their common origin. But this proposal

---

[16] For some discussion of these matters, see my "Formal Properties of Grammars," in R. D. Luce, R. Bush, and E. Galanter, eds., *Handbook of Mathematical Psychology*, Vol. II (New York: Wiley, 1963). For a more extensive discussion of the automata-theoretic framework, see R. J. Nelson, *Introduction to Automata* (New York: Wiley, 1968). A detailed presentation of properties of context-free grammars is given in S. Ginsburg, *The Mathematical Theory of Context-Free Languages* (New York: McGraw-Hill, 1966). There have been a number of studies of speed of computation, simplicity of algorithms, and so on, but none of them has any bearing on the issue under discussion.

[17] See note 10 of Lecture 2, p. 29, for further comment.

involves a serious misunderstanding of the problem at issue. The grammar of a language must be discovered by the child from the data presented to him. As noted earlier, the empirical problem is to find a hypothesis about initial structure rich enough to account for the fact that a specific grammar is constructed by the child, but not so rich as to be falsified by the known diversity of language. Questions of common origin are of potential relevance to this empirical issue in only one respect: if the existing languages are not a "fair sample" of the "possible languages," we may be led mistakenly to propose too narrow a schema for universal grammar. However, as I mentioned earlier, the empirical problem that we face today is that no one has been able to devise an initial hypothesis rich enough to account for the acquisition by the child of the grammar that we are, apparently, led to attribute to him when we try to account for his ability to use the language in the normal way. The assumption of common origin contributes nothing to explaining how this achievement is possible. In short, the language is "reinvented" each time it is learned, and the empirical problem to be faced by the theory of learning is how this invention of grammar can take place.

Putnam does face this problem and suggests that there might be "general multipurpose learning strategies" that account for this achievement. It is, of course, an empirical question whether the properties of the "language faculty" are specific to language or are merely a particular case of much more general mental faculties (or learning strategies). This is a problem that has been discussed earlier in this lecture, inconclusively and in a slightly different context. Putnam takes for granted that it is only general "learning strategies" that are innate but suggests no grounds for this empirical assumption. As I have argued earlier, a nondogmatic approach to this problem can be pursued, without reliance on unargued assumptions of this sort – that is, through the investigation of specific areas of human competence, such as language, followed by the attempt to devise a hypothesis that will account for the development of this competence. If we discover through such investigation that the same "learning strategies" are sufficient to account for the development of competence in various domains, we will have reason to believe that Putnam's assumption is correct. If we discover that the postulated innate structures differ from case to case, the only rational conclusion would be that a model of mind must involve separate "faculties," with unique or partially unique properties. I cannot see how anyone can resolutely insist on one or the other conclusion in the light of the evidence now available to us. But one thing is quite clear: Putnam has no justification for his final conclusion, that "invoking 'Innateness' only postpones the problem of learning; it does not solve it." Invoking an innate representation of universal grammar does solve the problem of learning, if it is true that this is the basis for language acquisition, as it well may be. If, on the other hand, there are general learning strategies that account for the acquisition of grammatical knowledge, then postulation of an innate universal grammar will not "postpone" the problem of learning, but will rather offer an incorrect solution to this problem. The issue is an empirical one of truth or falsity, not a methodological one of states of investigation.[18]

To summarize, it seems to me that neither Goodman nor Putnam offers a serious counterargument to the proposals concerning innate mental structure that have been advanced (tentatively, of course, as befits empirical hypotheses) or suggests a plausible alternative approach, with empirical content, to the problem of acquisition of knowledge.

Assuming the rough accuracy of conclusions that seem tenable today, it is reasonable to suppose that a generative grammar is a system of many hundreds of rules of several different types, organized in accordance with certain fixed principles of ordering and applicability and containing a certain fixed substructure which, along with the general principles of organization, is common to all languages. There is no a priori "naturalness" to such a system, any more than there is to the detailed structure of the visual cortex. No one who has given any serious thought to the problem of formalizing inductive procedures or "heuristic methods" is likely to set much store by the hope that such a system as a generative grammar can be constructed by methods of any generality.

To my knowledge, the only substantive proposal to deal with the problem of acquisition of knowledge of language is the rationalist conception that I have outlined. To repeat: suppose that we assign to the mind, as an innate property, the general theory of language that we have called "universal grammar." This theory encompasses the principles that I discussed in the preceding lecture and many others of the same sort, and it specifies a certain subsystem of rules that provides a skeletal structure for any language and a variety of conditions, formal and substantive, that any further elaboration of the grammar must meet. The theory of universal grammar, then, provides a schema to which any particular grammar must conform. Suppose, furthermore, that we can make this schema sufficiently restrictive so that very few possible grammars conforming to the schema will be consistent with the meager and degenerate data actually available to the language learner. His task, then, is to search among the possible grammars and select one that is not definitely rejected by the data available to him. What faces the language learner, under these assumptions, is not the impossible task of inventing a highly abstract and intricately structured theory on the basis of degenerate data, but rather the much more manageable task of determining whether these data belong to one or another of a fairly restricted set of potential languages.

---

[18] It is surprising to see that Putnam refers disparagingly to "vague talk of 'classes of hypotheses' – and 'weighting functions'" in the course of his discussion of "general learning strategies." For the moment, the latter is a mere phrase without any describable content. On the other hand, there is a substantial literature detailing the properties of the classes of hypotheses and weighting functions to which Putnam refers. Hence, the shoe seems to be on the other foot in this case.

The tasks of the psychologist, then, divide into several subtasks. The first is to discover the innate schema that characterizes the class of potential languages – that defines the "essence" of human language. This subtask falls to that branch of human psychology known as linguistics; it is the problem of traditional universal grammar, of contemporary linguistic theory. The second subtask is the detailed study of the actual character of the stimulation and the organism–environment interaction that sets the innate cognitive mechanism into operation. This is a study now being undertaken by a few psychologists, and it is particularly active right here in Berkeley. It has already led to interesting and suggestive conclusions. One might hope that such study will reveal a succession of maturational stages leading finally to a full generative grammar.[19]

A third task is that of determining just what it means for a hypothesis about the generative grammar of a language to be "consistent" with the data of sense. Notice that it is a great oversimplification to suppose that a child must discover a generative grammar that accounts for all the linguistic data that has been presented to him and that "projects" such data to an infinite range of potential sound–meaning relations. In addition to achieving this, he must also differentiate the data of sense into those utterances that give direct evidence as to the character of the underlying grammar and those that must be rejected by the hypothesis he selects as ill-formed, deviant, fragmentary, and so on. Clearly, everyone succeeds in carrying out this task of differentiation – we all know, within tolerable limits of consistency, which sentences are well formed and literally interpretable, and which must be interpreted as metaphorical, fragmentary, and deviant along many possible dimensions. I doubt that it has been fully appreciated to what extent this complicates the problem of accounting for language acquisition. Formally speaking, the learner must select a hypothesis regarding the language to which he is exposed that rejects a good part of the data on which this hypothesis must rest. Again, it is reasonable to suppose this is possible only if the range of tenable hypotheses is quite limited – if the innate schema of universal grammar is highly restrictive. The third subtask, then, is to study what we might think of as the problem of "confirmation" – in this context, the problem of what relation must hold between a potential grammar and a set

[19] It is not unlikely that detailed investigation of this sort will show that the conception of universal grammar as an innate schematism is only valid as a first approximation; that, in fact, an innate schematism of a more general sort permits the formulation of tentative "grammars" which themselves determine how later evidence is to be interpreted, leading to the postulation of richer grammars, and so on. I have so far been discussing language acquisition on the obviously false assumption that it is an instantaneous process. There are many interesting questions that arise when we consider how the process extends in time. For some discussion relating to problems of phonology, see my paper "Phonology and Reading," in H. Levin, ed., *Basic Studies on Reading*. Notice also that it is unnecessary to suppose, even in the first approximation, that "very few possible grammars conforming to the schema" will be available to the language learner. It is enough to suppose that the possible grammars consistent with the data will be "scattered" in terms of an evaluation procedure.

of data for this grammar to be confirmed as the actual theory of the language in question.

I have been describing the problem of acquisition of knowledge of language in terms that are more familiar in an epistemological than a psychological context, but I think that this is quite appropriate. Formally speaking, acquisition of "common-sense knowledge" – knowledge of a language, for example – is not unlike theory construction of the most abstract sort. Speculating about the future development of the subject, it seems to me not unlikely, for the reasons I have mentioned, that learning theory will progress by establishing the innately determined set of possible hypotheses, determining the conditions of interaction that lead the mind to put forth hypotheses from this set, and fixing the conditions under which such a hypothesis is confirmed – and, perhaps, under which much of the data is rejected as irrelevant for one reason or another.

Such a way of describing the situation should not be too surprising to those familiar with the history of psychology at Berkeley, where, after all, Edward Tolman has given his name to the psychology building; but I want to stress that the hypotheses I am discussing are qualitatively different in complexity and intricacy from anything that was considered in the classical discussions of learning. As I have now emphasized several times, there seems to be little useful analogy between the theory of grammar that a person has internalized and that provides the basis for his normal, creative use of language, and any other cognitive system that has so far been isolated and described; similarly, there is little useful analogy between the schema of universal grammar that we must, I believe, assign to the mind as an innate character, and any other known system of mental organization. It is quite possible that the lack of analogy testifies to our ignorance of other aspects of mental function, rather than to the absolute uniqueness of linguistic structure; but the fact is that we have, for the moment, no objective reason for supposing this to be true.

The way in which I have been describing acquisition of knowledge of language calls to mind a very interesting and rather neglected lecture given by Charles Sanders Peirce more than fifty years ago, in which he developed some rather similar notions about acquisition of knowledge in general.[20] Peirce argued that the general limits of human intelligence are much more narrow than might be suggested by romantic assumptions about the limitless perfectibility of man (or, for that matter, than are suggested by his own "pragmaticist" conceptions of the course of scientific progress in his better-known philosophical studies). He held that innate limitations on admissible hypotheses are a precondition for successful theory construction, and that the "guessing instinct" that provides hypotheses makes use of inductive procedures only for "corrective action."

---

[20] C. S. Peirce, "The Logic of Abduction," in V. Tomas, ed., *Peirce's Essays in the Philosophy of Science* (New York: Liberal Arts Press, 1957).

Peirce maintained in this lecture that the history of early science shows that something approximating a correct theory was discovered with remarkable ease and rapidity, on the basis of highly inadequate data, as soon as certain problems were faced; he noted "how few were the guesses that men of surpassing genius had to make before they rightly guessed the laws of nature." And, he asked, "How was it that man was ever led to entertain that true theory? You cannot say that it happened by chance, because the chances are too overwhelmingly against the single true theory in the twenty or thirty thousand years during which man has been a thinking animal, ever having come into any man's head." A fortiori, the chances are even more overwhelmingly against the true theory of each language ever having come into the head of every four-year-old child. Continuing with Peirce: "Man's mind has a natural adaptation to imagining correct theories of some kinds . . . If man had not the gift of a mind adapted to his requirements, he could not have acquired any knowledge." Correspondingly, in our present case, it seems that knowledge of a language – a grammar – can be acquired only by an organism that is "preset" with a severe restriction on the form of grammar. This innate restriction is a precondition, in the Kantian sense, for linguistic experience, and it appears to be the critical factor in determining the course and result of language learning. The child cannot know at birth which language he is to learn, but he must know that its grammar must be of a predetermined form that excludes many imaginable languages. Having selected a permissible hypothesis, he can use inductive evidence for corrective action, confirming or disconfirming his choice. Once the hypothesis is sufficiently well confirmed, the child knows the language defined by this hypothesis; consequently, his knowledge extends enormously beyond his experience and, in fact, leads him to characterize much of the data of experience as defective and deviant.

Peirce regarded inductive processes as rather marginal to the acquisition of knowledge; in his words, "Induction has no originality in it, but only tests a suggestion already made." To understand how knowledge is acquired, in the rationalist view that Peirce outlined, we must penetrate the mysteries of what he called "abduction," and we must discover that which "gives a rule to abduction and so puts a limit upon admissible hypotheses." Peirce maintained that the search for principles of abduction leads us to the study of innate ideas, which provide the instinctive structure of human intelligence. But Peirce was no dualist in the Cartesian sense; he argued (not very persuasively, in my opinion) that there is a significant analogy between human intelligence, with its abductive restrictions, and animal instinct. Thus, he maintained that man discovered certain true theories only because his "instincts must have involved from the beginning certain tendencies to think truly" about certain specific matters; similarly, "You cannot seriously think that every little chicken that is hatched, has to rummage through all possible theories until it lights upon the good idea of picking up something and eating it. On the contrary, you think that the chicken has an innate idea of doing this; that is to say, that it can think of this, but has no faculty of thinking anything else . . . But if you are going to think every poor chicken endowed with an innate tendency towards a positive truth, why should you think to man alone this gift is denied?"

No one took up Peirce's challenge to develop a theory of abduction, to determine those principles that limit the admissible hypotheses or present them in a certain order. Even today, this remains a task for the future. It is a task that need not be undertaken if empiricist psychological doctrine can be substantiated; therefore, it is of great importance to subject this doctrine to rational analysis, as has been done, in part, in the study of language. I would like to repeat that it was the great merit of structural linguistics, as of Hullian learning theory in its early stages and of several other modern developments, to have given precise form to certain empiricist assumptions.[21] Where this step has been taken, the inadequacy of the postulated mechanisms has been clearly demonstrated, and, in the case of language at least, we can even begin to see just why any methods of this sort must fail – for example, because they cannot, in principle, provide for the properties of deep structures and the abstract operations of formal grammar. Speculating about the future, I think it is not unlikely that the dogmatic character of the general empiricist framework and its inadequacy to

---

[21]   In contrast, the account of language acquisition presented by B. F. Skinner in his *Verbal Behavior* (New York: Appleton-Century-Crofts, 1957) seems to me either devoid of content or clearly wrong, depending on whether one interprets it metaphorically or literally (see my review of this book in *Language*, Vol. 35, No. 1, 1959, pp. 26–58). It is quite appropriate when a theory is disproven in a strong form to replace it by a weaker variant. However, not infrequently this step leads to vacuity. The popularity of Skinner's concept of "reinforcement," after the virtual collapse of Hullian theory, seems to me a case in point. (Note that the Skinnerian concepts can be well defined and can lead to interesting results, in a particular experimental situation – what is at issue is the Skinnerian "extrapolation" to a wider class of cases.)

Another example appears in K. Salzinger, "The Problem of Response Class in Verbal Behavior," in K. Salzinger and S. Salzinger, eds., *Research in Verbal Behavior and Some Neurophysiological Implications* (New York: Academic Press, 1967), pp. 35–54. Salzinger argues that George Miller is not justified in criticizing learning theory for its inability to explain linguistic productivity – that is, the ability of a speaker to determine, of a sequence of words that he has never heard, whether or not it is a well-formed sentence and what it means. The defect can be overcome, he argues, by making use of the notion of "response class." True, it cannot be that each response is reinforced, but the class of acceptable sentences constitutes a response class, like the set of bar-presses in a particular Skinnerian experiment. Unfortunately, this is empty verbiage until the condition that defines membership in this class is established. If the condition involves the notion "generation by a given grammar," then we are back where we started.

Salzinger also misconstrues the attempts to provide an experimental test that will distinguish grammatical from ungrammatical strings. He states that such tests have failed to confirm such a division and therefore concludes, apparently, that the distinction does not exist. Obviously, the failure indicates nothing more than that the tests were ineffective. One can invent innumerable tests that would fail to provide some given classification. Surely the classification itself is not in question. Thus, Salzinger would agree, quite apart from any experimental test that might be devised, that the sentences of this footnote share an important property that does not hold of the set of strings of words formed by reading each of these sentences, word by word, from right to left.

human and animal intelligence will gradually become more evident as specific realizations, such as taxonomic linguistics, behaviorist learning theory, and the perception models,[22] heuristic methods, and "general problem solvers" of the early enthusiasts of "artificial intelligence," are successively rejected on empirical grounds when they are made precise and on grounds of vacuity when they are left vague. And – assuming this projection to be accurate – it will then be possible to undertake a general study of the limits and capacities of human intelligence, to develop a Peircean logic of abduction.

Modern psychology is not devoid of such initiatives. The contemporary study of generative grammar and its universal substructure and governing principles is one such manifestation. Closely related is the study of the biological bases of human language, an investigation to which Eric Lenneberg has made substantial contributions.[23] It is tempting to see a parallel development in the very important work of Piaget and others interested in "genetic epistemology," but I am not sure that this is accurate. It is not clear to me, for example, what Piaget takes to be the basis for the transition from one of the stages that he discusses to the next, higher stage. There is, furthermore, a possibility, suggested by recent work of Mehler and Bever,[24] that the deservedly well-known results on conservation, in particular, may not demonstrate successive stages of intellectual development in the sense discussed by Piaget and his coworkers, but something rather different. If the preliminary results of Mehler and Bever are correct, then it would follow that the "final stage," in which conservation is properly understood, was already realized at a very early period of development. Later, the child develops a heuristic technique that is largely adequate but that fails under the conditions of the conservation experiment. Still later, he adjusts this technique successfully and once again makes the correct judgments in the conservation experiment. If this analysis is correct, then what we are observing is not a succession of stages of intellectual development, in Piaget's sense, but rather slow progress in bringing heuristic techniques into line with general concepts that have always been present. These are interesting alternatives; either way, the results may bear in important ways on the topics we are considering.

Still more clearly to the point, I think, are the developments in comparative ethology over the past thirty years, and certain current work in experimental and physiological psychology. One can cite many examples: for example, in the

[22] For a discussion of such systems and their limitations, see M. Minsky and S. Papert, *Perceptions and Pattern Recognition*, Artificial Intelligence Memo No. 140, MAC-M-358, Project MAC, Cambridge, Mass., September 1967.

[23] See E. H. Lenneberg, *Biological Foundations of Language* (New York: Wiley, 1967). My contribution to this volume, "The Formal Nature of Language," appears as the fifth paper in this book.

[24] See J. Mehler and T. G. Bever, "Cognitive Capacities of Young Children," *Science*, Vol. 158, No. 3797, October 1967, pp. 141–42.

latter category, the work of Bower suggesting an innate basis for the perceptual constancies; studies in the Wisconsin primate laboratory on complex innate releasing mechanisms in rhesus monkeys; the work of Hubel, Barlow, and others on highly specific analyzing mechanisms in the lower cortical centers of mammals; and a number of comparable studies of lower organisms (for example, the beautiful work of Lettvin and his associates on frog vision). There is now good evidence from such investigations that perception of line, angle, motion, and other complex properties of the physical world is based on innate organization of the neural system.

In some cases at least, these built-in structures will degenerate unless appropriate stimulation takes place at an early stage in life, but although such experience is necessary to permit the innate mechanisms to function, there is no reason to believe that it has more than a marginal effect on determining *how* they function to organize experience. Furthermore, there is nothing to suggest that what has so far been discovered is anywhere near the limit of complexity of innate structures. The basic techniques for exploring the neural mechanisms are only a few years old, and it is impossible to predict what order of specificity and complexity will be demonstrated when they come to be extensively applied. For the present, it seems that most complex organisms have highly specific forms of sensory and perceptual organization that are associated with the *Umwelt* and the manner of life of the organism. There is little reason to doubt that what is true of lower organisms is true of humans as well. Particularly in the case of language, it is natural to expect a close relation between innate properties of the mind and features of linguistic structure; for language, after all, has no existence apart from its mental representation. Whatever properties it has must be those that are given to it by the innate mental processes of the organism that has invented it and that invents it anew with each succeeding generation, along with whatever properties are associated with the conditions of its use. Once again, it seems that language should be, for this reason, a most illuminating probe with which to explore the organization of mental processes.

Turning to comparative ethology, it is interesting to note that one of its earliest motivations was the hope that through the "investigation of the a priori, of the innate working hypotheses present in subhuman organisms," it would be possible to shed light on the a priori forms of human thought. This formulation of intent is quoted from an early and little-known paper by Konrad Lorenz.[25] Lorenz goes on to express views very much like those Peirce had expressed a generation earlier. He maintains:

[25] K. Lorenz, "Kants Lehre vom apriorischen in Lichte gegenwärtiger Biologie," in *Blätter für Deutsche Philosophie*, Vol. 15, 1941, pp. 94–125. I am indebted to Donald Walker of the MITRE Corporation, Bedford, Mass., for bringing this paper to my attention.

One familiar with the innate modes of reaction of subhuman organisms can readily hypothesize that the a priori is due to hereditary differentiations of the central nervous system which have become characteristic of the species, producing hereditary dispositions to think in certain forms . . . Most certainly Hume was wrong when he wanted to derive all that is a priori from that which the senses supply to experience, just as wrong as Wundt or Helmholtz who simply explain it as an abstraction from preceding experience. Adaptation of the a priori to the real world has no more originated from "experience" than adaptation of the fin of the fish to the properties of water. Just as the form of the fin is given a priori, prior to any individual negotiation of the young fish with the water, and just as it is this form that makes possible this negotiation, so it is also the case with our forms of perception and categories in their relationship to our negotiation with the real external world through experience. In the case of animals, we find limitations specific to the forms of experience possible for them. We believe we can demonstrate the closest functional and probably genetic relationship between these animal a prioris and our human a priori. Contrary to Hume, we believe, just as did Kant, that a "pure" science of innate forms of human thought, independent of all experience, is possible.

Peirce, to my knowledge, is original and unique in stressing the problem of studying the rules that limit the class of possible theories. Of course, his concept of abduction, like Lorenz's biological a priori, has a strongly Kantian flavor, and all derive from the rationalist psychology that concerned itself with the forms, the limits, and the principles that provide "the sinews and connections" for human thought, that underlie "that infinite amount of knowledge of which we are not always conscious," of which Leibnitz spoke. It is therefore quite natural that we should link these developments to the revival of philosophical grammar, which grew from the same soil as an attempt, quite fruitful and legitimate, to explore one basic facet of human intelligence.

In recent discussion, models and observations derived from ethology have frequently been cited as providing biological support, or at least analogue, to new approaches to the study of human intelligence. I cite these comments of Lorenz's mainly in order to show that this reference does not distort the outlook of at least some of the founders of this domain of comparative psychology.

One word of caution is necessary in referring to Lorenz, now that he has been discovered by Robert Ardrey and Joseph Alsop and popularized as a prophet of doom. It seems to me that Lorenz's views on human aggression have been extended to near absurdity by some of his expositors. It is no doubt true that there are innate tendencies in the human psychic constitution that lead to aggressiveness under specific social and cultural conditions. But there is little reason to suppose that these tendencies are so dominant as to leave us forever tottering on the brink of a Hobbesian war of all against all – as, incidentally, Lorenz at least is fully aware, if I read him rightly. Skepticism is certainly in order when a doctrine of man's "inherent aggressiveness" comes to the surface in a society that glorifies competitiveness, in a civilization that has been distinguished by the brutality of the attack that it has mounted against less fortunate peoples. It is fair to ask to what extent the enthusiasm for this curious view of man's nature is attributable to fact and logic and to what extent it merely reflects the limited extent to which the general cultural level has advanced since the days when Clive and the Portuguese explorers taught the meaning of true savagery to the inferior races that stood in their way.

In any event, I would not want what I am saying to be confused with other, entirely different attempts to revive a theory of human instinct. What seems to me important in ethology is its attempt to explore the innate properties that determine how knowledge is acquired and the character of this knowledge. Returning to this theme, we must consider a further question: how did the human mind come to acquire the innate structure that we are led to attribute to it? Not too surprisingly, Lorenz takes the position that this is simply a matter of natural selection. Peirce offers a rather different speculation, arguing that "nature fecundates the mind of man with ideas which, when these ideas grow up, will resemble their father, Nature." Man is "provided with certain natural beliefs that are true" because "certain uniformities . . . prevail throughout the universe, and the reasoning mind is [it]self a product of this universe. These same laws are thus, by logical necessity, incorporated in his own being." Here, it seems clear that Peirce's argument is entirely without force and that it offers little improvement over the preestablished harmony that it was presumably intended to replace. The fact that the mind is a product of natural laws does not imply that it is equipped to understand these laws or to arrive at them by "abduction." There would be no difficulty in designing a device (say, programing a computer) that is a product of natural law, but that, given data, will arrive at any arbitrary absurd theory to "explain" these data.

In fact, the processes by which the human mind achieved its present stage of complexity and its particular form of innate organization are a total mystery, as much so as the analogous questions about the physical or mental organization of any other complex organism. It is perfectly safe to attribute this development to "natural selection," so long as we realize that there is no substance to this assertion, that it amounts to nothing more than a belief that there is some naturalistic explanation for these phenomena. The problem of accounting for evolutionary development is, in some ways, rather like that of explaining successful abduction. The laws that determine possible successful mutation and the nature of complex organisms are as unknown as the laws that determine the choice of hypotheses.[26] With no knowledge of the laws that determine the

---

[26] It has been argued on statistical grounds – through comparison of the known rate of mutation with the astronomical number of imaginable modifications of chromosomes and their parts – that such laws must exist and must vastly restrict the realizable possibilities. See the papers by Eden, Schützenberger, and Gavadan in *Mathematical Challenges to the Neo-Darwinian Interpretation of Evolution*, Wistar Symposium Monograph No. 5, 1967.

organization and structure of complex biological systems, it is just as senseless to ask what the "probability" is for the human mind to have reached its present state as it is to inquire into the "probability" that a particular physical theory will be devised. And, as we have noted, it is idle to speculate about laws of learning until we have some indication of what kind of knowledge is attainable – in the case of language, some indication of the constraints on the set of potential grammars.

In studying the evolution of mind, we cannot guess to what extent there are physically possible alternatives to, say, transformational generative grammar, for an organism meeting certain other physical conditions characteristic of humans. Conceivably, there are none – or very few – in which case talk about evolution of the language capacity is beside the point. The vacuity of such speculation, however, has no bearing one way or another on those aspects of the problem of mind that can be sensibly pursued. It seems to me that these aspects are, for the moment, the problems illustrated in the case of language by the study of the nature, the use, and the acquisition of linguistic competence.

There is one final issue that deserves a word of comment. I have been using mentalistic terminology quite freely, but entirely without prejudice as to the question of what may be the physical realization of the abstract mechanisms postulated to account for the phenomena of behavior or the acquisition of knowledge. We are not constrained, as was Descartes, to postulate a second substance when we deal with phenomena that are not expressible in terms of matter in motion, in his sense. Nor is there much point in pursuing the question of psychophysical parallelism, in this connection. It is an interesting question whether the functioning and evolution of human mentality can be accommodated within the framework of physical explanation, as presently conceived, or whether there are new principles, now unknown, that must be invoked, perhaps principles that emerge only at higher levels of organization than can now be submitted to physical investigation. We can, however, be fairly sure that there will be a physical explanation for the phenomena in question, if they can be explained at all, for an uninteresting terminological reason, namely that the concept of "physical explanation" will no doubt be extended to incorporate whatever is discovered in this domain, exactly as it was extended to accommodate gravitational and electromagnetic force, massless particles, and numerous other entities and processes that would have offended the common sense of earlier generations. But it seems clear that this issue need not delay the study of the topics that are now open to investigation, and it seems futile to speculate about matters so remote from present understanding.

I have tried to suggest that the study of language may very well, as was traditionally supposed, provide a remarkably favorable perspective for the study of human mental processes. The creative aspect of language use, when investigated with care and respect for the facts, shows that current notions of habit and generalization, as determinants of behavior or knowledge, are quite inadequate. The abstractness of linguistic structure reinforces this conclusion, and it suggests further that in both perception and learning the mind plays an active role in determining the character of the acquired knowledge. The empirical study of linguistic universals has led to the formulation of highly restrictive and, I believe, quite plausible hypotheses concerning the possible variety of human languages, hypotheses that contribute to the attempt to develop a theory of acquisition of knowledge that gives due place to intrinsic mental activity. It seems to me, then, that the study of language should occupy a central place in general psychology.

Surely the classical questions of language and mind receive no final solution, or even the hint of a final solution, from the work that is being actively pursued today. Nevertheless, these problems can be formulated in new ways and seen in a new light. For the first time in many years, it seems to me, there is some real opportunity for substantial progress in the study of the contribution of the mind to perception and the innate basis for acquisition of knowledge. Still, in many respects, we have not made the first approach to a real answer to the classical problems. For example, the central problems relating to the creative aspect of language use remain as inaccessible as they have always been. And the study of universal semantics, surely crucial to the full investigation of language structure, has barely advanced since the medieval period. Many other critical areas might be mentioned where progress has been slow or nonexistent. Real progress has been made in the study of the mechanisms of language, the formal principles that make possible the creative aspect of language use and that determine the phonetic form and semantic content of utterances. Our understanding of these mechanisms, though only fragmentary, does seem to me to have real implications for the study of human psychology. By pursuing the kinds of research that now seem feasible and by focusing attention on certain problems that are now accessible to study, we may be able to spell out in some detail the elaborate and abstract computations that determine, in part, the nature of percepts and the character of the knowledge that we can acquire – the highly specific ways of interpreting phenomena that are, in large measure, beyond our consciousness and control and that may be unique to man.

4 Form and meaning in natural languages

When we study human language, we are approaching what some might call the "human essence," the distinctive qualities of mind that are, so far as we know, unique to man and that are inseparable from any critical phase of human existence, personal or social. Hence the fascination of this study, and, no less, its frustration. The frustration arises from the fact that despite much progress, we remain as incapable as ever before of coming to grips with the core problem of human language, which I take to be this: having mastered a language, one is able to understand an indefinite number of expressions that are new to one's experience, that bear no simple physical resemblance and are in no simple way analogous to the expressions that constitute one's linguistic experience; and one is able, with greater or less facility, to produce such expressions on an appropriate occasion, despite their novelty and independently of detectable stimulus configurations, and to be understood by others who share this still mysterious ability. The normal use of language is, in this sense, a creative activity. This creative aspect of normal language use is one fundamental factor that distinguishes human language from any known system of animal communication.

It is important to bear in mind that the creation of linguistic expressions that are novel but appropriate is the normal mode of language use. If some individual were to restrict himself largely to a definite set of linguistic patterns, to a set of habitual responses to stimulus configurations, or to "analogies" in the sense of modern linguistics, we would regard him as mentally defective, as being less human than animal. He would immediately be set apart from normal humans by his inability to understand normal discourse, or to take part in it in the normal way – the normal way being innovative, free from control by external stimuli, and appropriate to new and ever changing situations.

It is not a novel insight that human speech is distinguished by these qualities, though it is an insight that must be recaptured time and time again. With each advance in our understanding of the mechanisms of language, thought, and behavior, comes a tendency to believe that we have found the key to understanding man's apparently unique qualities of mind. These advances are real, but an honest appraisal will show, I think, that they are far from providing such a key. We do not understand, and, for all we know, we may never come to understand what makes it possible for a normal human intelligence to use language as an instrument for the free expression of thought and feeling; or, for that matter, what qualities of mind are involved in the creative acts of intelligence that are characteristic, not unique and exceptional, in a truly human existence.

I think that this is an important fact to stress, not only for linguists and psychologists whose research centers on these issues, but, even more, for those who hope to learn something useful in their own work and thinking from research into language and thought. It is particularly important that the limitations of understanding be clear to those involved in teaching, in the universities, and even more important, in the schools. There are strong pressures to make use of new educational technology and to design curriculum and teaching methods in the light of the latest scientific advances. In itself, this is not objectionable. It is important, nevertheless, to remain alert to a very real danger: that new knowledge and technique will define the nature of what is taught and how it is taught, rather than contribute to the realization of educational goals that are set on other grounds and in other terms. Let me be concrete. Technique and even technology is available for rapid and efficient inculcation of skilled behavior, in language teaching, teaching of arithmetic, and other domains. There is, consequently, a real temptation to reconstruct curriculum in the terms defined by the new technology. And it is not too difficult to invent a rationale, making use of the concepts of "controlling behavior," enhancing skills, and so on. Nor is it difficult to construct objective tests that are sure to demonstrate the effectiveness of such methods in reaching certain goals that are incorporated in these tests. But successes of this sort will not demonstrate that an important educational goal has been achieved. They will not demonstrate that it is important to concentrate on developing skilled behavior in the student. What little we know about human intelligence would at least suggest something quite different: that by diminishing the range and complexity of materials presented to the inquiring mind, by setting behavior in fixed patterns, these methods may harm and distort the normal development of creative abilities. I do not want to dwell on the matter. I am sure that any of you will be able to find examples from your own experience. It is perfectly proper to try to exploit genuine advances in knowledge, and within some given field of study, it is inevitable, and quite proper, that research should be directed by considerations of feasibility as well as considerations of ultimate significance. It is also highly likely, if not inevitable, that considerations of feasibility and significance will lead in divergent paths. For those who wish to apply the achievements of one discipline to the problems of another, it is important to make very clear the exact nature not only of what has been achieved, but equally important, the limitations of what has been achieved.

I mentioned a moment ago that the creative aspect of normal use of language is not a new discovery. It provides one important pillar for Descartes' theory of mind, for his study of the limits of mechanical explanation. The latter, in turn, provides one crucial element in the construction of the anti-authoritarian social and political philosophy of the Enlightenment. And, in fact, there were even some efforts to found a theory of artistic creativity on the creative aspect of normal language use. Schlegel, for example, argues that poetry has a unique position among the arts, a fact illustrated, he claims, by the use of the term "poetical" to refer to the element of creative imagination in any artistic effort, as distinct, say, from the term "musical," which would be used metaphorically to refer to a sensual element. To explain this asymmetry, he observes that every mode of artistic expression makes use of a certain medium and that the medium of poetry – language – is unique in that language, as an expression of the human mind rather than a product of nature, is boundless in scope and is constructed on the basis of a recursive principle that permits each creation to serve as the basis for a new creative act. Hence the central position among the arts of the art forms whose medium is language.

The belief that language, with its inherent creative aspect, is a unique human possession did not go unchallenged, of course. One expositor of Cartesian philosophy, Antoine Le Grand, refers to the opinion "of some people of the East Indies, who think that Apes and Baboons, which are with them in great numbers, are imbued with understanding, and that they can speak but will not for fear they should be employed, and set to work." If there is a more serious argument in support of the claim that human language capacity is shared with other primates, then I am unaware of it. In fact, whatever evidence we do have seems to me to support the view that the ability to acquire and use language is a species-specific human capacity, that there are very deep and restrictive principles that determine the nature of human language and are rooted in the specific character of the human mind. Obviously arguments bearing on this hypothesis cannot be definitive or conclusive, but it appears to me, nevertheless, that even in the present stage of our knowledge, the evidence is not inconsiderable.

There are any number of questions that might lead one to undertake a study of language. Personally, I am primarily intrigued by the possibility of learning something, from the study of language, that will bring to light inherent properties of the human mind. We cannot now say anything particularly informative about the normal creative use of language in itself. But I think that we are slowly coming to understand the mechanisms that make possible this creative use of language, the use of language as an instrument of free thought and expression. Speaking again from a personal point of view, to me the most interesting aspects of contemporary work in grammar are the attempts to formulate principles of organization of language which, it is proposed, are universal reflections of properties of mind; and the attempt to show that on this assumption, certain facts about particular languages can be explained. Viewed in this way, linguistics is simply a part of human psychology: the field that seeks to determine the nature of human mental capacities and to study how these capacities are put to work. Many psychologists would reject a characterization of their discipline in these terms, but this reaction seems to me to indicate a serious inadequacy in their conception of psychology, rather than a defect in the formulation itself. In any event, it seems to me that these are proper terms in which to set the goals of contemporary linguistics, and to discuss its achievements and its failings.

I think it is now possible to make some fairly definite proposals about the organization of human language and to put them to empirical test. The theory of transformational-generative grammar, as it is evolving along diverse and sometimes conflicting paths, has put forth such proposals; and there has been, in the past few years, some very productive and suggestive work that attempts to refine and reconstruct these formulations of the processes and structures that underlie human language.

The theory of grammar is concerned with the question, What is the nature of a person's knowledge of his language, the knowledge that enables him to make use of language in the normal, creative fashion? A person who knows a language has mastered a system of rules that assigns sound and meaning in a definite way for an infinite class of possible sentences. Each language thus consists (in part) of a certain pairing of sound and meaning over an infinite domain. Of course, the person who knows the language has no consciousness of having mastered these rules or of putting them to use, nor is there any reason to suppose that this knowledge of the rules of language can be brought to consciousness. Through introspection, a person may accumulate various kinds of evidence about the sound–meaning relation determined by the rules of the language that he has mastered; there is no reason to suppose that he can go much beyond this surface level of data so as to discover, through introspection, the underlying rules and principles that determine the relation of sound and meaning. Rather, to discover these rules and principles is a typical problem of science. We have a collection of data regarding sound–meaning correspondence, the form and interpretation of linguistic expressions, in various languages. We try to determine, for each language, a system of rules that will account for such data. More deeply, we try to establish the principles that govern the formation of such systems of rules for any human language.

The system of rules that specifies the sound–meaning relation for a given language can be called the "grammar" – or, to use a more technical term, the "generative grammar" – of this language. To say that a grammar "generates" a certain set of structures is simply to say that it specifies this set in a precise way. In this sense, we may say that the grammar of a language generates an infinite set of "structural descriptions," each structural description being an abstract object of some sort that determines a particular sound, a particular meaning, and whatever formal properties and configurations serve to mediate the relation between sound and meaning. For example, the grammar of English generates structural descriptions for the sentences I am now speaking; or, to take a simpler case for purposes of illustration, the grammar of English would generate a structural description for each of these sentences:

1   John is certain that Bill will leave.

2   John is certain to leave.

Each of us has mastered and internally represented a system of grammar that assigns structural descriptions to these sentences; we use this knowledge, totally without awareness or even the possibility of awareness, in producing these sentences or understanding them when they are produced by others. The structural descriptions include a phonetic representation of the sentences and a specification of their meaning. In the case of the cited examples 1 and 2, the structural descriptions must convey roughly the following information: they must indicate that in the case of 1, a given psychological state (namely, being certain that Bill will leave) is attributed to John; whereas in the case of 2, a given logical property (namely, the property of being certain) is attributed to the proposition that John will leave. Despite the superficial similarity of form of these two sentences, the structural descriptions generated by the grammar must indicate that their meanings are very different: one attributes a psychological state to John, the other attributes a logical property to an abstract proposition. The second sentence might be paraphrased in a very different form:

3   That John will leave is certain.

For the first there is no such paraphrase. In the paraphrase 3 the "logical form" of 2 is expressed more directly, one might say. The grammatical relations in 2 and 3 are very similar, despite the difference of surface form; the grammatical relations in 1 and 2 are very different, despite the similarity of surface form. Such facts as these provide the starting point for an investigation of the grammatical structure of English – and more generally, for the investigation of the general properties of human language.

To carry the discussion of properties of language further, let me introduce the term "surface structure" to refer to a representation of the phrases that constitute a linguistic expression and the categories to which these phrases belong. In sentence 1, the phrases of the surface structure include: "that Bill will leave," which is a full proposition; the noun phrases "Bill" and "John"; the verb phrases "will leave" and "is certain that Bill will leave," and so on. In sentence 2, the surface structure includes the verb phrases "to leave" and "is certain to leave"; but the surface structure of 2 includes no proposition of the form "John will leave," even though this proposition expresses part of the meaning of "John is certain to leave," and appears as a phrase in the surface structure of its paraphrase, "that John will leave is certain." In this sense, surface structure does not necessarily provide an accurate indication of the structures and relations that determine the meaning of a sentence; in the case of sentence 2, "John is certain to leave," the surface structure fails to indicate that the proposition "John will leave" expresses a part of the meaning of the sentence – although in the other two examples that I gave the surface structure comes rather close to indicating the semantically significant relations.

Continuing, let me introduce the further technical term "deep structure" to refer to a representation of the phrases that play a more central role in the semantic interpretation of a sentence. In the case of 1 and 3, the deep structure might not be very different from the surface structure. In the case of 2, the deep structure will be very different from the surface structure, in that it will include some such proposition as "John will leave" and the predicate "is certain" applied to this proposition, though nothing of the sort appears in the surface structure. In general, apart from the simplest examples, the surface structures of sentences are very different from their deep structures.

The grammar of English will generate, for each sentence, a deep structure, and will contain rules showing how this deep structure is related to a surface structure. The rules expressing the relation of deep and surface structure are called "grammatical transformations." Hence the term "transformational-generative grammar." In addition to rules defining deep structures, surface structures, and the relation between them, the grammar of English contains further rules that relate these "syntactic objects" (namely, paired deep and surface structures) to phonetic representations on the one hand, and to representations of meaning on the other. A person who has acquired knowledge of English has internalized these rules and makes use of them when he understands or produces the sentences just given as examples, and an indefinite range of others.

Evidence in support of this approach is provided by the observation that interesting properties of English sentences can be explained directly in terms of the deep structures assigned to them. Thus consider once again the two sentences 1 ("John is certain that Bill will leave") and 2 ("John is certain to leave"). Recall that in the case of the first, the deep structure and surface structure are virtually identical, whereas in the case of the second, they are very different. Observe also that in the case of the first, there is a corresponding nominal phrase, namely, "John's certainty that Bill will leave (surprised me)"; but in the case of the second, there is no corresponding nominal phrase. We cannot say "John's certainty to leave surprised me." The latter nominal phrase is intelligible, I suppose, but it is not well formed in English. The speaker of English can easily make himself aware of this fact, though the reason for it will very likely escape him. This fact is a special case of a very general property of English: namely, nominal phrases exist corresponding to sentences that are very close in surface form to deep structure, but not corresponding to such sentences that are remote in surface form from deep structure. Thus "John is certain that Bill will leave," being close in surface form to its deep structure, corresponds to the nominal phrase "John's certainty that Bill will leave"; but there is no such phrase as "John's certainty to leave" corresponding to "John is certain to leave," which is remote from its deep structure.

The notions of "closeness" and "remoteness" can be made quite precise. When we have made them precise, we have an explanation for the fact that nominalizations exist in certain cases but not in others – though were they to exist in these other cases, they would often be perfectly intelligible. The explanation turns on the notion of deep structure: in effect, it states that nominalizations must reflect the properties of deep structure. There are many examples that illustrate this phenomenon. What is important is the evidence it provides in support of the view that deep structures which are often quite abstract exist and play a central role in the grammatical processes that we use in producing and interpreting sentences. Such facts, then, support the hypothesis that deep structures of the sort postulated in transformational-generative grammar are real mental structures. These deep structures, along with the transformation rules that relate them to surface structure and the rules relating deep and surface structures to representations of sound and meaning, are the rules that have been mastered by the person who has learned a language. They constitute his knowledge of the language; they are put to use when he speaks and understands.

The examples I have given so far illustrate the role of deep structure in determining meaning, and show that even in very simple cases, the deep structure may be remote from the surface form. There is a great deal of evidence indicating that the phonetic form of a sentence is determined by its surface structure, by principles of an extremely interesting and intricate sort that I will not try to discuss here. From such evidence it is fair to conclude that surface structure determines phonetic form, and that the grammatical relations represented in deep structure are those that determine meaning. Furthermore, as already noted, there are certain grammatical processes, such as the process of nominalization, that can be stated only in terms of abstract deep structures.

The situation is complicated, however, by the fact that surface structure also plays a role in determining semantic interpretation.[1] The study of this question is one of the most controversial aspects of current work, and, in my opinion, likely to be one of the most fruitful. As an illustration, consider some of the properties of the present perfect aspect in English – for example, such sentences as "John has lived in Princeton." An interesting and rarely noted feature of this

---

[1] I discuss this matter in some detail in "Deep Structure and Semantic Interpretation," in R. Jakobson and S. Kawamoto, eds., *Studies in General and Oriental Linguistics*, commemorative volume for Shiro Hattori, TEC Corporation for Language and Educational Research, Tokyo, 1970.

aspect is that in such cases it carries the presupposition that the subject is alive. Thus it is proper for me to say "I have lived in Princeton" but, knowing that Einstein is dead, I would not say "Einstein has lived in Princeton." Rather, I would say "Einstein lived in Princeton." (As always, there are complications, but this is accurate as a first approximation.) But now consider active and passive forms with present perfect aspect. Knowing that John is dead and Bill alive, I can say "Bill has often been visited by John, but not "John has often visited Bill"; rather, "John often visited Bill." I can say "I have been taught physics by Einstein" but not "Einstein has taught me physics"; rather, "Einstein taught me physics." In general, active and passive are synonymous and have essentially the same deep structures. But in these cases, active and passive forms differ in the presuppositions they express; put simply, the presupposition is that the person denoted by the surface subject is alive. In this respect, the surface structure contributes to the meaning of the sentence in that it is relevant to determining what is presupposed in the use of a sentence.

Carrying the matter further, observe that the situation is different when we have a conjoined subject. Thus given that Hilary is alive and Marco Polo dead, it is proper to say "Hilary has climbed Mt. Everest" but not "Marco Polo has climbed Mt. Everest"; rather, again, "Marco Polo climbed Mt. Everest." (Again, I overlook certain subtleties and complications.) But now consider the sentence "Marco Polo and Hilary (among others) have climbed Mt. Everest." In this case, there is no expressed presupposition that Marco Polo is alive, as there is none in the passive "Mt. Everest has been climbed by Marco Polo (among others)."

Notice further that the situation changes considerably when we shift from the normal intonation, as in the cases I have just given, to an intonation contour that contains a contrastive or expressive stress. The effect of such intonation on presupposition is fairly complex. Let me illustrate with a simple case. Consider the sentence "The Yankees played the Red Sox in Boston." With normal intonation, the point of main stress and highest pitch is the word "Boston" and the sentence might be an answer to such questions as "where did the Yankees play the Red Sox?" ("in Boston"); "what did the Yankees do?" ("they played the Red Sox in Boston"); "what happened?" ("the Yankees played the Red Sox in Boston"). But suppose that contrastive stress is placed on "Red Sox," so that we have "The Yankees played the RED SOX in Boston." Now, the sentence can be the answer only to "Who did the Yankees play in Boston?" Note that the sentence presupposes that the Yankees played someone in Boston; if there was no game at all, it is improper, not just false, to say "The Yankees played the RED SOX in Boston." In contrast, if there was no game at all, it is false, but not improper, to say "The Yankees played the Red Sox in Boston," with normal intonation. Thus contrastive stress carries a presupposition in a sense in which normal intonation does not, though normal intonation also carries a presupposition in another sense; thus it would be improper to answer the question "Who played the Red Sox in Boston?" with "The Yankees played the Red Sox in Boston" (normal intonation). The same property of contrastive stress is shown by the so-called cleft sentence construction. Thus the sentence "It was the YANKEES who played the Red Sox in Boston" has primary stress on "Yankees," and presupposes that someone played the Red Sox in Boston. The sentence is improper, not just false, if there was no game at all. These phenomena have generally been overlooked when the semantic role of contrastive stress has been noted.

To further illustrate the role of surface structure in determining meaning, consider such sentences as this: "John is tall for a pygmy." This sentence presupposes that John is a pygmy, and that pygmies tend to be short; hence given our knowledge of the Watusi, it would be anomalous to say "John is tall for a Watusi." On the other hand, consider what happens when we insert the word "even" in the sentence. Inserting it before "John" we derive: "Even John is tall for a pygmy." Again, the presupposition is that John is a pygmy and that pygmies are short. But consider: "John is tall even for a pygmy." This presupposes that pygmies are tall; it is therefore a strange sentence, given our knowledge of the facts, as compared, say, to "John is tall even for a Watusi," which is quite all right. The point is that the position of "even" in the sentence "John is tall for a pygmy" determines the presupposition with respect to the average height of pygmies.

But the placement of the word "even" is a matter of surface structure. We can see this from the fact that the word "even" can appear in association with phrases that do not have any representation at the level of deep structure: Consider, for example, the sentence "John isn't certain to leave at 10; in fact, he isn't even certain to leave at all." Here, the word "even" is associated with "certain to leave," a phrase which, as noted earlier, does not appear at the level of deep structure. Hence in this case as well properties of surface structure play a role in determining what is presupposed by a certain sentence.

The role of surface structure in determining meaning is illustrated once again by the phenomenon of pronominalization.[2] Thus if I say "Each of the men hates his brothers," the word "his" may refer to one of the men; but if I say "The men each hate his brothers," the word "his" must refer to some other person, not otherwise referred to in the sentence. However, the evidence is strong that "each of the men" and "the men each" derive from the same deep structure. Similarly, it has been noted that placement of stress plays an important role in determining pronominal reference. Consider the following discourse: "John washed the car; I was afraid someone ELSE would do it." The sentence implies that I hoped

---

[2] The examples that follow are due to Ray Dougherty, Adrian Akmajian, and Ray Jackendoff. See my article in Jakobson and Kawamoto, eds., *Studies in General and Oriental Linguistics*, for references.

that John would wash the car, and I'm happy that he did. But now consider the following: "John washed the car; I was AFRAID someone else would do it." With stress on "afraid," the sentence implies that I hoped that John would not wash the car. The reference of "someone else" is different in the two cases. There are many other examples that illustrate the role of surface structure in determining pronominal reference.

To complicate matters still further, deep structure too plays a role in determining pronominal reference. Thus consider the sentence "John appeared to Bill to like him." Here, the pronoun "him" may refer to Bill but not John. Compare "John appealed to Bill to like him." Here, the pronoun may refer to John but not Bill. Thus we can say "John appealed to Mary to like him," but not "John appeared to Mary to like him," where "him" refers to "John"; on the other hand, we can say "John appeared to Mary to like her," but not "John appealed to Mary to like her," where "her" refers to Mary. Similarly, in "John appealed to Bill to like himself," the reflexive refers to Bill; but in "John appeared to Bill to like himself," it refers to John. These sentences are approximately the same in surface structure; it is the differences in deep structure that determine the pronominal reference.

Hence pronominal reference depends on both deep and surface structure. A person who knows English has mastered a system of rules which make use of properties of deep and surface structure in determining pronominal reference. Again, he cannot discover these rules by introspection. In fact, these rules are still unknown, though some of their properties are clear.

To summarize: the generative grammar of a language specifies an infinite set of structural descriptions, each of which contains a deep structure, a surface structure, a phonetic representation, a semantic representation, and other formal structures. The rules relating deep and surface structure – the so-called "grammatical transformations" – have been investigated in some detail, and are fairly well understood. The rules that relate surface structure and phonetic representation are also reasonably well understood (though I do not want to imply that the matter is beyond dispute: far from it). It seems that both deep and surface structure enter into the determination of meaning. Deep structure provides the grammatical relations of predication, modification, and so on, that enter into the determination of meaning. On the other hand, it appears that matters of focus and presupposition, topic and comment, the scope of logical elements, and pronominal reference are determined, in part at least, by surface structure. The rules that relate syntactic structures to representations of meaning are not at all well understood. In fact, the notion "representation of meaning" or "semantic representation" is itself highly controversial. It is not clear at all that it is possible to distinguish sharply between the contribution of grammar to the determination of meaning, and the contribution of so-called "pragmatic considerations," questions of fact and belief and context of utterance. It is perhaps worth mentioning that rather similar questions can be raised about the notion "phonetic representation." Although the latter is one of the best-established and least controversial notions of linguistic theory, we can, nevertheless, raise the question whether or not it is a legitimate abstraction, whether a deeper understanding of the use of language might not show that factors that go beyond grammatical structure enter into the determination of perceptual representations and physical form in an inextricable fashion, and cannot be separated, without distortion, from the formal rules that interpret surface structure as phonetic form.

So far, the study of language has progressed on the basis of a certain abstraction: namely, we abstract away from conditions of use of language and consider formal structures and the formal operations that relate them. Among these formal structures are those of syntax, namely, deep and surface structures; and also the phonetic and semantic representations, which we take to be certain formal objects related to syntactic structures by certain well-defined operations. This process of abstraction is in no way illegitimate, but one must understand that it expresses a point of view, a hypothesis about the nature of mind, that is not a priori obvious. It expresses the working hypothesis that we can proceed with the study of "knowledge of language" – what is often called "linguistic competence" – in abstraction from the problems of how language is used. The working hypothesis is justified by the success that is achieved when it is adopted. A great deal has been learned about the mechanisms of language, and, I would say, about the nature of mind, on the basis of this hypothesis. But we must be aware that in part, at least, this approach to language is forced upon us by the fact that our concepts fail us when we try to study the use of language. We are reduced to platitudes, or to observations which, though perhaps quite interesting, do not lend themselves to systematic study by means of the intellectual tools presently available to us. On the other hand, we can bring to the study of formal structures and their relations a wealth of experience and understanding. It may be that at this point we are facing a problem of conflict between significance and feasibility, a conflict of the sort that I mentioned earlier in this paper. I do not believe that this is the case, but it is possible. I feel fairly confident that the abstraction to the study of formal mechanisms of language is appropriate; my confidence arises from the fact that many quite elegant results have been achieved on the basis of this abstraction. Still, caution is in order. It may be that the next great advance in the study of language will require the forging of new intellectual tools that permit us to bring into consideration a variety of questions that have been cast into the waste-bin of "pragmatics," so that we could proceed to study questions that we know how to formulate in an intelligible fashion.

As noted, I think that the abstraction to linguistic competence is legitimate. To go further, I believe that the inability of modern psychology to come to grips with the problems of human intelligence is in part, at least, a result of its unwillingness to undertake the study of abstract structures and mechanisms of mind. Notice that the approach to linguistic structure that I have been outlining has a highly traditional flavor to it. I think it is no distortion to say that this approach makes precise a point of view that was inherent in the very important work of the seventeenth- and eighteenth-century universal grammarians, and that was developed, in various ways, in rationalist and romantic philosophy of language and mind. The approach deviates in many ways from a more modern, and in my opinion quite erroneous, conception that knowledge of language can be accounted for as a system of habits, or in terms of stimulus-response connections, principles of "analogy" and "generalization," and other notions that have been explored in twentieth-century linguistics and psychology, and that develop from traditional empiricist speculation. The fatal inadequacy of all such approaches, I believe, results from their unwillingness to undertake the abstract study of linguistic competence. Had the physical sciences limited themselves by similar methodological strictures, we would still be in the era of Babylonian astronomy.

One traditional concept that has reemerged in current work is that of "universal grammar," and I want to conclude by saying just a word about this topic. There are two kinds of evidence suggesting that deep-seated formal conditions are satisfied by the grammars of all languages. The first kind of evidence is provided by the study of a wide range of languages. In attempting to construct generative grammars for languages of widely varied kinds, investigators have repeatedly been led to rather similar assumptions as to the form and organization of such generative systems. But a more persuasive kind of evidence bearing on universal grammar is provided by the study of a single language. It may at first seem paradoxical that the intensive study of a single language should provide evidence regarding universal grammar, but a little thought about the matter shows that this is a very natural consequence.

To see this, consider the problem of determining the mental capacities that make language acquisition possible. If the study of grammar – of linguistic competence – involves an abstraction from language use, then the study of the mental capacities that make acquisition of grammar possible involves a further, second-order abstraction. I see no fault in this. We may formulate the problem of determining the intrinsic characteristics of a device of unknown properties that accepts as "input" the kind of data available to the child learning his first language, and produces as "output" the generative grammar of that language. The "output," in this case, is the internally represented grammar, mastery of which constitutes knowledge of the language. If we undertake to study the intrinsic structure of a language-acquisition device without dogma or prejudice, we arrive at conclusions which, though of course only tentative, still seem to me both significant and reasonably well-founded. We must attribute to this device enough structure so that the grammar can be constructed within the empirically given constraints of time and available data, and we must meet the empirical condition that different speakers of the same language, with somewhat different experience and training, nevertheless acquire grammars that are remarkably similar, as we can determine from the ease with which they communicate and the correspondences among them in the interpretation of new sentences. It is immediately obvious that the data available to the child is quite limited – the number of seconds in his lifetime is trivially small as compared with the range of sentences that he can immediately understand and can produce in the appropriate manner. Having some knowledge of the characteristics of the acquired grammars and the limitations on the available data, we can formulate quite reasonable and fairly strong empirical hypotheses regarding the internal structure of the language-acquisition device that constructs the postulated grammars from the given data. When we study this question in detail, we are, I believe, led to attribute to the device a very rich system of constraints on the form of a possible grammar; otherwise, it is impossible to explain how children come to construct grammars of the kind that seem empirically adequate under the given conditions of time and access to data. But if we assume, furthermore, that children are not genetically predisposed to learn one rather than another language, then the conclusions we reach regarding the language-acquisition device are conclusions regarding universal grammar. These conclusions can be falsified by showing that they fail to account for the construction of grammars of other languages, for example. And these conclusions are further verified if they serve to explain facts about other languages. This line of argument seems to me very reasonable in a general way, and when pursued in detail it leads us to strong empirical hypotheses concerning universal grammar, even from the study of a particular language.

I have discussed an approach to the study of language that takes this study to be a branch of theoretical human psychology. Its goal is to exhibit and clarify the mental capacities that make it possible for a human to learn and use a language. As far as we know, these capacities are unique to man, and have no significant analogue in any other organism. If the conclusions of this research are anywhere near correct, then humans must be endowed with a very rich and explicit set of mental attributes that determine a specific form of language on the basis of very slight and rather degenerate data. Furthermore, they make use of the mentally represented language in a highly creative way, constrained by its rules but free to express new thoughts that relate to past experience or present sensations only in a remote and abstract fashion. If this is correct, there is no hope in the study of the "control" of human behavior by stimulus conditions, schedules of reinforcement, establishment of habit structures, patterns of behavior, and so on. Of course, one can design a restricted environment in which such control and such patterns can be demonstrated, but there is no reason to suppose that any more is learned about the range of human potentialities by such methods than would be learned by observing humans in a prison or an army – or in many a schoolroom. The essential properties of the human mind will always escape such investigation. And if I can be pardoned a final "nonprofessional" comment, I am very happy with this outcome.

5   The formal nature of language

General properties of language

Many generations of productive scholarship notwithstanding, the questions to which this paper is addressed can receive only quite tentative answers. There are few languages for which descriptions in depth are available, and only selected aspects of language have been studied with sufficient care and success to provide support for conclusions of a general nature. Still, it is possible, with some degree of confidence, to outline certain properties and conditions that distinguish human languages among arbitrary systems of symbolic manipulation, communication, and self-expression.

Competence and performance

At the crudest level of description, we may say that a language associates sound and meaning in a particular way; to have command of a language is to be able, in principle, to understand what is said and to produce a signal with an intended semantic interpretation. But aside from much unclarity, there is also a serious ambiguity in this crude characterization of command of language. It is quite obvious that sentences have an intrinsic meaning determined by linguistic rule and that a person with command of a language has in some way internalized the system of rules that determine both the phonetic shape of the sentence and its intrinsic semantic content – that he has developed what we will refer to as a specific *linguistic competence.* However, it is equally clear that the actual observed use of language – actual *performance* – does not simply reflect the intrinsic sound–meaning connections established by the system of linguistic rules. Performance involves many other factors as well. We do not interpret what is said in our presence simply by application of the *linguistic* principles that determine the phonetic and semantic properties of an utterance. Extralinguistic beliefs concerning the speaker and the situation play a fundamental role in determining how speech is produced, identified, and understood. Linguistic performance is, furthermore, governed by principles of cognitive structure (for example, by memory restrictions) that are not, properly speaking, aspects of language.

To study a language, then, we must attempt to disassociate a variety of factors that interact with underlying competence to determine actual performance; the technical term "competence" refers to the ability of the idealized speaker–hearer to associate sounds and meanings strictly in accordance with the rules of his language. The grammar of a language, as a model for idealized competence,[1] establishes a certain relation between sound and meaning – between phonetic and semantic representations. We may say that the grammar of the language L generates a set of pairs (s, I), where s is the phonetic representation of a certain signal[2] and I is the semantic interpretation assigned to this signal by the rules of the language. To discover this grammar is the primary goal of the linguistic investigation of a particular language.

The general theory of linguistic structure is concerned with discovering the conditions that any such grammar must meet. This general theory will be concerned with conditions of three kinds: conditions on the class of admissible phonetic representations, the class of admissible semantic representations, and the systems of rules that generate paired phonetic and semantic representations. In all three respects, human languages are subject to stringent limiting conditions. There is no difficulty in constructing systems that do not meet these conditions, and that do not, therefore, qualify as potential human languages despite the fact that they associate sound and meaning in some definite way. Human languages are systems of a highly specific kind. There is no a priori necessity for a system relating sound and meaning to be of this kind. As this paper proceeds, we shall mention some of the highly restrictive conditions that appear to be essential properties of human language.

A grammar generates a certain set of pairs (s, I), where s is a phonetic representation and I its associated semantic interpretation. Similarly, we might think of a performance model as relating sound and meaning in a specific way. A perceptual model, PM, for example, might be described, as in 1, as a device that accepts a signal as input (along with much else) and assigns various grammatical representations as "output."

1

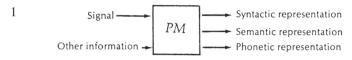

---

[1] The term "grammar" is often used ambiguously to refer both to the internalized system of rules and to the linguist's description of it.
[2] To be more precise, a certain class of signals that are repetitions of one another, in a sense to which we return subsequently.

A central problem for psychology is to discover the characteristics of a system *PM* of this sort. Clearly, in understanding a signal, a hearer brings to bear information about the structure of his language. In other words, the model *PM* incorporates the grammar *G* of a language. The study of how sentences are understood – the general problem of speech perception – must, obviously, remain within narrow limits unless it makes use of this basic property of a perceptual model. But it is important to distinguish clearly between the function and properties of the perceptual model *PM* and the competence model *G* that it incorporates. Both *G* and *PM* relate sound and meaning; but *PM* makes use of much information beyond the intrinsic sound–meaning association determined by the grammar *G*, and it operates under constraints of memory, time, and organization of perceptual strategies that are not matters of grammar. Correspondingly, although we may describe the grammar *G* as a system of processes and rules that apply in a certain order to relate sound and meaning, we are not entitled to take this as a description of the successive acts of a performance model such as *PM* – in fact, it would be quite absurd to do so. What we have said regarding perceptual models is equally applicable to production models. The grammatical rules that generate phonetic representations of signals with their semantic interpretations do not constitute a model for the production of sentences, although any such model must incorporate the system of grammatical rules. If these simple distinctions are overlooked, great confusion must result.

In this paper, attention is focused on competence and the grammars that characterize it; when speaking of semantic and phonetic interpretation of sentences, we refer exclusively to the idealized representations determined by this underlying system. Performance provides data for the study of linguistic competence. Competence, in the sense just described, is one of many factors that interact to determine performance. In general, we would expect that in studying the behavior of a complex organism, it will be necessary to isolate such essentially independent underlying systems as the system of linguistic competence, each with its intrinsic structure, for separate attention.

Initial steps toward a study of competence

Turning to the study of underlying competence, let us first take note of a few very obvious properties of the grammar of a human language. It is, first of all, quite clear that the set of paired phonetic and semantic representations generated by the grammar will be infinite. There is no human language in which it is possible, in fact or in principle, to specify a certain sentence as the longest sentence meaningful in this language. The grammar of any language contains devices that make it possible to form sentences of arbitrary complexity, each with its intrinsic semantic interpretation. It is important to realize that this is no mere logical nicety. The normal use of language relies in an essential way on this unboundedness, on the fact that language contains devices for generating sentences of arbitrary complexity. Repetition of sentences is a rarity; innovation, in accordance with the grammar of the language, is the rule in ordinary day-by-day performance. The idea that a person has a "verbal repertoire" – a stock of utterances that he produces by "habit" on an appropriate occasion – is a myth, totally at variance with the observed use of language. Nor is it possible to attach any substance to the view that the speaker has a stock of "patterns" in which he inserts words or morphemes. Such conceptions may apply to greetings, a few cliches, and so on, but they completely misrepresent the normal use of language, as the reader can easily convince himself by unprejudiced observation.[3]

To discover the grammar of some language user, we must begin by obtaining information that bears on his interpretation of sentences, on the semantic, grammatical, and phonetic structure that he assigns to them. For example, for the study of English, it would be important to discover such facts as the following. Consider the sentence frames 2 and the words "persuaded," "expected," and "happened":

2   a. John – Bill that he should leave
         b. John – Bill to leave
         c. John – to leave
         d. It is – that Bill will leave

The word "persuaded" can be inserted in a and b, but not c or d; "expected" can be inserted in b, c, d, but not a; "happened" can be inserted only in c. Inserting "persuaded" in a, we derive an ambiguous sentence, the interpretation of which depends on the reference of "he"; under one interpretation, the sentence is a near paraphrase of b, with "persuaded" inserted. When "expected" appears in b and c, the subject–verb relation holds between "Bill" and "leave" in b, but between "John" and "leave" in c. The sentence "John happened to leave" has roughly the same meaning as "It happened that John left," but "John expected to leave" is not even a remote paraphrase of "It expected that John left." Such facts as these can be stated in many ways, and we might use one or another technique to make sure of their accuracy. These are facts about the competence of the speaker of English. They can be used as a basis for discovering his internalized grammar.

Let us consider the status of such observations with slightly greater care. These observations actually bear directly on the output of a perceptual model

---

[3] Or by some simple calculations of the number of sentences and "patterns" that might be needed, for empirical adequacy, in such repertoires. For some relevant comments, see G. A. Miller, E. Galanter, and K. H. Pribram, *Plans and the Structure of Behavior* (New York: Holt, Rinehart and Winston, 1960), pp. 145 f.; G. A. Miller and N. Chomsky, "Finitary Models of Language Users," in R. D. Luce, R. Bush, and E. Galanter, eds., *Handbook of Mathematical Psychology* (New York: Wiley, 1963), Vol. II, p. 430.

such as 1; they relate to the structures assigned to signals by the hearer. Our characterization of the output of 1 is a construct based on evidence of this sort. Then, the perceptual model *PM* itself is a second-order construct. Abstracting further, we can study the grammar that constitutes one fundamental component of 1 as a third-order construct. Thus the evidence cited in the preceding paragraph actually has a bearing on grammar only indirectly. We must, in other words, presuppose the legitimacy of each abstraction. There seems little question of the legitimacy of abstraction in such cases as these, and there is an overwhelming mass of evidence of the sort cited. Once again, we note that idealization of the kind just described is inescapable if a complex organism is to be studied in a serious way.

This process of abstraction can be carried one step further. Consider an acquisition model *AM* that uses linguistic data to discover the grammar of the language to which this data pertains.

3

Just how the device *AM* selects a grammar will be determined by its internal structure, by the methods of analysis available to it, and by the initial constraints that it imposes on any possible grammar. If we are given information about the pairing of linguistic data and grammars, we may try to determine the nature of the device *AM*. Although these are not the terms that have been used, linguistics has always been concerned with this question. Thus modern structural linguistics has attempted to develop methods of analysis of a general nature, independent of any particular language, and an older and now largely forgotten tradition attempted to develop a system of universal constraints that any grammar must meet. We might describe both these attempts as concerned with the internal structure of the device *AM*, with the innate conception of "human language" that makes language acquisition possible.[4]

Universal grammar

Let us now turn to the study of underlying competence, and consider the general problem of how a sound–meaning pairing might be established. As a preliminary to this investigation of universal grammar, we must ask how sounds and meanings are to be represented. Since we are interested in human languages in general, such systems of representation must be independent of any particular language. We must, in other words, develop a universal phonetics and a

---

[4] The existence of innate mental structure is, obviously, not a matter of controversy. What we may question is just what it is and to what extent it is specific to language.

universal semantics that delimit, respectively, the set of possible signals and the set of possible semantic representations for any human language. It will then be possible to speak of a language as a particular pairing of signals with semantic interpretations, and to investigate the rules that establish this pairing. Our review of the general properties of language thus falls naturally into three parts: a discussion of universal phonetics, of universal semantics, and of the overarching system of universal grammar. The first two topics involve the representation of idealized form and semantic content; the theory of universal grammar deals with the mechanisms used in natural languages to determine the form of a sentence and its semantic content.

The importance of developing a universal semantics and universal phonetics, in the sense of the last paragraph, was clearly recognized long before the development of modern linguistics. For example, Bishop Wilkins in his *Essay Towards a Real Character and a Philosophical Language* (1668) attempted to develop a universal phonetic alphabet and a universal catalogue of concepts in terms of which, respectively, the signals and semantic interpretations for any language can be represented. The phonetic alphabet is based on a system of phonetic properties developed in terms of point and manner of articulation. Each phonetic symbol is analyzable as a set of such properties; in modern terms, it is analyzable as a set of *distinctive features.* It is furthermore tacitly assumed that the physical signal is determined, by language-independent principles, from its representation in terms of phonetic symbols. The concepts that are proposed as units of semantic interpretation are also analyzable into fixed properties (semantic features) of some sort, for example, animate-inanimate, relational-absolute, agent-instrument, etc. It is tacitly assumed that the semantic interpretation of a sentence is determined by universal, language-independent principles from the concepts comprised in the utterance and the manner in which they are grammatically related (for example, as subject-predicate).[5] Although the defects in execution in such pioneering studies as that of Wilkins are obvious, the general approach is sound. The theory of universal phonetics has been intensively pursued along the lines just indicated with considerable success; the parallel theory of universal semantics has, in contrast, been very little studied.

Universal grammar: universal phonetics

The theory of universal phonetics attempts to establish a universal phonetic alphabet and a system of laws. The alphabet defines the set of possible signals from which the signals of a particular language are drawn. If the theory is correct, each signal of a language can be represented as a sequence of symbols of

[5] This assumption is not explicit in Wilkins, but is developed in other seventeenth- and eighteenth-century work. See my *Cartesian Linguistics* (New York: Harper & Row, 1966) for references and discussion.

the phonetic alphabet. Suppose that two physical events are represented as the same sequence. Then in any language they must be repetitions of one another.[6] On the other hand, two physical events might be regarded by speakers of one language as repetitions and by speakers of another language as nonrepetitions. In this case, the universal alphabet must provide the means for distinguishing them. Representation in terms of the universal alphabet should provide whatever information is necessary to determine how the signal may be produced, and it should, at the same time, correspond to a refined level of perceptual representation. We stress once again, however, that actual performance involves other factors beyond ideal phonetic representation.

The symbols of the universal phonetic alphabet are not the "primitive elements" of universal phonetic theory. These primitive elements include, rather, what have been called (*phonetic*) *distinctive features*, properties such as voicing, frontness–backness, stress, etc.[7] Each of these features can be thought of as a scale in terms of which two or more values can be distinguished (how many values need be distinguished is an open question, but the number is apparently quite small for each feature). A symbol of the phonetic alphabet is properly to be regarded as a set of features, each with a specified value. A signal, then, is represented as a sequence of such sets.

Three obvious properties of language are reflected in a phonetic theory of this sort. The first is its discreteness – the fact that only a determinable finite number of signals of any given length can be nonrepetitions. The second property is the unboundedness of language – the fact that a signal can be of arbitrary length, so that a language will contain infinitely many semantically interpreted signals. In addition to these formal properties, a phonetic theory of this sort reflects the fact that two segments of a signal, represented by two symbols of the universal alphabet, may be alike in certain respects and distinct in others; and that there are, furthermore, a fixed number of such dimensions of sameness and difference and a fixed number of potentially significant points along these dimensions. Thus, the initial segments of *pin* and *bin*[8] differ with respect to voicing and aspiration but not (significantly) with respect to point of articulation; the two consonants of *cocoa* differ with respect to neither point of articulation nor voicing, but only with respect to aspiration; etc.

---

[6] In an appropriate sense of repetition. Thus any two physical signals are in some way distinct, but some of the differences are irrelevant in a particular language, and others are irrelevant in any language.

[7] A theory of phonetic distinctive features is developed in R. Jakobson, G. Fant, and M. Halle, *Preliminaries to Speech Analysis*, 2nd edn (Cambridge, Mass.: MIT. Press, 1963). A revised and, we think, improved version appears in N. Chomsky and M. Halle, *Sound Pattern of English* (New York: Harper & Row, 1968).

[8] Observe that although the order of phonetic segments is a significant fact, there is no reason to assume that the physical event represented by a particular sequence of phonetic symbols can be analyzed into successive parts, each associated with a particular symbol.

It is important to note that the distinctive features postulated in universal phonetic theory are absolute in several senses but relative in others. They are absolute in the sense that they are fixed for all languages. If phonetic representation is to provide sufficient information for identification of a physical signal, then specification of feature values must also be absolute. On the other hand, the features are relative when considered in terms of the notion of repetition–nonrepetition. For example, given three absolute values designated 1, 2, 3 in terms of the feature front–back, we might find that in language $L1$ two utterances that differ only in the values 1, 2 of frontness–backness are distinguished as nonrepetitions but utterances differing only in the values 2, 3 are not; whereas in language $L2$ the opposite might be the case. Each language would use the feature front–back to distinguish nonrepetitions, but the absolute value 2 that is "front" in one language would be "back" in the other.

In addition to a system of distinctive features, a universal phonetic theory will also attempt to formulate certain laws that govern the permitted sequences and permitted variety of selection in a particular language. For example, Jakobson has observed that no language uses both the feature labialization and the feature velarization for distinguishing nonrepetitions, and he has suggested a more general formulation in terms of which these two features can be regarded as variants of a single, more abstract feature. Generalizations of this sort – particularly when they can be supported by rational argument – can be proposed as laws of universal phonetics.

Universal grammar: universal semantics

Although universal phonetics is a fairly well-developed subject, the same cannot be said of universal semantics. Here, too, we might hope to establish a universal system of semantic features and laws regarding their interrelations and permitted variety. In fact, the problem of determining such features and such laws has once again become a topic of serious investigation in the past few years,[9] and there is some promise of fruitful development. It can be seen at once that an analysis of concepts in terms of such features as animateness, action, etc. (see p. 107), will hardly be adequate, and that certain features must be still more abstract. It is, for example, a fact of English that the phrase "a good knife" means "a knife which cuts well." Consequently the concept "knife" must be specified in part

---

[9] See J. Katz, *The Philosophy of Language* (New York: Harper & Row, 1965), for a review of some recent work. For another view, see U. Weinreich, "Explorations in Semantic Theory," in T. A. Sebeok, ed., *Current Trends in Linguistics*, Vol. III of *Linguistic Theory* (The Hague: Mouton, 1966); and for comments on this and more extensive development of the topic, see J. Katz, *Semantic Theory* (New York: Harper & Row, Publishers, 1972). In addition, there has been quite a bit of recent work in descriptive semantics, some of which is suggestive with respect to the problems discussed here.

in terms of features having to do with characteristic functions (not just physical properties), and in terms of an abstract "evaluation feature"[10] that is determined by such modifiers as "good," "terrible," etc. Only by such an analysis can the semantic relationship between "this is a good knife" and "this knife cuts well" be established. In contrast, the irrelevance of "this is a good knife for digging with" to "this knife cuts well" shows that the semantic interpretation of a sentence is determined by grammatical relations of a sort that are by no means transparent.

As in the case of universal phonetics, we might hope to establish general principles regarding the possible systems of concepts that can be represented in a human language and the intrinsic connections that may exist among them. With the discovery of such principles, universal semantics would become a substantive discipline.

Universal grammar: universal syntax

Suppose that a satisfactory theory of universal phonetics and of universal semantics were at hand. We could then define a language as a set of sentences, where a sentence is a particular kind of sound–meaning pair, and go on to study the systems of rules that define human languages. But in fact only the theory of universal phonetics is sufficiently well established to support this enterprise. Consequently, we must approach the study of language structure in a slightly more indirect way.

Notice that although the notion "semantic representation" is itself far from clear, we can, nevertheless, find innumerable empirical conditions that an explication of this notion must meet. Consider, for example, the following sentence:

4   What disturbed John was being disregarded by everyone.

It is clear, first of all, that this expression has two distinct interpretations. Under one interpretation, it means that John was disturbed by the fact that everyone disregarded him; under the second, it means that everyone was disregarding the things that disturb John. Under the first of these interpretations, a certain grammatical relation holds between "disregard" and "John," namely the same relation that holds between these items in "Everyone disregards John" (the "verb–object" relation). Under the second interpretation neither this nor any other grammatically significant relation holds between "disregard" and "John." On the other hand, if we insert the word "our" between "was" and "being," the sentence is unambiguous, and no grammatical relation holds between "disregard" and "John," although the verb–object relation now holds between "disregard" and "we" (an underlying element of "our").

---

[10] For discussion of this notion, see J. Katz, "Semantic Theory and the Meaning of 'Good,'" *Journal of Philosophy*, Vol. 61, No. 23, 1964.

Examples of this sort can be elaborated indefinitely. They provide conditions of adequacy that the notion "semantic interpretation" must meet (for example, relations of paraphrase and implication and the property of ambiguity must be correctly reflected), and they illustrate clearly some of the ways in which the semantic interpretations of linguistic expressions must be determined from those of their grammatically related parts.

From such considerations, we are led to formulate a more restricted but quite significant immediate goal for the study of linguistic structure. Still taking a language to be a set of sentences, let us consider each abstract "sentence" to be a specific pairing of a phonetic representation with an abstract structure of some sort (let us call it a *deep structure*) that incorporates information relevant to semantic interpretation. We can then study the system of rules that determines this pairing, in a particular language, and the general characteristics of such rules. This enterprise will be significant to the extent that these underlying deep structures do actually provide a way to meet the empirical conditions on semantic interpretation. Semantic theory, as it progresses, will then provide means for enriching deep structures and associating semantic interpretations with them. The empirical significance of a full theory of grammar, comprising a universal phonetics, semantics, and syntax, will depend in part on the extent to which conditions on semantic interpretation can be satisfied by systematic use of the devices and principles that this theory supplies.

Summarizing these remarks, let us establish the following frame-work for the study of linguistic structure. The *grammar* of a language is a system of rules that determines a certain pairing of sound and meaning. It consists of a *syntactic component*, a *semantic component*, and a *phonological component*. The syntactic component defines a certain (infinite) class of abstract objects (*D*, *S*), where *D* is a *deep structure* and *S* a *surface structure*. The deep struc-ture contains all information relevant to semantic interpretation; the surface structure, all information relevant to phonetic interpretation. The semantic and phonological components are purely interpretive. The former assigns semantic interpretations to deep structures; the latter assigns phonetic interpretations to surface structures. Thus the grammar as a whole relates semantic and phonetic interpretations, the association being mediated by the rules of the syntactic com-ponent that define paired deep and surface structures. The study of the three components will, of course, be highly integrated; each can be investigated to the extent that it is clear what conditions the others impose upon it.

This formulation should be regarded as an informal first approximation. When we develop a precise theory of grammatical structure – for example, the particular version of the theory of transformational grammar sketched below – we will provide a technical meaning for the terms "deep structure" and "sur-face structure," and in terms of these technical meanings, we can then raise the empirical (not conceptual) question of how deep and surface structures contribute to and determine semantic and phonetic interpretations. In the technical sense that is given to the concepts of deep and surface structure in the theory outlined below, it seems to me that present information suggests that surface structure completely determines phonetic interpretation and that deep structure completely determines certain highly significant aspects of semantic interpretation. But the looseness of the latter term makes a more definite statement impossible. In fact, I think that a reasonable explication of the term "semantic interpretation" would lead to the conclusion that surface structure also contributes in a restricted but important way to semantic interpretation, but I will say no more about this matter here.

Universal grammar might be defined as the study of the conditions that must be met by the grammars of all human languages. Universal semantics and phonetics, in the sense described earlier, will then be a part of universal grammar. So defined, universal grammar is nothing other than the theory of language structure. This seems in accord with traditional usage. However, only certain aspects of universal grammar were studied until quite recently. In particular, the problem of formulating the conditions that must be met by the rules of syntax, phonology, and semantics was not raised in any explicit way in traditional linguistics, although suggestive and nontrivial steps toward the study of this problem are implicit in much traditional work.[11]

A grammar of the sort described previously, which attempts to characterize in an explicit way the intrinsic association of phonetic form and semantic content in a particular language, might be called a *generative grammar*[12] to distinguish it from descriptions that have some different goal (for example, pedagogic grammars). In intention, at least, traditional scholarly grammars are generative grammars, although they fall far short of achieving the goal of determining how sentences are formed or interpreted. A good traditional grammar gives a full exposition of exceptions to rules, but it provides only hints and examples to illustrate regular structures (except for trivial cases – for example, inflectional paradigms). It is tacitly presumed that the intelligent reader will use his "linguistic intuition" – his latent, unconscious knowledge of universal grammar – to determine the regular structures from the presented examples and remarks. The grammar itself does not express the deep-seated regularities of the language. For the purpose of the study of linguistic structure, particular or universal, such grammars are, therefore, of limited value. It is necessary to

[11] See Chomsky, *Cartesian Linguistics*, for discussion.
[12] See p. 91. In general, a set of rules that recursively define an infinite set of objects may be said to *generate* this set. Thus a set of axioms and rules of inference for arithmetic may be said to generate a set of proofs and a set of theorems of arithmetic (last lines of proofs). Similarly, a (generative) grammar may be said to generate a set of structural descriptions, each of which, ideally, incorporates a deep structure, a surface structure, a semantic interpretation (of the deep structure), and a phonetic interpretation (of the surface structure).

extend them to full generative grammars if the study of linguistic structure is to be advanced to the point where it deals significantly with regularities and general principles. It is, however, important to be aware of the fact that the concept "generative grammar" itself is no very great innovation. The fact that every language "makes infinite use of finite means" (Wilhelm von Humboldt) has long been understood. Modern work in generative grammar is simply an attempt to give an explicit account of how these finite means are put to infinite use in particular languages and to discover the deeper properties that define "human language," in general (that is, the properties that constitute universal grammar).

We have been concerned thus far only with clarification of concepts and setting of goals. Let us now turn to the problem of formulating hypotheses of universal grammar.

Structure of the phonological component

The syntactic component of a generative grammar defines (generates) an infinite set of pairs (D, S), where D is a deep structure and S is a surface structure; the interpretive components of the grammar assign a semantic representation to D and a phonetic representation to S.

Let us first consider the problem of assigning phonetic representations to surface structures. As in the previous discussion of universal phonetics, we take a phonetic representation to be a sequence of symbols of the universal phonetic alphabet, each symbol being analyzed into distinctive features with specific values. Stating the same idea slightly differently, we may think of a phonetic representation as a matrix in which rows correspond to features of the universal system, columns correspond to successive segments (symbols of the phonetic alphabet), and each entry is an integer that specifies the value of a particular segment with respect to the feature in question. Our problem, then, is to determine what information must be contained in the surface structure, and how the rules of the phonological component of the grammar use this information to specify a phonetic matrix of the sort just described.

Consider once again the example 4, which we repeat in 5 for ease of reference:

5   What # disturb-ed # John # was # be-ing # dis-regard-ed # by # every-one.

To first approximation,[13] we may think of 5 as a sequence of the *formatives* "what," "disturb," "ed," "John," "was," "be," "ing," "dis," "regard," "ed," "by," "every," "one," with the *junctures* represented by the symbols # and – in the

---

[13] The analysis that is presented here for purposes of exposition would have to be refined for empirical adequacy.

positions indicated in 5. These junctures specify the manner in which formatives are combined; they provide information which is required by the interpretive rules of the phonological component. A juncture must, in fact, be analyzed as a set of features, that is, as a single-column matrix in which the rows correspond to certain features of the junctural system and each entry is one of two values which we may represent as + or −. Similarly, each formative will be analyzed as a matrix in which columns stand for successive segments, rows correspond to certain *categorial features*, and each entry is either + or −. Therefore, the entire sentence 5 can be regarded as a single matrix with the entries + and −.[14]

The categorial features include the universal features of the phonetic system, along with *diacritic* features which essentially indicate exceptions to rules. Thus the matrix corresponding to "what," in the dialect in which the corresponding phonetic representation is [wat], will contain three segments, the first specified as a labial glide, the second as a low back unrounded vowel, the third as an unvoiced dental stop consonant (these specifications given completely in terms of the + and − values of features supplied by the universal phonetic system). The rules of the phonological component, in this case, will convert this specification in terms of + and − values into a more detailed specification in terms of integers, in which the value of each segment with respect to the phonetic features (for example, tongue height, degree of aspiration, etc.) is indicated to whatever degree of accuracy is required by the presupposed theory of universal phonetics, and with whatever range of variation is allowed by the language. In this example, the assigned values will simply refine the bifurcation into + and − values given in the underlying matrix for "what" in 5.

The example just cited is unusually simple, however. In general, the rules of the phonological component will not only give a finer specification of the underlying division into + and − values, but will also change values significantly and, perhaps, insert, delete, or rearrange segments. For example, the formative "by" will be represented with an underlying matrix consisting of two columns, the second of which is specified as a high front-vowel (specification given in terms of values of features). The corresponding phonetic matrix, however, will consist of three columns, the second of which is specified as a low back-vowel and the third as a palatal glide (the specification here being in terms of integral valued entries in a phonetic matrix).[15]

The surface structure of 5, then, is represented as a matrix in which one of two values appears in each entry. The fact that only two values may appear indicates

---

[14] Notice that every two successive formatives are separated by a juncture, as is necessary if the representation of 5 as a single matrix is to preserve the formative structure. For present purposes, we may think of each segment of a formative as unmarked for all junctural features and each juncture as unmarked for each formative feature.

[15] The reasons for this analysis go beyond the scope of this discussion. For details see Chomsky and Halle, *Sound Pattern of English.*

that this underlying matrix really serves a purely classificatory function. Each sentence is classified in such a way as to distinguish it from all other sentences, and in such a way as to determine just how the rules of the phonological component assign specific positional phonetic values. We see, then, that the distinctive features of the universal phonetic system have a *classificatory function* in the underlying matrix constituting a part of the surface structure, and a *phonetic function* in the matrix constituting the phonetic representation of the sentence in question. Only in the former function are the distinctive features uniformly binary; only in the latter do they receive a direct physical interpretation.

The underlying classificatory matrix just described does not exhaust the information required by the interpretive phonological rules. Beyond this, it is necessary to know how the sentence in question is subdivided into phrases of varying size, and what types of phrase these are. In the case of 5, for example, phonological interpretation requires the information that "disturb" and "disregard" are verbs, that "what disturbed John" is a noun phrase, that "John was being" is not a phrase at all, and so on. The relevant information can be indicated by a proper bracketing of the sentence with labeled brackets.[16] The unit contained within paired brackets [$_A$ and] $_A$ will be referred to as a phrase of the category A. For example, the sequence "what # disturbed # John" in 5 will be enclosed within the brackets [$_{NP}$,]$_{NP}$, indicating that it is a noun phrase; the formative "disturb" will be enclosed within the brackets [$_V$,]$_V$, indicating that it is a verb; the whole expression 5 will be enclosed within the brackets [$_S$,]$_S$, indicating that it is a sentence; the sequence "John was being" will not be enclosed within paired brackets, since it is no phrase at all. To take an extremely simple example, the sentence "John saw Bill" might be represented in the following way as a surface structure, where each orthographically represented item is to be regarded as a classificatory matrix:

$$6 \qquad \left[_S\left[_{NP}\left[_N{}^{John}\right]_N\right]_{NP}\left[_{VP}\left[_V{}^{saw}\right]_V\left[_{NP}\left[_N{}^{Bill}\right]_N\right]_{NP}\right]_{VP}\right]_S$$

This representation indicates that "John" and "Bill" are nouns (N's) and "saw" a verb (V); that "John" and "Bill" are, furthermore, noun phrases (NP's); that "saw Bill" is a verb phrase (VP); and that "John saw Bill" is a sentence (S). It seems that interpretation of a sentence by the phonological component of the grammar invariably requires information which can be represented in the way just described. We therefore postulate that the surface structure of a sentence is a properly labeled bracketing of a classificatory matrix of formatives and junctures.

---

[16] In the obvious sense. Thus [$_A$ ... [$_B$ ...] $_B$ ... [$_C$ ...] $_C$ ...] $_A$ would, for example, be a proper bracketing of the string ... in terms of the labeled brackets [$_A$,] $_A$, [$_B$,] $_B$, [$_C$,] $_C$, but neither of the following would be proper bracketing:
[$_A$ ... [$_B$ ...] $_A$; [$_A$ ... [$_B$ ...] $_A$ ...] $_B$

The phonological component of a grammar converts a surface structure into a phonetic representation. We have now given a rough specification of the notions "surface structure" and "phonetic representations." It remains to describe the rules of the phonological component and the manner in which they are organized.

The evidence presently available suggests that the rules of the phonological component are linearly ordered in a sequence $R_1, \ldots R_n$, and that this sequence of rules applies in a cyclic fashion to a surface structure in the following way. In the first cycle of application, the rules $R_1, \ldots, R_n$ apply in this order to a maximal continuous part of the surface structure containing no internal brackets. After the last of these rules has applied, innermost brackets are erased and the second cycle of application is initiated. In this cycle, the rules again apply in the given order to a maximal continuous part of the surface structure containing no internal brackets. Innermost brackets are then erased, and the third cycle is initiated. The process continues until the maximal domain of phonological processes (in simple cases, the entire sentence) is reached. Certain of the rules are restricted in application to the level of word-boundary – they apply in the cycle only when the domain of application is a full word. Others are free to iterate at every stage of application. Notice that the principle of cyclic application is highly intuitive. It states, in effect, that there is a fixed system of rules that determines the form of large units from the (ideal) form of their constituent parts.

We can illustrate the principle of cyclic application with some rules of stress assignment in English. It seems to be a fact that although phonetic representations for English must allow five or six different values along the distinctive feature of stress, nevertheless, all segments can be unmarked with respect to stress in surface structures – that is, stress has no categorial function (except highly marginally) as a distinctive feature for English. The complex stress contours of the phonetic representation are determined by such rules as 7 and 8.[17]

7   Assign primary stress to the left-most of two primary stressed vowels, in nouns.

8   Assign primary stress to the right-most stress-peak, where a vowel V is a stress-peak in a certain domain if this domain contains no vowel more heavily stressed than V.

Rule 7 applies to nouns with two primary stresses; rule 8 applies to a unit of any other kind. The rules apply in the order 7, 8, in the cyclic manner described above. By convention, when primary stress is assigned in a certain position, all

---

[17] These are simplified, for expository purposes. See Chomsky and Halle, *Sound Pattern of English*, for a more accurate account. Notice that in this exposition we are using the term "applies" ambiguously, in the sense of "available for application" and also in the sense of "actually modifies the sequence under consideration."

other stresses are weakened by one. Notice that if a domain contains no stressed vowel, then rule 8 will assign primary stress to its right-most vowel.

To illustrate these rules, consider first the surface structure 6. In accordance with the general principle of cyclic application, the rules 7 and 8 first apply to the innermost units [N John]N, [V saw]V, and [N Bill]N. Rule 7 is inapplicable; rule 8 applies, assigning primary stress to the single vowel in each case. Innermost

brackets are then erased. The next cycle deals with the units [NP John]NP and
$$\overset{1}{}$$

[NP Bill]NP and simply reassigns primary stress to the single vowel, by rule 8

Innermost brackets are then erased, and we have the unit [VP saw Bill]VP as the domain of application of the rules. Rule 7 is again inapplicable, since this is not a noun; rule 8 assigns primary stress to the vowel of "Bill," weakening the stress on "saw" to secondary. Innermost brackets are erased, and we have the unit

[s John $\overset{1}{\text{saw}}$ $\overset{2}{}$ Bill $\overset{1}{}$]s as the domain of application. Rule 7 is again inapplicable, and rule 8 assigns primary stress to "Bill," weakening the other stresses and

giving "John $\overset{2}{}$ saw $\overset{3}{}$ Bill $\overset{1}{}$" which can be accepted as an ideal representation of the stress contour.

Consider now the slightly more complex example "John's black-board eraser." In the first application of the cycle, rules 7 and 8 apply to the innermost bracketed units "John," "black," "board," "erase"; rule 7 is inapplicable, and rule 8 assigns primary stress in each case to the right-most vowel (the only vowel, in the first three). The next cycle involves the units "John's" and "eraser," and is vacuous.[18] The domain of application for the next cycle is

[N $\overset{1}{\text{black}}$ $\overset{1}{\text{board}}$]N. Being a noun, this unit is subject to rule 7, which assigns primary stress to "black," weakening the stress on "board" to secondary. Innermost brackets are erased, and the domain of application for the next cycle is

[N $\overset{1}{\text{balck}}$ $\overset{2}{\text{board}}$ $\overset{1}{\text{eraser}}$]N. Again rule 7 applies, assigning primary stress to "black" and weakening all other stresses by one. In the final cycle, the domain

of application of the rules is [NP $\overset{1}{\text{John's}}$ $\overset{1}{\text{black}}$ $\overset{3}{\text{board}}$ $\overset{2}{\text{eraser}}$]NP. Rule 7 is inapplicable, since this is a full noun phrase. Rule 8 assigns primary stress to the right-most primary stressed vowel, weakening all the others and giving

"John's $\overset{2}{}$ blackboard $\overset{1}{}$ $\overset{4}{}$ eraser $\overset{3}{}$." In this way, a complex phonetic representation

[18] The word "eraser" is, at this stage, bisyllabic.

is determined by independently motivated and very simple rules, applying in accordance with the general principle of the cycle.

This example is characteristic and illustrates several important points. The grammar of English must contain the rule 7 so as to account for the fact that the stress contour is falling in the case of the noun "blackboard," and it must contain rule 8, to account for the rising contour of the phrase "black board" ("board which is black"). The principle of the cycle is not, strictly speaking, part of the grammar of English but is rather a principle of universal grammar that determines the application of the particular rules of English or any other language, whatever these rules may be. In the case illustrated, the general principle of cyclic application assigns a complex stress contour, as indicated. Equipped with the principle of the cycle and the two rules 7 and 8, a person will know[19] the proper stress contour for "John's blackboard eraser" and innumerable other expressions which he may never have heard previously. This is a simple example of a general property of language; *certain universal principles must interrelate with specific rules to determine the form (and meaning) of entirely new linguistic expressions.*

This example also lends support to a somewhat more subtle and far-reaching hypothesis. There is little doubt that such phenomena as stress contours in English are a perceptual reality; trained observers will, for example, reach a high degree of unanimity in recording new utterances in their native language. There is, however, little reason to suppose that these contours represent a *physical* reality. It may very well be the case that stress contours are not represented in the physical signal in anything like the perceived detail. There is no paradox in this. If just two levels of stress are distinguished in the physical signal, then the person who is learning English will have sufficient evidence to construct the rules 7 and 8 (given the contrast "blackboard," "black board," for example). Assuming then that he knows the principle of the cycle, he will be able to perceive the stress contour of "John's blackboard eraser" even if it is not a physical property of the signal. The evidence now available strongly suggests that this is an accurate description of how stress is perceived in English.

It is important to see that there is nothing mysterious in this description. There would be no problem in principle in designing an automaton that uses the rules 7 and 8, the rules of English syntax, and the principle of the transformational cycle to assign a multi-leveled stress contour even to an utterance in which stress is not represented at all (for example, a sentence spelled in conventional orthography). The automaton would use the rules of syntax to determine the surface structure of the utterance, and would then apply the rules 7 and 8, in accordance with the principle of the cycle, to determine the multi-leveled contour. Taking such an automaton as a first approximation to a model for speech perception (see 1,

---

[19] As earlier, we refer here to "tacit" or "latent knowledge," which can, perhaps, be brought to consciousness with proper attention but is surely not presented to "unguided intuition."

p. 103), we might propose that the hearer uses certain selected properties of the physical signal to determine which sentence of the language was produced and to assign to it a deep and surface structure. With careful attention, he will then be able to "hear" the stress contour assigned by the phonological component of his grammar, whether or not it corresponds to any physical property of the presented signal. Such an account of speech perception assumes, putting it loosely, that syntactic interpretation of an utterance may be a prerequisite to "hearing" its phonetic representation in detail; it rejects the assumption that speech perception requires a full analysis of phonetic form followed by a full analysis of syntactic structure followed by semantic interpretation, as well as the assumption that perceived phonetic form is an accurate point-by-point representation of the signal. But it must be kept in mind that there is nothing to suggest that either of the rejected assumptions is correct, nor is there anything at all mysterious in the view just outlined that rejects these assumptions. In fact, the view just outlined is highly plausible, since it can dispense with the claim that some presently undetectable physical properties of utterances are identified with an accuracy that goes beyond anything experimentally demonstrable even under ideal conditions, and it can account for the perception of stress contours of novel utterances[20] on the very simple assumption that rules 7 and 8 and the general principle of cyclic application are available to the perceptual system.

There is a great deal more to be said about the relative merits of various kinds of perceptual models. Instead of pursuing this topic, let us consider further the hypothesis that rules 7 and 8, and the principle of cyclic application, are available to the perceptual system and are used in the manner suggested. It is clear how rules 7 and 8 might be learned from simple examples of rising and falling contour (for example, "black board" contrasted with "blackboard"). But the question then arises: how does a person learn the principle of cyclic application? Before facing this question, it is necessary to settle one that is logically prior to it: why assume that the principle is learned at all? There is much evidence that the principle is used, but from this it does not follow that it has been learned. In fact, it is difficult to imagine how such a principle might be learned, uniformly by all speakers, and it is by no means clear that sufficient evidence is available in the physical signal to justify this principle. Consequently, the most reasonable conclusion seems to be that the principle is not learned at all, but rather that it is simply part of the conceptual equipment that the learner brings to the task of language acquisition. A rather similar argument can be given with respect to other principles of universal grammar.

Notice again that there should be nothing surprising in such a conclusion. There would be no difficulty, in principle, in designing an automaton which

---

[20] And other aspects. The argument is, in fact, much more general. It must be kept in mind that speech perception is often impaired minimally, or not at all, even by significant distortion of the signal, a fact difficult to reconcile with the view that phonetic analysis in detail is a prerequisite for analysis of the syntactic and semantic structure.

incorporates the principles of universal grammar and puts them to use to determine which of the possible languages is the one to which it is exposed. A priori, there is no more reason to suppose that these principles are themselves learned than there is to suppose that a person learns to interpret visual stimuli in terms of line, angle, contour, distance, or, for that matter, that he learns to have two arms. It is completely a question of empirical fact; there is no information of any general extralinguistic sort that can be used, at present, to support the assumption that some principle of universal grammar is learned, or that it is innate, or (in some manner) both. If linguistic evidence seems to suggest that some principles are unlearned, there is no reason to find this conclusion paradoxical or surprising.

Returning to the elaboration of principles of universal grammar, it seems that the phonological component of a grammar consists of a sequence of rules that apply in a cyclic manner, as just described, to assign a phonetic representation to a surface structure. The phonetic representation is a matrix of phonetic feature specifications and the surface structure is a properly labeled bracketing of formatives which are, themselves, represented in terms of marking of categorial distinctive features. What evidence is now available supports these assumptions; they provide the basis for explaining many curious features of phonetic fact.

It is important to notice that there is no a priori necessity for the phonological component of a grammar to have just these properties. These assumptions about universal grammar restrict the class of possible human languages to a very special subset of the set of imaginable "languages." The evidence available to us suggests that these assumptions pertain to the language acquisition device *AM* of 3, p. 106, that is that they form one part of the schematism that the child brings to the problem of language learning. That this schematism must be quite elaborate and highly restrictive seems fairly obvious. If it were not, language acquisition, within the empirically known limits of time, access, and variability, would be an impenetrable mystery. Considerations of the sort mentioned in the foregoing discussion are directly relevant to the problem of determining the nature of these innate mechanisms, and, therefore, deserve extremely careful study and attention.

Structure of the semantic component

Let us now consider the second interpretive component of a generative grammar, the system of rules that converts a deep structure into a semantic representation that expresses the intrinsic meaning of the sentence in question. Although many aspects of semantic interpretation remain quite obscure, it is still quite possible to undertake a direct investigation of the theory of deep structures and their interpretation, and certain properties of the semantic component seem fairly clear. In particular, as we have noted earlier, many empirical conditions on semantic interpretation can be clearly formulated. For example, we know that sentence 4 on p. 110 must be assigned at least two semantic representations, and that one of these must be essentially the same as the interpretation assigned to both 9 and 10.

9   Being disregarded by everyone disturbed John.

10   The fact that everyone disregarded John disturbed him.[21]

Furthermore, it is clear that the semantic representation of a sentence depends on the representation of its parts, as in the parallel case of phonetic interpretation. For example, in the case of 10, it is obvious that the semantic interpretation depends, in part, on the semantic interpretation of "Everyone disregarded John"; if the latter were replaced in 10 by "Life seemed to pass John by," the interpretation of the whole would be changed in a fixed way. This much is transparent, and it suggests that a principle like the principle of cyclic application in phonology should hold in the semantic component.

A slightly more careful look at the problem shows that semantic interpretation must be significantly more abstract than phonological interpretation with respect to the notion of "constituent part." Thus the interpretation of "Everyone disregarded John" underlies not only 10, but also 9 and 4, and in exactly the same way. But neither 4 nor 9 contains "everyone disregarded John" as a constituent part, as does 10 . In other words, the deep structures underlying 9 and 10 should both be identical (or very similar) to one of two deep structures underlying 4, despite the wide divergence in surface structure and phonetic form. It follows that we cannot expect deep structure to be very close to surface structure in general.

In the case of a sentence like 6 ("John saw Bill"), there is little difference between deep and surface structure. Semantic interpretation would not be far from the mark, in this case, if it were quite parallel to phonetic interpretation. Thus the interpretation of "saw Bill" can be derived from that of "saw"[22] and that of "Bill," and the interpretation of 6 can be determined from that of "John" and that of "saw Bill." To carry out such interpretation we must know not only the bracketing of 6 into constituents, but also the grammatical relations that are represented; that is, we must know that "Bill" is the *direct-object* of "saw" and that the subject–predicate relation holds between "John" and "saw Bill" in "John saw Bill." Similarly, in the slightly more complex case of "John saw Bill leave," we must know that the subject–predicate relation holds between "John" and "saw Bill leave" and also between "Bill" and "leave."

[21] The latter is again ambiguous in an entirely different way from 4, depending on the reference of "him." We will assume, throughout, that it refers to *John.*

[22] But the interpretation of this depends on that of "see" and that of "past tense"; hence, these separate items must be represented in the deep structure, though not, in this case, in the surface structure.

Notice that at least in such simple cases as 6, we already have a mechanism for representing grammatical relations of just the sort that are required for semantic interpretation. Suppose that we define the relations *subject-of* as the relation holding between a noun phrase and a sentence of which it is an immediate constituent[23] and the relation *predicate-of* as holding between a verb phrase and a sentence of which it is an immediate constituent. The subject–predicate relation can then be defined as the relation holding between the subject of a sentence and the predicate of this sentence. Thus, in these terms, "John" is the subject and "saw Bill (leave)" the predicate of "John saw Bill (leave)," and the subject–predicate relation holds between the two. In the same way, we can define the relation *direct-object* (in terms of the immediate constituency of verb and noun phrase in verb phrase) and others in a perfectly appropriate and satisfactory way. But returning now to 6, this observation implies that a *labeled bracketing* will serve as the deep structure (just as a labeled bracketing will serve as the surface structure); it contains just the information about constituency and about grammatical relations that is required for semantic interpretation.

We noted that in "John saw Bill leave" the subject–predicate relation holds between "Bill" and "leave," as well as between "John" and "saw Bill leave." If 6 or something very much like it – see, for example, note 22 – is to be taken as the deep structure, with grammatical relations defined as previously, then the deep structure of "John saw Bill leave" will have to be something like 11 (many details omitted):

11     $[_S[_{NP}John]_{NP}[_{VP}[_V saw]_V[_S[_{NP}Bill]_{NP}[_{VP}[_V leave]_V]_{VP}]_S]_{VP}]_S$

The labeled bracketing 11 expresses the subject–predicate relation between "John" and "saw Bill leave" and between "Bill" and "leave," as required.

Moving to a somewhat more complex example, the sentences 9 and 10 (as well as 4 under one interpretation) will each have to contain something like 12 in the deep structure:

12     $[_S[_{NP}everyone]_{NP}[_{VP}[_V disregards]_V[_{NP}John]_{NP}]_{VP}]_S$

If this requirement is met, then we will be able to account for the fact that, obviously, the meaning of 4 (= "what disturbed John was being disregarded by everyone") in one interpretation of 9 (= "being disregarded by everyone disturbed John") is determined in part by the fact that the direct-object relation holds between "disregard" and "John" and the subject–predicate relation

---

[23] A phrase *X* is an immediate constituent of the phrase *Y* containing *X* if there is no phrase *Z* which contains *X* and is contained in *Y*. Thus, the noun phrase "John" is an immediate constituent of the sentence "John saw Bill" [analyzed as in 6], but the noun phrase "Bill" is not, being contained in the intervening phrase "saw Bill." "John saw" is not an immediate constituent of the sentence, since it is not a phrase; "John" is not an immediate constituent of "John saw," since the latter is not a phrase. Notice that the definitions proposed here for grammatical functions and relations make sense only when restricted to deep structures, in general.

between "everyone" and "disregards John," despite the fact that these relations are in no way indicated in the surface structure in 4 or 9.

From many such examples, we are led to the following conception of how the semantic component functions. This interpretive component of the full generative grammar applies to a deep structure and assigns to it a semantic representation, formulated in terms of the still quite obscure notions of universal semantics. The deep structure is a labeled bracketing of minimal "meaning-bearing" elements. The interpretive rules apply cyclically, determining the semantic interpretation of a phrase X of the deep structure from the semantic interpretations of the immediate constituents of X and the grammatical relation represented in this configuration of X and its parts.

Superficially, at least, the two interpretive components of the grammar are rather similar in the way in which they operate, and they apply to objects of essentially the same sort (labeled bracketings). But the deep structure of a sentence will, in nontrivial cases, be quite different from its surface structure.

Notice that if the notions "noun phrase," "verb phrase," "sentence," "verb," can receive a language-independent characterization within universal grammar, then the grammatical relations defined above (similarly, others that we might define in the same way) will also receive a universal characterization. It seems that this may be possible, and certain general lines of approach to such a characterization seem clear (see p. 139). We might then raise the question of whether the semantic component of a grammar contains such particular rules as the rules 7 and 8 of the phonological component of English or whether, alternatively, the principles of semantic interpretation belong essentially to universal grammar. However, we will put aside these and other questions relating to the semantic component, and turn next to the discussion of the one noninterpretive component of the grammar – which we have called its "syntactic component." Notice that as in the case of the phonological component, insofar as principles of interpretation can be assigned to universal rather than particular grammar, there is little reason to suppose that they are learned or that they could in principle be learned.

Structure of the syntactic component

The syntactic component of a grammar must generate (see note 12) pairs (D, S), where D is a deep structure and S an associated surface structure. The surface structure S is a labeled bracketing of a sequence of formatives and junctures. The deep structure D is a labeled bracketing that determines a certain network of grammatical functions and grammatical relations among the elements and groups of elements of which it is composed. Obviously, the syntactic component must have a finite number of rules (or rule schemata), but these must be so organized that an infinite number of pairs (D, S) of deep and surface structures can be generated, one corresponding to each interpreted sentence (phonetically and semantically interpreted, that is) of the language.[24] In principle, there are various ways in which such a system might be organized. It might, for example, consist of independent rules generating deep and surface structures and certain conditions of compatibility relating them, or of rules generating surface structures combined with rules mapping these into the associated deep structure, or of rules generating deep structures combined with rules mapping these into surface structures.[25] Choice among these alternatives is a matter of fact, not decision. We must ask which of the alternatives makes possible the deepest generalizations and the most far-reaching explanation of linguistic phenomena of various sorts. As with other aspects of universal grammar, we are dealing here with a set of empirical questions; crucial evidence may be difficult to obtain, but we cannot conclude from this that there is, in principle, no right and wrong in the matter.

Of the many alternatives that might be suggested, the linguistic evidence now available seems to point consistently to the conclusion that the syntactic component consists of rules that generate deep structures combined with rules mapping these into associated surface structures. Let us call these two systems of rules the *base* and the *transformational* components of the syntax, respectively. The base system is further subdivided into two parts: the *categorial* system and the *lexicon*. Each of these three subparts of the syntax has a specific function to perform, and there seem to be heavy universal constraints that determine their form and interrelation. The general structure of a grammar would, then, be as depicted in diagram 13:

13

$$B \longrightarrow \text{Deep structure} \left< \begin{array}{l} S \nearrow \text{Semantic representation} \\[2ex] T \searrow \\ \text{Surface structure} \xrightarrow{P} \text{Phonetic representation} \end{array} \right.$$

The mapping S is carried out by the semantic component; T by the transformational component; and P by the phonological component. Generation of deep structures by the base system (by operation B) is determined by the categorial system and the lexicon.

The lexicon is a set of lexical entries; each lexical entry, in turn, can be regarded as a set of features of various sorts. Among these are the phonological

---

[24] In fact, we might think of a grammar as assigning a semantic interpretation to all possible sentences (this being a clear notion, given theories of universal phonetics and semantics), including those that deviate from rules of the language. But this is a matter that we will not go into any further here.

[25] The question of how the syntactic component is organized should not be confused, as it all too often is, with the problem of developing a model of performance (production or perception). In fact, any of the kinds of organization just described (and others) could be used as the basis for a theory of performance of either kind.

features and the semantic features that we have already mentioned briefly. The phonological features can be thought of as indexed as to position (that is, first, second, etc.); aside from this, each is simply an indication of marking with respect to one of the universal distinctive features (regarded here in their categorial function) or with respect to some diacritic feature (see p. 114), in the case of irregularity. Thus the positionally indexed phonological features constitute a distinctive feature matrix with the entries given as + or − values, as described earlier. The semantic features constitute a "dictionary definition." As noted previously, some of these at least must be quite abstract; there may, furthermore, be intrinsic connections of various sorts among them that are sometimes referred to as "field structure." In addition, the lexical entry contains syntactic features that determine the positions in which the entry in question may appear, and the rules that may apply to structures containing it as these are converted into surface structures. In general, the lexical entry contains all information about the item in question that cannot be accounted for by general rule.

Aside from lexical entries, the lexicon will contain redundancy rules that modify the feature content of a lexical entry in terms of general regularities. For example, the fact that vowels are voiced or that humans are animate requires no specific mention in particular lexical entries. Much of the redundant lexical information can, no doubt, be provided by general conventions (that is, rules of universal grammar) rather than by redundancy rules of the language.

The lexicon is concerned with all properties, idiosyncratic or redundant, of individual lexical items. The categorial component of the base determines all other aspects of deep structure. It seems that the categorial component is what is called a *simple* or *context-free phrase-structure grammar.* Just what such a system is can be understood quite easily from a simple example. Suppose that we have the *rules* 14:

14   S   → NP VP
        VP → V NP
        NP → N
        N → Δ
        V → Δ

With these rules we construct the derivation 15 in the following way. First write down the symbol *S* as the first line of the derivation. We interpret the first rule of 14 as permitting *S* to be replaced by NP VP, giving the second line of 15. Interpreting the second rule of 14 in a similar way, we form the third line of the derivation 15 with VP replaced by V NP. We form the fourth line of 15 by applying the rule NP → N of 14, interpreted the same way, to both of the occurrences of NP in the third line. Finally, we form the final two lines of 15 by applying the rules N → Δ and V → Δ.

15   *S*
      NP VP
      NP V NP
      N V N
      Δ V Δ
      Δ Δ Δ

Clearly, we can represent what is essential to the derivation 15 by the tree diagram 16.

16

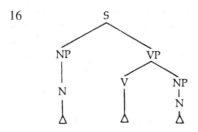

In the diagram 16, each symbol dominates the symbols by which it was replaced in forming 15. In fact, we may think of the rules of 14 as simply describing the way in which a tree diagram such as 16 can be constructed. Evidently, 16 is just another notation for the labeled bracketing 17:

17    $[_S[_{NP}[_N \Delta]_N]_{NP}[_{VP}[_V \Delta]_V[_{NP}[_N \Delta]_N]_{NP}]_{VP}]_S$

Domination of some element by a symbol A in 16 (as, for example, V NP is dominated by VP) is indicated in 17 by enclosing this element by the labeled brackets [A,]A. If we have a lexicon which tells us that "John" and "Bill" can replace the symbol Δ when this symbol is dominated by N (that is, is enclosed by [N,]N), and that "saw" can replace Δ when it is dominated by V, then we can extend the derivation 15 to derive "John saw Bill," with the associated structure that we have given as 6. In fact, 6, derives from 17 by replacing the first occurrence of Δ by "John," the second by "saw," and the third by "Bill."

Notice that the rules 14 in effect define grammatical relations, where the definitions are given as on pp. 121–22. Thus, the first rule of 14 defines the subject–predicate relation and the second, the verb–object relation. Similarly, other semantically significant grammatical functions and relations can be defined by rules of this form, interpreted in the manner indicated.

Restating these notions in a more formal and general way, the categorial component of the base is a system of rules of the form $A \rightarrow Z$, where A is a category symbol such as S (for "sentence"), NP (for "noun phrase"), N (for "noun"), etc., and Z is a string of one or more symbols which may again be category symbols or which may be *terminal* symbols (that is, symbols which do not appear on the left-hand side of the arrow in any base rule). Given such a system, we can form *derivations*, a derivation being a sequence of lines that meets the following conditions: the first line is simply the symbol S (standing for sentence); the last line contains only terminal symbols; if X, Y are two successive lines, then X must be of the form $\ldots A \ldots$ and Y of the form $\ldots Z \ldots$, where $A \to Z$ is one of the rules. A derivation imposes a labeled bracketing on its terminal string in the obvious way. Thus given the successive lines $X = \ldots A \ldots$, $Y = \ldots Z \ldots$, where Y was derived from X by the rule $A \to Z$, we will say that the string derived from Z (or Z itself, if it is terminal) is bracketed by [A,]A. Equivalently, we can represent the labeled bracketing by a tree diagram in which a node labeled A (in this example) dominates the successive nodes labeled by the successive symbols of Z.

We assume that one of the terminal symbols of the categorial component is the dummy symbol Δ. Among the nonterminal symbols are several that stand for *lexical categories*, in particular N (for "noun"), V (for "verb"), ADJ (for "adjective"). A lexical category A can appear on the left-hand side of a rule $A \to Z$ only if Z is Δ. Lexical entries will then be inserted in derivations in place of Δ by rules of a different sort, extending the derivations provided by the categorial component. Aside from Δ, indicating the position in which an item from the lexicon may appear, the terminal symbols of the categorial component are grammatical elements such as *be*, *of*, etc. Some of the terminal symbols introduced by categorial rules will have an intrinsic semantic content.

A labeled bracketing generated by base rules (that is, by the phrase-structure rules of the categorial component and by the rule of lexical insertion mentioned in the preceding paragraph) will be called a *base phrase-marker*. More generally, we will use the term "phrase-marker" here to refer to any string of elements properly bracketed with labeled brackets.[26] The rules of the transformational component modify phrase-markers in certain fixed ways. These rules are arranged in a sequence $T_1, \ldots, T_m$. This sequence of rules applies to a base phrase-marker in a cyclic fashion. First, it applies to a configuration dominated by S (that is, a configuration [s . . .]s) and containing no other occurrence of S. When the transformational rules have applied to all such configurations, then they next apply to a configuration dominated by S and containing only S-dominated configurations to which the rules have already applied. This process continues until the rules apply to the full phrase-marker dominated by the initial occurrence of S in the base phrase-marker. At this point, we have a surface structure. It may be that the ordering conditions on transformations are looser – that there are certain ordering conditions on the set $\{T_1, \ldots, T_m\}$, and that at a given stage in the cycle, a sequence of transformations can apply if it does not violate these conditions – but I will not go into this matter here.

---

[26] It may be that a slightly more general notion of "phrase-marker" is needed, but we will put this question aside here.

The properties of the syntactic component can be made quite clear by an example (which, naturally, must be much oversimplified). Consider a subpart of English with the lexicon 18 and the categorial component 19.

18   *Lexicon: it, fact, John, Bill, boy,*   (Noun)
            future
            dream, see, persuade,   (Verb)
            annoy
            sad   (Adjective)
            will   (Modal)
            the   (Determiner)

19   S → (Q) NP AUX VP
        VP → be ADJ
        VP → V (NP) (of NP)
        NP → (DET) N (that S)
        AUX → past
        AUX → M
        N, V, ADJ, DET, M → Δ

In 19, parentheses are used to indicate an element that may or may not be present in the rule. Thus the first line of 19 is an abbreviation for two rules, one in which *S* is rewritten *Q NP AUX VP*, the other in which *S* is rewritten *NP AUX VP*. Similarly, the third line of 19 is actually an abbreviation for four rules, etc. The last line of 19 stands for five rules, each of which rewrites one of the categorial symbols on the left as the dummy terminal symbol Δ.

This categorial component provides such derivations as the following:

20   a. S
            NP AUX VP
            NP AUX be ADJ
            N AUX be ADJ
            N past be ADJ
            Δ past be Δ

        b. S
            NP AUX VP
            NP AUX V NP of NP
            DET N AUX V N of DET N that S
            DET N M V N of DET N that S
            Δ   ΔΔΔΔ of   Δ   Δ that S
            Δ   ΔΔΔΔ of   Δ   Δ that NP VP
            Δ   ΔΔΔΔ of   Δ   Δ that NP AUX V
            Δ   ΔΔΔΔ of   Δ   Δ that N AUX V
            Δ   ΔΔΔΔ of   Δ   Δ that N past V
            Δ   ΔΔΔΔ of   Δ   Δ that Δ past Δ

These derivations are constructed in the manner just described. They impose labeled bracketings which, for clarity, we will give in the equivalent tree representation:

21   a.

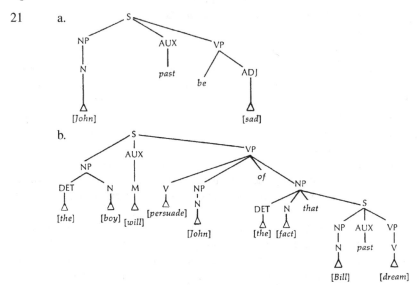

b.

We now use the lexicon to complete the base derivations 20a, 20b. Each entry in the lexicon contains syntactic features which identify the occurrences of Δ that it can replace in a derivation. For example, the items of the five rows of 18 can replace occurrences of Δ that are dominated, in the tree representations of 21, by the categorial symbols N, V, ADJ, M, DET, respectively.

But the restrictions are much narrower than this. Thus of the verbs in 18 (line 2), only *persuade* can replace an occurrence of Δ dominated by V when this occurrence of V is followed in the VP by: NP of NP. We can form "... *persuade John of the fact*," but not "... *dream (see, annoy) John of the fact*." Similarly, of the nouns in 18 (first line) only *fact* can appear in the context DET − *that* S (that is, "the fact that John left"); only *it* in a NP of the form − *that* S;[27] only *fact, boy*, and *future* in a NP of the form DET − ("the fact," "the boy," "the future"), etc. Details aside, the general character of such restrictions is quite clear. Assuming, then, that the lexical entries contain the appropriate lexical features, we can extend the base derivations of 20 to give the terminal strings 22, inserting the items enclosed in brackets in 21.

22   a. *John past be sad*
        b. *the boy will persuade John of the fact that Bill past dream*

[27] This may not seem obvious. We return to the example directly.

We can also form such terminal strings as 23, with other choices in derivations.

23   *Q the boy will dream of the future*
       it that John past see Bill past annoy the boy
       John will be sad
       John past see the future

In this way, we form full base derivations, using the rules of the categorial component and then substituting lexical entries for particular occurrences of the dummy symbol Δ in accordance with the syntactic features of these lexical entries. Correspondingly, we have the labeled brackets represented as 21, with lexical entries substituted for occurrences of Δ in the permitted ways. These are the base phrase-markers.

Notice that the rules that introduce lexical entries into base phrase-markers are entirely different in character from the rules of the categorial component. The rules of 19 that were used to form 20 are of a very elementary sort. Each such rule allows a certain symbol *A* in the string . . . *A* . . . to be rewritten as a certain string *Z*, *independently of the context of A and the source of A in the derivation*. But in introducing lexical entries in place of Δ, we must consider selected aspects of the phrase-marker in which Δ appears. For example, an occurrence of Δ can be replaced by "John" if it is dominated in the phrase-marker by N, but not by V. Thus the rules of lexical insertion really apply not to strings of categorial and terminal symbols, as do the rules of the categorial component, but to phrase-markers such as 21. Rules which apply to phrase-markers, modifying them in some specific way, are referred to in current terminology as *(grammatical) transformations*. Thus the rules of lexical insertion are transformational rules, whereas the rules of the categorial component are simply rewriting rules.

Let us now return to the examples 22a, 22b. Consider first 22a, with the base phrase-marker 21a.[28] We see at once that 21 contains just the information required in the deep structure of the sentence "John was sad." Clearly, the string *past be* is simply a representation of the formative "was," just as *past see* represents "saw," *past persuade* represents "persuaded," etc. With a rule that converts *past be* to the formative "was," we form the surface structure of the sentence "John was sad." Furthermore, if we define grammatical functions and relations in the manner described earlier (see pp. 121–22), 21 expresses the fact that the subject–predicate relation holds between *John* and *past be sad*, and it also contains semantic information about the meaning-bearing items *John*, *past*, *sad*; we may assume, in fact, that *past* is itself a symbol of a universal terminal alphabet with a fixed semantic interpretation, and the semantic features of the lexical entries of *John* and *sad* can also be assumed to be selected, like the phonological features of these entries, from some universal system of

---

[28] We henceforth suppose 21a and 21b to be extended to full phrase-markers by insertion of appropriate lexical entries, as indicated.

representation of the sort discussed above. In short, 21a contains all information required for semantic interpretation, and we can, therefore, take it to be the deep structure underlying the sentence "John was sad."

What is true of this example is true quite generally. That is, the base phrase-markers generated by the categorial component and the lexicon are the deep structures that determine semantic interpretation. In this simple case, only one rule is needed to convert the deep structure to a surface structure, namely, the rule converting *past be* to the formative *was*. Since this rule is clearly a special case of a rule that applies as well to any string of the form *past V*, it is really a very simple transformational rule (in the terminology just given) rather than an elementary rule of the type that we find in the categorial component. This observation can be generalized. The rules that convert deep structures to surface structures are transformational rules.

Suppose now that instead of the derivation 20a we had formed the very similar derivation 20:

24   S
        Q NP AUX VP
        Q NP AUX be ADJ
        Q N AUX be ADJ
        Q N M be ADJ
        Q Δ Δ be Δ
        Q John will be sad

with its associated phrase-marker. We intend the symbol Q to be a symbol of the universal terminal alphabet with a fixed semantic interpretation, namely, that the associated sentence is a question. Suppose that the transformational component of the syntax contains rules that convert phrase-markers of the form Q *NP AUX* . . . to corresponding phrase-markers of the form *AUX NP* . . . (that is, the transformation replaces Q by *AUX*, leaving the phrase-marker otherwise unchanged). Applied to the phrase-marker corresponding to 24, this rule gives the labeled bracketing of the sentence "Will John be sad?"; that is, it forms the surface structure for this sentence.

Suppose that in place of 24 we had used the rule rewriting AUX as *past*. The question transformation of the preceding paragraph would give a phrase-marker with the terminal string "past John be sad," just as it gives "Will John be sad?" in the case of 24. Evidently, we must modify the question transformation so that it inverts not just *past*, in this case, but the string *past be*, so that we derive finally, "Was John sad?" This modification is, in fact, straightforward, when the rules are appropriately formulated.

Whether we select M or *past* in 24, the generated base phrase-marker once again qualifies as a deep structure. The grammatical relation of *John* to *will* (*past*) *be sad* is exactly the same in 24 as in 20a, with the definitions proposed previously, as required for empirical adequacy. Of course, the surface forms do not express these grammatical relations, directly; as we have seen earlier, significant grammatical relations are rarely expressed directly in the surface structure.

Let us now turn to the more complex example 20b – 21b – 22b. Once again, the base phrase-marker 21b of 22b expresses the information required for the semantic interpretation of the sentence "The boy will persuade John of the fact that Bill dreamt," which derives from 22b by a transformational rule that forms "dreamt" from *past dream*. Therefore, 21b can serve as the deep structure underlying this sentence, exactly as 21a can serve for "John was sad," and the phrase-marker corresponding to 24 for "Will John be sad?"

Suppose that in rewriting NP in the third line of 20b, we had selected not DET N *that* S but N *that* S [see the fourth line of 19]. The only lexical item of 18 that can appear in the position of this occurrence of N is *it*. Therefore, instead of 22b, we would have derived

25   the boy will persuade John of it that Bill past dream,

with grammatical relations and lexical content otherwise unmodified. Suppose now that the transformational component of the syntax contains rules with the following effect:

26   a. *it* is deleted before *that* S
       b. *of* is deleted before *that* S

Applying 26a and 26b to 25 in that order, with the rule that converts *past dream* to "dreamt," we derive the surface structure of "The boy will persuade John that Bill dreamt." The base phrase-marker corresponding to 25 serves as the deep structure underlying this sentence.

Notice that the rule 26a is much more general. Thus suppose we select the NP *it that Bill past dream* as the subject of *past annoy John*, as is permitted by the rules 18, 19. This gives

27   it that Bill past dream past annoy John

Applying the rule 26a (and the rules for forming past tense of verbs), we derive, "That Bill dreamt annoyed John." Alternatively, we might have applied the transformational rule with the effect of 28:

28   A phrase-marker of the form *it that S X* is restructured as the corresponding phrase-marker of the form *it X that S*.

Applying 28 to 27, we derive "It annoyed John that Bill dreamt." In this case, 26a is inapplicable. Thus 27 underlies two surface structures, one determined by 28 and the other by 26a; having the same deep structure, these are synonymous. In the case of 25, 28 is inapplicable and, therefore, we have only one corresponding surface structure.

We can carry the example 25 further by considering additional transformational rules. Suppose that instead of selecting *Bill* in the embedded sentence of

25, we had selected *John* a second time. There is a very general transformational rule in English and other languages providing for the deletion of repeated items. Applying this rule along with other minor ones of an obvious sort, we derive

29   The boy will persuade John to dream

from a deep structure that contains, as it must, a subphrase-marker that expresses the fact that *John* is the subject of *dream*. Actually, in this case the deep phrase-marker would be slightly different, in ways that need not concern us here, in this rough expository sketch.

Suppose now that we were to add a transformation that converts a phrase-marker of the form NP AUX V NP into the corresponding passive, in the obvious way.[29] Applying to phrase-markers very much like 21b, this rule would provide surface structures for the sentences "John will be persuaded that Bill dreamt (by the boy)" [from 25] and "John will be persuaded to dream (by the boy)" [from 29]. In each case, the semantic interpretation will be that of the underlying deep phrase-marker. In certain cases, the significant grammatical relations are entirely obscured in the surface structure. Thus in the case of the sentence "John will be persuaded to dream," the fact that "John" is actually the subject of "dream" is not indicated in the surface structure, although the underlying deep structure, as we have noted, expresses this fact directly.

From these examples we can see how a sequence of transformations can form quite complicated sentences in which significant relations among the parts are not represented in any direct way. In fact, it is only in artificially simple examples that deep and surface structure correspond closely. In the normal sentences of everyday life, the relation is much more complex; long sequences of transformations apply to convert underlying deep structures into the surface form.

The examples that we have been using are stilted and unnatural. With a less rudimentary grammar, quite natural ones can be provided. For example, in place of the sentences formed from 27 by 26 or 28 we could use more acceptable sentences such as "That you should believe this is not surprising," "It is not surprising that you should believe this," etc. Actually, the unnaturalness of the examples we have used illustrates a simple but often neglected point, namely, that the intrinsic meaning of a sentence and its other grammatical properties are determined by rule, not by conditions of use, linguistic context, frequency of parts, etc.[30] Thus the examples of the last few paragraphs may never have been

---

[29] Notice that this transformation would modify the phrase-marker to which it applies in a more radical way than those discussed above. The principles remain the same, however.

[30] These factors may affect performance, however. Thus they may affect the physical signal and play a role in determining how a person will interpret sentences. In both producing and understanding sentences, the speaker–hearer makes use of the ideal phonetic and semantic interpretations, but other factors also play a role. The speaker may be simply interested in making himself understood–the hearer, in determining what the speaker intended (which may not be identical

produced in the experience of some speaker (or, for that matter, in the history of the language), but their status as English sentences and their ideal phonetic and semantic interpretations are unaffected by this fact.

Since the sequence of transformations can effect drastic modifications in a phrase-marker, we should not be surprised to discover that a single structure[31] may result from two very different deep structures – that is, that certain sentences are ambiguous (for example, sentence 4 on p. 110). Ambiguous sentences provide a particularly clear indication of the inadequacy of surface structure as a representation of deeper relations.[32]

More generally, we can easily find paired sentences with essentially the same surface structure but entirely different grammatical relations. To mention just one such example, compare the sentences of 30:

30   a. I persuaded the doctor to examine John.
        b. I expected the doctor to examine John.

The surface structures are essentially the same. The sentence 30a is of the same form as 29. It derives from a deep structure which is roughly of the form 31:

31   *I past persuade the doctor of it that the doctor AUX examine John*

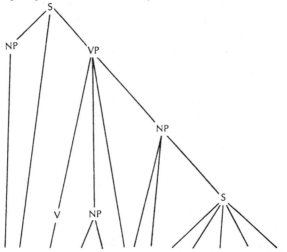

I past persuade the doctor of it that the doctor AUX examine John

with the literal semantic interpretation of the sentence or sentence fragment that he produced). Once again, we must insist on the necessity for distinguishing performance from competence if either is to be studied in a serious way.

31 More accurately, surface structures that are sufficiently close so as to determine the same phonetic representation.

32 Modern linguistics has made occasional use of this property of language as a research tool. The first general discussion of how ambiguity can be used to illustrate the inadequacy of certain conceptions of syntactic structure is in C. F. Hockett's "Two Models for Grammatical Description," *Word*, Vol. 10, 1954, pp. 210–31, reprinted in M. Joos, ed., *Readings in Linguistics One*, 4th edn. (Chicago: University of Chicago Press, 1966).

This deep structure is essentially the same as 21b, and by the transformational process described in connection with 29, we derive from it the sentence 30a. But in the case of 30b there are no such related structures as "I expected the doctor of the fact that he examined John," ". . . of the necessity (for him) to examine John," etc., as there are in the case of 30a. Correspondingly, there is no justification for an analysis of 30b as derived from a structure like 31. Rather, the deep structure underlying 30b will be something like 32 (again omitting details):

32   *I past expect it that the doctor AUX examine John*

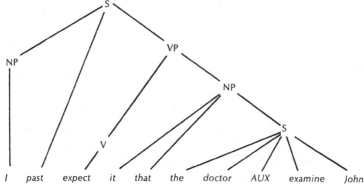

There are many other facts that support this analysis of 30a and 30b. For example, from a structure like 32 we can form "What I expected was that the doctor (will, should, etc.) examine John," by the same rule that forms "What I saw was the book," from the underlying NP-V-NP structure "I saw the book." But we cannot form "What I persuaded was that the doctor should examine John," corresponding to 30a, because the underlying structure 31 is not of the form NP-V-NP as required by this transformation. Applying rule 26a to 32, we derive "I expected that the doctor (will, should, etc.) examine John." We derive 30b, instead, by the use of the same rule that gives 29, with "to" rather than "that" appearing with the embedded sentence, which, in this case, contains no other representative of the category AUX.

Details aside, we see that 30a is derived from 31 and 30b from 32, so that despite near identity of surface structure, the deep structures underlying 30a and 30b are very different. That there must be such a divergence in deep structure is not at all obvious.[33] It becomes clear, however, if we consider the effect of replacing "the doctor to examine John" by its passive, "John to be examined by the doctor," in 30a and 30b. Thus we have under examination the sentences 33 and 34:

---

[33] It seems, in fact, that this phenomenon has escaped the attention of English grammarians, both traditional and modern.

33   a. I persuaded the doctor to examine John [= 30a].
        b. I persuaded John to be examined by the doctor.

34   a. I expected the doctor to examine John [= 30b].
        b. I expected John to be examined by the doctor.

The semantic relation between the paired sentences of 34 is entirely different from the relation between the sentences of 33. We can see this by considering the relation in truth value. Thus 34a and 34b are necessarily the same in truth value; if I expected the doctor to examine John then I expected John to be examined by the doctor, and conversely. But there is no necessary relation in truth value between 33a and 33b. If I persuaded the doctor to examine John, it does not follow that I persuaded John to be examined by the doctor, or conversely.

In fact, exchange of active and passive in the embedded sentence preserves meaning, in a rather clear sense, in the case of 30b but not 30a. The explanation is immediate from consideration of the deep structures underlying these sentences. Replacing active by passive in 32, we then go on to derive 34b in just the way that 30b is derived from 32. But to derive 33b, we must not only passivize the embedded sentence in 31, but we must also select "John" instead of "the doctor" as the object of the verb "persuade"; otherwise, the conditions for deletion of the repeated noun phrase, as in the derivation of 29, will not be met. Consequently, the deep structure underlying 33b is quite different from that underlying 33a. Not only is the embedded sentence passivized, but the object "the doctor" must be replaced in 31 by "John." The grammatical relations are, consequently, quite different, and the semantic interpretation differs correspondingly. It remains true, in both cases, that passivization does not affect meaning (in the sense of "meaning" relevant here). The change of meaning in 30a when "the doctor to examine John" is replaced by "John to be examined by the doctor" is occasioned by the change of grammatical relations, "John" now being the direct object of the verb phrase in the underlying structure rather than "the doctor." There is no corresponding change in the case of 34a, so that the meaning remains unaltered when the embedded sentence is passivized.

The example 30a, 30b illustrates, once again, the inadequacy (and, quite generally, irrelevance) of surface structure for the representation of semantically significant grammatical relations. The labeled bracketing that conveys the information required for phonetic interpretation is in general very different from the labeled bracketing that provides the information required for semantic interpretation. The examples 30a, 30b also illustrate how difficult it may be to bring one's "linguistic intuition" to consciousness. As we have seen, the grammar of English, as a characterization of competence (see pp. 102f.), must, for descriptive adequacy, assign different deep structures to the sentences 30a and 30b. The grammar that each speaker has internalized does distinguish these deep structures, as we can see from the fact that any speaker of English is capable of understanding the effect of replacing the embedded sentence by its passive in the two cases of 30. But this fact about his internalized grammatical competence may escape even the careful attention of the native speaker (see note 33).

Perhaps such examples as these suffice to give something of the flavor of the syntactic structure of a language. Summarizing our observations about the syntactic component, we conclude that it contains a base and a transformational part. The base generates deep structures, and the transformational rules convert them to surface structures. The categorial component of the base defines the significant grammatical relations of the language, assigns an ideal order to underlying phrases, and, in various ways, determines which transformations will apply.[34] The lexicon specifies idiosyncratic properties of individual lexical items. Together, these two components of the base seem to provide the information relevant for semantic interpretation in the sense in which we have been using this term, subject to the qualifications mentioned earlier. The transformational rules convert phrase-markers to new phrase-markers, affecting various kinds of reordering and reorganization. The kinds of changes that can be effected are quite limited; we will, however, not go into this matter here. Applying in sequence, the transformations may affect the organization of a base phrase-marker quite radically, however. Thus the transformations provide a wide variety of surface structures that have no direct or simple relation to the base structures from which they originate and which express their semantic content.

It is a fact of some significance that the mapping of deep to surface structures is not a matter of a single step but is, rather, analyzable into a sequence of successive transformational steps. The transformations that contribute to this mapping of deep to surface structures can be combined in many different ways, depending on the form of the deep structure to which they apply. Since these transformations apply in sequence, each must produce a structure of the sort to which the next can apply. This condition is met in our formulation, since transformations apply to phrase-markers and convert them into new phrase-markers. But there is very good empirical evidence that the surface structures that determine phonetic form are, in fact, phrase-markers (that is, labeled bracketing of formatives). It follows, then, that the deep structures to which transformations originally apply should themselves be phrase-markers, as in our formulation.

In principle, there are many ways in which a network of grammatical relations might be represented. One of the major reasons for selecting the method of phrase-markers generated by base rules is precisely the fact that transformations must apply in sequence and therefore must apply to objects of the sort that they

---

[34] It is an open question whether this determination is unique.

themselves produce, ultimately, to phrase-markers that have the same formal properties as surface structures.[35]

Concluding observations

The grammatical theory just presented calls for several comments. We pointed out earlier that the grammar of a language must, for empirical adequacy, allow for infinite use of finite means, and we assigned this recursive property to the syntactic component, which generates an infinite set of paired deep and surface structures. We have now further localized the recursive property of the grammar, assigning it to the categorial component of the base. Certain base rules introduce the initial symbol S that heads derivations, for example, the fourth rule of 19. It may be that introduction of "propositional content" in deep structures by this means is the only recursive device in the grammar apart from the rules involved in forming coordinated constructions, which raise various problems going beyond what we have been discussing here.

It is reasonable to ask why human languages should have a design of this sort – why, in particular, they should use grammatical transformations of the sort described to convert deep structures to surface form. Why should they not make use of deep structures in a more direct way?[36] Two reasons suggest themselves at once. We have already observed that the conditions of lexical insertion are essentially transformational rather than phrase-structural (see p. 130). More generally, we find many nonphrase-structural constraints (for example, those involved in deletion of identical items – see pp. 132 and 136) when we study a language carefully. Thus transformations not only convert a deep structure to a surface structure, but they also have a "filtering effect," ruling out certain potential deep structures as not well-formed.[37] Apart from this, we would naturally be inclined to seek an explanation for the use of grammatical transformations in the empirical constraints that linguistic communication must meet. Even the simple fact that sound is unrecoverable imposes conditions on speech that need not, for example, be imposed on a linguistic system designed only for writing (for example, the artificial systems mentioned in note 36). A written system provides an "external memory" that changes the perceptual problem in quite a significant way. We would expect a system designed for the

---

[35] There are other supporting reasons. For one thing, grammatical relations are not among words or morphemes but among phrases, in general. For another, empirical investigation has uniformly shown that there is an optimal ideal order of phrases in underlying structures, consistent with the assumption that these are generated by a base system of the sort discussed above.

[36] It is interesting to observe, in this connection, that the theory of context-free phrase-structure grammar (see p. 125) is very close to adequate for "artificial languages" invented for various purposes, for example, for mathematics or logic or as computer languages.

[37] And hence, in certain cases, as underlying "semigrammatical sentences" that deviate, in the indicated way, from grammatical rule. This suggests one approach to the problem touched on in note 24.

conditions of speech communication to be somehow adapted to the load on memory. In fact, grammatical transformations characteristically reduce the amount of grammatical structure in phrase-markers in a well-defined way, and it may be that one consequence of this is to facilitate the problem of speech perception by a short-term memory of a rather limited sort.[38] This observation suggests some promising directions for further research, but little of substance can be said with any confidence on the basis of what is understood today.

One further point requires some clarification. We noted at the outset that performance and competence must be sharply distinguished if either is to be studied successfully. We have now discussed a certain model of competence. It would be tempting, but quite absurd, to regard it as a model of performance as well. Thus we might propose that to produce a sentence, the speaker goes through the successive steps of constructing a base-derivation, line by line from the initial symbol S, then inserting lexical items and applying grammatical transformations to form a surface structure, and finally applying the phonological rules in their given order, in accordance with the cyclic principle discussed earlier. There is not the slightest justification for any such assumption. In fact, in implying that the speaker selects the general properties of sentence structure before selecting lexical items (before deciding what he is going to talk about), such a proposal seems not only without justification but entirely counter to whatever vague intuitions one may have about the processes that underlie production. A theory of performance (production or perception) will have to incorporate the theory of competence – the generative grammar of a language – as an essential part. But models of performance can be constructed in many different ways, consistently with fixed assumptions about the competence on which they are based. There is much that can be said about this topic, but it goes beyond the bounds of this paper.

Specifying the properties of the various components and subcomponents of a grammar precisely, along the lines outlined in this discussion, we formulate a highly restrictive hypothesis about the structure of any human language. As we have remarked several times, it is far from necessary, on any a priori grounds, that a language must have a structure of this sort. Furthermore, it seems quite likely that very heavy conditions can be placed on grammars beyond those outlined above. For example, it may be (as, in fact, was traditionally assumed) that base structures can vary only very slightly from language to language; and, by sufficiently restricting the possible range of base structures, it may be possible to arrive at quite general definitions for the categories that function as "nonterminal symbols" in the rules of the categorial component. As observed previously, this

---

[38] For some speculations about this matter and discussion of the general problem, see G. A. Miller and N. Chomsky, "Finitary Models for the User," in R. D. Luce, E. Galanter, and R. Bush, eds., *Handbook of Mathematical Psychology* (New York: Wiley, 1963), Vol. II. The suggestion that transformations may facilitate performance is implicit in V. Yngve, "A Model and a Hypothesis for Language Structure," *Proceedings of the American Philosophical Society*, 1960, pp. 444–66.

would provide language-independent definitions of grammatical relations, and would raise the possibility that there exist deep-seated universal principles of semantic interpretation.

In mentioning such possibilities, we must take note of the widespread view that modern investigations have not only conclusively refuted the principles of traditional universal grammar but have, moreover, shown that the search for such principles was ill-conceived from the start. But it seems to me that such conclusions are based on a serious misunderstanding of traditional universal grammar, and on an erroneous interpretation of the results of modern work. Traditional universal grammar tried to demonstrate, on the basis of what information was then available, that deep structures vary little from language to language. That surface structures might be highly diverse was never doubted. It was also assumed that the categories of syntax, semantics, and phonetics are universal and quite restricted in variety. Actually, modern "anthropological linguistics" has provided little evidence that bears on the assumption of uniformity of deep structures, and insofar as the universality of categories is concerned, conclusions rather like the traditional ones are commonly accepted in practice in descriptive work.[39]

Modern linguistics and anthropological linguistics have concerned themselves only marginally with deep structure, either in theory or practice. A great diversity of surface structures has been revealed in descriptive work, as anticipated in traditional universal grammar. Nevertheless, a good case can be made for the conclusion that the fundamental error of traditional universal grammar was that it was not sufficiently restrictive in the universal conditions it proposed for human language – that much heavier constraints must be postulated to account for the empirical facts.

Our discussion of the structure of English in the illustrative examples given previously has necessarily been quite superficial and limited to very simple phenomena. But even a discussion of the topics we have touched on requires a fairly intimate knowledge of the language and a reasonably well-articulated theory of generative grammar. Correspondingly, it is only when problems of the sort illustrated are seriously studied that any contribution can be made to the theory of universal grammar. Under these circumstances, it is not too surprising that even today, the hypotheses of universal grammar that can be formulated with any conviction are supported by evidence from a fairly small number of studies of very few of the languages of the world, and that they must therefore be highly tentative. Still, the inadequacy of the evidence should not be overstated. Thus it is surely true – and there is nothing paradoxical

[39] Traditional theories of universal phonetics have been largely accepted as a basis for modern work, and have been refined and amplified in quite important ways. See the references in note 7.

in this – that a single language can provide strong evidence for conclusions regarding universal grammar. This becomes quite apparent when we consider again the problem of language acquisition (see p. 106). The child must acquire a generative grammar of his language on the basis of a fairly restricted amount of evidence.[40] To account for this achievement, we must postulate a sufficiently rich internal structure – a sufficiently restricted theory of universal grammar that constitutes his contribution to language acquisition.

For example, it was suggested earlier that in order to account for the perception of stress contours in English, we must suppose that the user of the language is making use of the principle of cyclic application. We also noted that he could hardly have sufficient evidence for this principle. Consequently, it seems reasonable to assume that this principle is simply part of the innate schematism that he uses to interpret the limited and fragmentary evidence available to him. It is, in other words, part of universal grammar. Similarly, it is difficult to imagine what "inductive principles" might lead the child unerringly to the assumptions about deep structure and about organization of grammar that seem to be necessary if we are to account for such facts as those we have mentioned. Nor is a search for such principles particularly well-motivated. It seems reasonable to assume that these properties of English are, in reality, facts of universal grammar. If such properties are available to the child, the task of language acquisition becomes feasible. The problem for the child is not the apparently insuperable inductive feat of arriving at a transformational generative grammar from restricted data, but rather that of discovering which of the possible languages he is being exposed to. Arguing in this way, we can arrive at conclusions about universal grammar from study of even a single language.

The child is presented with data, and he must inspect hypotheses (grammars) of a fairly restricted class to determine compatibility with these data. Having selected a grammar of the predetermined class, he will then have command of the language generated by this grammar.[41] Thus he will know a great deal about

---

[40] Furthermore, evidence of a highly degraded sort. For example, the child's conclusions about the rules of sentence formation must be based on evidence that consists, to a large extent, of utterances that break rules, since a good deal of normal speech consists of false starts, disconnected phrases, and other deviations from idealized competence.

The issue here is not one of "normative grammar." The point is that a person's normal speech departs from the rules of his own internalized grammar in innumerable ways, because of the many factors that interact with underlying competence to determine performance. Correspondingly, as a language learner, he acquires a grammar that characterizes much of the evidence on which it was based as deviant and anomalous.

[41] We are presenting an "instantaneous model" of language acquisition which is surely false in detail, but can very well be accepted as a reasonable first approximation. This is not to deny that the fine structure of learning deserves study. The question, rather, is what the range of possibilities may be within which experience can cause knowledge and belief to vary. If the range is quite narrow (as, it seems to me, is suggested by considerations of the sort mentioned above), then a first approximation of the sort suggested will be a prerequisite to any fruitful

142   Language and Mind

phenomena to which he has never been exposed, and which are not "similar" or "analogous" in any well-defined sense to those to which he has been exposed.[42] He will, for example, know the relations among the sentences 33 and 34, despite their novelty; he will know what stress contours to assign to utterances, despite the novelty and lack of physical basis for these phonetic representations; and so on, for innumerable other similar cases. This disparity between knowledge and experience is perhaps the most striking fact about human language. To account for it is the central problem of linguistic theory.

The basic conclusion that seems to be emerging with increasing clarity from contemporary work in linguistics is that very restrictive initial assumptions about the form of generative grammar must be imposed if explanations are to be forthcoming for the facts of language use and language acquisition. Furthermore, there is, so far, no evidence to suggest that the variety of generative grammars for human languages is very great. The theory of universal grammar suggested by the sketchy description that we have just given will no doubt be proven incorrect in various respects. But it is not unlikely that its fundamental defect will be that it permits far too much latitude for the construction of grammars, and that the kinds of languages that can be acquired by humans in the normal way are actually of a much more limited sort than this theory would suggest. Yet even as the theory of generative grammar stands today, it imposes fairly narrow conditions on the structure of human language. If this general conclusion can be firmly established – and, furthermore, significantly strengthened – this will be a highly suggestive contribution to theoretical psychology. It is hardly open to controversy that today, as in the seventeenth century, the central and critical problem for linguistics is to use empirical evidence from particular languages to refine the principles of universal grammar. I have tried, in this paper, to suggest some of the principles that seem well established and to illustrate some of the empirical considerations that bear on such principles.[43]

investigation of learning. Given an instantaneous model that is empirically well supported, as a first approximation, there are many questions that can immediately be raised: for example, what are the strategies by which hypotheses are sampled, how does the set of hypotheses available at one stage depend on those tested at earlier stages, etc.

[42] Except, tautologically, in the sense that they are accounted for by the same theory.

[43] In addition to works mentioned in earlier notes the following books can be consulted for further development of topics touched on in this paper: N. Chomsky, *Syntactic Structures* (The Hague: Mouton, 1957); N. Chomsky, *Aspects of the Theory of Syntax* (Cambridge, Mass.: MIT Press, 1965); M. Halle, *Sound Pattern of Russian* (The Hague: Mouton, 1959); J. Katz and P. Postal, *An Integrated Theory of Linguistic Descriptions* (Cambridge, Mass.: MIT Press, 1964). See also many papers in J. Fodor and J. Katz, eds., *Structure of Language: Readings in the Philosophy of Language* (Englewood Cliffs, N.J.: Prentice-Hall, 1964). For more information on aspects of English structure touched on here, see also R. Lees, *Grammar of English Nominalizations* (New York: Humanities Press, 1963), and P. Rosenbaum, "Grammar of English Predicate Complement Constructions," unpublished Ph.D. dissertation, MIT, 1965. For further material see the bibliographies of the works cited.

6 Linguistics and philosophy

The methods and concerns of linguists and philosophers are similar in so many respects that it would be folly, I believe, to insist on a sharp separation of these disciplines, or for either to maintain a parochial disregard for insights achieved in the other. A number of examples might be cited to illustrate the possibility of fruitful interchange between the two. Zeno Vendler, in his recent book *Linguistics and Philosophy*, goes so far as to maintain that "the science of structural linguistics" provides "a new technique" for analytic philosophy, one that "is nothing but the natural continuation of the line of development that goes through the philosophers of ordinary language to J. L. Austin." For reasons to which I will return in a moment, I am a bit skeptical about the contribution that linguistics might make to philosophy along the lines that he sketches, but I think that he has shown that certain concepts of linguistics can be used in a rewarding way in the investigation of problems that have arisen in analytic philosophy.

Conversely, as the attention of linguists begins to turn to problems of meaning and use, there is no question that they can learn much from the long tradition of philosophical investigation of such problems, although here too, I think, a note of skepticism is in order.

To facilitate the discussion of this and other topics, let me present a small illustration of a problem that is at the frontier of research today. In the descriptive study of any language a central problem is to formulate a set of rules that generate what we may call the "surface structures" of utterances. By the term "surface structure," I refer to the analysis of an utterance into a hierarchy of phrases, each belonging to a specific category. This hierarchy can be represented as a labeled bracketing of the utterance, in an obvious sense. For example, consider the two sentences:

1   John is certain that Bill will leave.

2   John is certain to leave.

The surface structures of these utterances can be represented, in a natural way, with the following labeled bracketing:

1' $\left[_S\left[_{NP}{}^{John}\right]\left[_{VP}{}^{is}\left[_{AP}{}^{certain}\right.\right.\right.$
       $\left.\left.\left.\left[_S{}^{that}\left[_{NP}{}^{Bill}\right]_{VP}{}^{will\ leave}\right]\right]\right]\right]$

2' $\left[_S\left[_{NP}{}^{John}\right]\left[_{VP}{}^{is}\left[_{AP}{}^{certain}\right]\left[_{VP}{}^{to\ leave}\right]\right]\right]$

Paired brackets bound phrases; the label assigned to a pair of brackets indicates the category of the bounded phrase. Thus in 1, "certain that Bill will leave" is a phrase of the category Adjective Phrase; in both 1 and 2, "John" is a phrase of the category Noun Phrase; "will leave" is a Verb Phrase in 1; and both 1 and 2 are phrases of the category Sentence. One may question the details of these particular analyses, but there is little doubt that at some level of description, these, or representations very much like them, constitute a significant aspect of the structure of the sentences 1 and 2, and, more generally, that every sentence of the language has a surface structure of roughly this sort. There is, for example, strong evidence that the perceived phonetic form of the utterance is determined, by phonological rules of considerable generality, from representations of essentially this sort.

Granting this much, the linguist studying English will try to formulate a set of rules that generate an infinite number of surface structures, one for each sentence of English. Correspondingly, linguistic theory will be concerned with the problem of how such structures are generated in any human language, and will try to formulate general principles governing the systems of rules that express the facts of one or another such language.

Given the evidence available to us today, it seems to me reasonable to propose that in every human language surface structures are generated from structures of a more abstract sort, which I will refer to as "deep structures," by certain formal operations of a very special kind generally called "grammatical transformations." Each transformation is a mapping of labeled bracketings onto labeled bracketings. Deep structures are themselves labeled bracketings. The infinite class of deep structures is specified by a set of "base rules." Transformations applied in sequence to deep structures in accordance with certain fixed conventions and principles ultimately generate the surface structures of the sentences of the language. Thus a set of base rules defining an infinite class of deep structures and a set of grammatical transformations can serve to generate the surface structures.

To illustrate, consider sentences 1 and 2 again. The underlying deep structures might be represented roughly in the form 1'', 2'':

1''   same as 1'

2'' $\left[_S\left[_{NP}\left[_S\left[_{NP}{}^{John}\right]\left[_{VP}{}^{to\ leave}\right]\right]\right]\left[_{VP}{}^{is}\left[_{AP}{}^{certain}\right]\right]\right]$

We may think of these deep structures as expressing the fact that in 1, we predicate of John that he is certain that Bill will leave, whereas in 2, which is rather similar to 1 in surface structure, we predicate of the proposition that John leaves, that it is certain, in a very different sense of "certain." There is no difficulty in defining the concepts Subject and Predicate, in terms of configurations in deep structures, so that they express the intended interpretation. The operations that derive 2′ from 2″ include an operation of "extraposition," which from a structure very much like 2″ would yield the structure 3, and an operation of "it-replacement" which derives 2′ from a structure almost exactly like 3, but with "to" in place of "will" and "that" deleted:

3 $$\left[_S\left[_{NP}{}^{it}\right]\left[_{VP}{}^{is}\left[_{AP}{}^{certain}\right]\right.\right.$$
$$\left.\left[_S{}^{that}\left[_{NP}{}^{John}\right]\left[_{VP}{}^{will\ leave}\right]\right]\right]\right]$$

Details aside, the theory of "transformational-generative grammar" maintains that all surface structures are formed by application of such transformations – each of which maps labeled bracketings onto labeled bracketings – from deep structures that are often quite abstract. The sentences 1 and 2 are similar in surface structure, but very different in deep structure; the sentences 2 and 3 are very similar in deep structure, but quite different in surface structure. The deep structures of the language are quite restricted in their variety, and it appears that there are universal conditions that sharply restrict the class of possible rules.

Consider now the matter of semantic interpretation. It is clear from these quite typical examples that the surface structures give little indication of the semantic interpretation, whereas the deep structures are quite revealing in this respect. Pursuing this line of reasoning, one might propose a further elaboration of the theory just outlined, in the following terms. Let us suppose that there is a system of "universal semantics" that specifies the class of possible semantic representations for a natural language much in the way that universal phonetics specifies the class of possible phonetic representations, by specifying a class of distinctive features and certain conditions on their combination. Observe that it would be perfectly reasonable to study universal semantics even without any clear idea as to what its constituent elements might be, just as one could draw fairly persuasive conclusions regarding universal phonetics from consideration of the slow growth of the number of distinct sentences with increasing length, the phenomena of rhyme and assonance, the lack of slow drift through the "space" of sentences under chains of repetition, etc., even without any conception of what the distinctive features of this system might be. In any event, still supposing this to be a reasonable approach, one might propose that a language contains rules associating deep structures with representations drawn from universal semantics, as it contains phonological rules relating surface structures to representations drawn from universal phonetics.

At this point in the development of such a theory, the linguist would do well to turn to work in analytic philosophy, particularly to the many studies of referential opacity. One essential empirical assumption in the preceding account is that surface structure cannot contribute to meaning; whatever contribution the expression P makes to the meaning of the sentence XPY must be determined by the deep structure underlying P. The investigation of referential opacity has turned up a great number of examples illustrating how replacement of one expression by another changes meaning, even when the semantic connection between the two is very close. The approach just outlined would have to guarantee that in each such case there is a corresponding difference in deep structure to which the difference in meaning can be attributed. Without pursuing the matter, I would simply note that the nature of these examples makes it appear very unlikely that such an approach can succeed; but, in any event, the study of this aspect of linguistic theory must certainly take into account a mass of evidence that has been accumulated in the course of philosophical investigation.

I have mentioned the possibility that insights developed in the course of philosophical analysis might be relevant to the study of a central part of linguistic theory, and that concepts of linguistics might be useful to the philosopher in his work. Nevertheless, it seems to me that one should not expect too much from an interchange of this sort, for a number of reasons. In the cases I have mentioned, what is proposed is that the incidental by-products of research in one field will be of use for the central concerns of another. Furthermore, it is a fact that neither field makes use of research techniques of a sophisticated or specialized nature. Thus one would expect that in each field, it would be quite possible to collect and analyze the information relevant to its specific concerns directly. It is, therefore, something of an accident when one field can build directly on results of the other.

For these reasons, I think that Vendler may be expecting too much of the method he suggests, namely, "an appeal to the facts of language already organized by the science of structural linguistics." I believe that modern linguistics has real achievements to its credit, and that some of these do have relevance to philosophical questions. But it must be kept in mind that these achievements owe little to modern science and less to modern technology. The gathering of data is informal; there has been very little use of experimental approaches (outside of phonetics) or of complex techniques of data collection and data analysis of a sort that can easily be devised, and that are widely used in the behavioral sciences. The arguments in favor of this informal procedure seem to me quite compelling; basically, they turn on the realization that for the theoretical problems that seem most critical today, it is not at all difficult to obtain a mass of crucial data without use of such techniques. Consequently, linguistic work, at what I believe to be its best, lacks many of the features of the behavioral sciences. Nor is it obvious that the development of explanatory theories in linguistics merits the honorific designation "scientific." I think that these intellectual constructions are nontrivial and often illuminating. However, apart from certain insights owed to modern logic and mathematics, there is no reason why they could not have been developed many years ago. In fact, were it not for the dominance of certain empiricist assumptions to which I will return directly, I suspect that they would have been developed long before now and that much of what is new and exciting in linguistics today would be taken for granted by any educated person.

There are many questions about language that a philosopher might ask to which linguistics provides no answer and no reasonable hope for an answer. For example, a philosopher concerned with problems of knowledge, or causality (to take an example of Vendler's), might well be interested in investigating in detail the properties of the words "know" and "cause." Since linguistics offers no privileged access to data of this sort, it would be merely a lucky accident if acquaintance with linguistics proved to be of substantial help in this inquiry. A linguistic form is not of importance to linguistics because of the intrinsic interest of the concept or proposition it expresses (if any), but because of the evidence it provides concerning some assumption about the nature of language. Thus the analysis of sentences 1, 2, and 3 has been of interest to linguistics because of the light it sheds on the nature of deep and surface structures and the grammatical transformations that link them. Such data are of importance to linguistics insofar as they can be explained on the basis of some interesting assumptions about the organization of grammar, and are inconsistent with other such assumptions. In themselves, these facts are of no more interest than the fact that certain marks appear on a photographic plate at the base of a South African mine shaft. The latter is critical for elementary particle theory for the same reason that the facts related to sentences 1–3 are important for the theory of language. Similar remarks can be made about the likelihood that the conclusions of philosophers or the data they accumulate will be important for linguistics.

To make the matter more concrete, consider again the examples 1–3. Conceivably, such sentences, and others like them, might be of some interest to a philosopher concerned with the various concepts of certainty. These examples are of interest to linguistics, at the moment, for entirely different reasons. Thus it is interesting that there is a nominalized expression corresponding to 1, but no nominalized expression corresponding to 2; 4 is a nominalized form of 1, but we cannot form 5, corresponding to 2:

4   John's certainty that Bill would leave

5   John's certainty to leave

The distinction is more general; thus consider 6 and 7:

6   John is eager to leave.

7   John is easy to leave.

Corresponding to 6, we have the nominal phrase 8; but we cannot form 9 corresponding to 7:

8   John's eagerness to leave

9   John's easiness to leave

Notice that sentence 6 is like 1 in that the deep structure is very close to the surface structure; whereas 7 is like 2 in that the deep structure is very different from the surface structure. In fact, the surface of 7 would be formed by operations much like those that form 2 from 2″ and 3, by a derivation of roughly the form 10:

10   a. $\left[_S$ for one to leave John$\right]_S$ is easy (analogous to 2″)

      b. it is easy $\left[_S$ for one to leave John$\right]_S$ (analogous to 3)

      c. John is easy to leave (=7, analogous to 2).

The generalization exemplified by 1, 2, 4–9 is that a nominal phrase can be formed corresponding to a base structure but not to a surface structure. Thus we have 4 corresponding to 1″ and 8 corresponding to 6 (more properly, to the deep structure underlying 6 as 1′ underlies 1, but no nominalized expression such as 5 and 9, corresponding to the surface structures 2 and 7. This general observation can be illustrated by many other examples. It is interesting because of the support it lends to the assumption that abstract deep structures of the sort illustrated play a role in the mental representation of sentences. We find that when we study English grammar on the basis of this and related assumptions, we are able to characterize quite readily the class of sentences to which there correspond nominal phrases of the sort under discussion. There is no natural way to characterize this class in terms of surface structure, since, as we have seen, sentences that are very similar in surface structure behave quite differently with respect to the formal processes involved in the construction of nominal expressions. We might go on to try to explain these facts at a deeper level by formulating a principle of universal grammar from which it would follow that the nominal phrases in question will correspond only to deep structures.

To summarize, the examples in question are important for the study of language because of the evidence that they provide in support of a particular theory of linguistic structure, not because of the fact that the various concepts of certainty are of interest in their own right. The philosopher concerned with certainty would learn very little from a collection of data that is of great interest for linguistic research.

Apart from accident or matters of personal history, linguistics will be of relevance to philosophy only insofar as its conclusions about the nature of language bear on questions that concern the philosopher. One cannot predict to what extent this will be true in the future; it might turn out, for example, that linguistic study of semantic and syntactic structure in the future will provide a firm basis for certain kinds of philosophical investigation – one thinks, for example, of the potential relevance of a systematic classification of verbs that would have cross-language validity. For the moment, this is more a hope for the future than a present reality, however. Still, I think that a case can be made that certain well-founded conclusions about the nature of language do bear on traditional philosophical questions, but in ways rather different from those just mentioned. Specifically, I think that these conclusions are relevant to the problem of how knowledge is acquired and how the character of human knowledge is determined by certain general properties of the mind. What I would like to do, for the remainder of this paper, is to restate certain proposals about this matter that have been developed elsewhere,[1] and then to consider a variety of problems and objections that have been raised by several philosophers with respect to these proposals.[2]

One might adopt the following research strategy for the study of cognitive processes in humans. A person is presented with a physical stimulus that he interprets in a certain way. Let us say that he constructs a certain "percept" that represents certain of his conclusions (unconscious, in general) about the source of stimulation. To the extent that we can characterize this percept, we can proceed to investigate the process of interpretation. We can, in other words, proceed to develop a model of perception that takes stimuli as inputs and assigns percepts as "outputs," a model that will meet certain given empirical conditions on the actual pairing of stimuli with interpretations of these stimuli. For example, the person who understands sentences 1 and 2 knows (whether he is aware of it or not) that in the case of 2 it is a proposition that is certain and in the case of 1 it is a person who is certain of something, in a very different sense of "certain." If we are interested in studying perception of language – specifically, the processes by which sentences are understood – we can begin by describing the percepts in such a way as to bring out this difference, as we did in proposing that $1''$ and $2''$, interpreted in the suggested manner, are essential components of the percept. We can then ask how these percepts are constructed by the hearer, given the input stimuli 1 and 2.

A perceptual model that relates stimulus and percept might incorporate a certain system of beliefs, certain strategies that are used in interpreting stimuli, and other factors – for example, organization of memory. In the case of language,

[1] See, for example, my contribution to the symposium on innate ideas published in *Synthese*, Vol. 17, No. 1, March 1967, pp. 2–11, and the references cited there on p. 11.

[2] Specifically, the contributions by Nelson Goodman and Hilary Putnam to the symposium in *Synthese*, Vol. 17, No. 1, March 1967, pp. 12–28, and the review articles by Henry Hiż and Gilbert Harman in the issue of the *Journal of Philosophy* devoted to "Some Recent Issues in Linguistics," Vol. 64, No. 2, February 2, 1967, pp. 67–87. The latter two are largely devoted to critical analysis of Chapter 1 of my *Aspects of the Theory of Syntax* (Cambridge, Mass.: MIT Press, 1965).

the technical term for the underlying system of beliefs is "grammar," or "generative grammar." A grammar is a system of rules that generates an infinite class of "potential percepts," each with its phonetic, semantic, and syntactic aspects, the class of structures that constitute the language in question. The percepts themselves are first-order constructs; we determine their properties by experiment and observation. The grammar that underlies the formation of percepts is a second-order construct. To study it, we must abstract away from the other factors that are involved in the use and understanding of language, and concentrate on the knowledge of language[3] that has been internalized in some manner by the language user.

Concentrating on this system, we can then inquire into the means by which it was acquired and the basis for its acquisition. We can, in other words, attempt to construct a second model, a learning model, which takes certain data as input and gives, as "output," the system of beliefs that is one part of the internal structure of the perceptual model. The "output," in this case, is represented in the "final state" of the organism that has acquired this system of beliefs; we are asking, then, how this final state was achieved, through the interplay of innate factors, maturational processes, and organism–environment interaction.

In short, we can begin by asking "what is perceived" and move from there to a study of perception. Focusing on the role of belief (in our case, knowledge of language) in perception, we can try to characterize "what is learned" and move from there to the study of learning. One might, of course, decide to study some other topic, or to proceed in some different manner. Thus much of modern psychology has decided, for reasons that do not impress me, to limit itself to the study of behavior and control of behavior. I do not want to pursue the matter here, but I will merely state my own opinion: that this approach has proven quite barren, and that it is irrational to limit one's objectives in this way. One cannot hope to study learning or perception in any useful way by adhering to methodological strictures that limit the conceptual apparatus so narrowly as to disallow the concept "what is perceived" and the concept "what is learned."

I think that interesting conclusions can be reached when one studies human language along the lines just outlined. In the areas of syntax and phonetics at least, a plausible general account can be given of the system of representation for percepts in any human language. Furthermore, there has been substantial progress in constructing generative grammars that express the knowledge of language that is the "output" of a learning model and a fundamental component of a perceptual model. There is, I believe, good evidence that a generative grammar for a human language contains a system of base rules of a highly restricted sort, a set of grammatical transformations that map the deep structures

---

[3] Since the language has no objective existence apart from its mental representation, we need not distinguish between "system of beliefs" and "knowledge," in this case.

formed in accordance with base rules onto surface structures, and a set of phonological rules that assign phonetic interpretations, in a universal phonetic alphabet, to surface structures. Furthermore, there is also good evidence that certain highly restrictive principles determine the functioning of these rules, conditions of ordering and organization of a complex and intricate sort. There is a considerable literature dealing with these matters, and I will not try to review it here. I only wish to emphasize that there is no a priori necessity for a language to be organized in the highly specific manner proposed in these investigations. Hence if this theory of linguistic structure is correct, or near correct, some nontrivial problems arise for the theory of human learning. Specifically, we must ask how, on the basis of the limited data available to him, the child is able to construct a grammar of the sort that we are led to ascribe to him, with its particular choice and arrangement of rules and with the restrictive principles of application of such rules. What, in other words, must be the internal structure of a learning model that can duplicate this achievement? Evidently, we must try to characterize innate structure in such a way as to meet two kinds of empirical conditions. First, we must attribute to the organism, as an innate property, a structure rich enough to account for the fact that the postulated grammar is acquired on the basis of the given conditions of access to data; second, we must not attribute to the organism a structure so rich as to be incompatible with the known diversity of languages. We cannot attribute knowledge of English to the child as an innate property, because we know that he can learn Japanese as well as English. We cannot attribute to him merely the ability to form associations, or to apply the analytic procedures of structural linguistics, because (as is easy to show when these proposals are made precise) the structures they yield are not those that we must postulate as generative grammars. Within the empirical bounds just stated, we are free to construct theories of innate structure and to test them in terms of their empirical consequences. To say this is merely to define the problem. Substantive questions arise only when a specific theory is proposed.

By investigating sentences and their structural descriptions, speech signals and the percepts to which they give rise, we can arrive at detailed conclusions regarding the generative grammar that is one fundamental element in linguistic performance, in speech and understanding of speech. Turning then to the next higher level of abstraction, we raise the question of how this generative grammar is acquired. From a formal point of view, the grammar that is internalized by every normal human can be described as a theory of his language, a theory of a highly intricate and abstract form that determines, ultimately, a connection between sound and meaning by generating structural descriptions of sentences ("potential percepts"), each with its phonetic, semantic, and syntactic aspects. From this point of view, one can describe the child's acquisition of knowledge of language as a kind of theory construction. Presented with highly restricted data, he constructs a theory of the language of which this data is a sample (and, in fact, a highly degenerate sample, in the sense that much of it must be excluded as irrelevant and incorrect – thus the child learns rules of grammar that identify much of what he has heard as ill-formed, inaccurate, and inappropriate). The child's ultimate knowledge of language obviously extends far beyond the data presented to him. In other words, the theory he has in some way developed has a predictive scope of which the data on which it is based constitute a negligible part. The normal use of language characteristically involves new sentences, sentences that bear no point-by-point resemblance or analogy to those in the child's experience. Furthermore, the task of constructing this system is carried out in a remarkably similar way by all normal language learners, despite wide differences in experience and ability. The theory of human learning must face these facts.

I think that these facts suggest a theory of human intelligence that has a distinctly rationalist flavor. Using terms suggested by Peirce, in his lectures on "the logic of abduction," the problem of the theory of learning is to state the condition that "gives a rule to abduction and so puts a limit on admissible hypotheses." If "man's mind has a natural adaptation to imagining correct theories of some kinds," then acquisition of knowledge of a sort that we are considering is possible. The problem for the psychologist (or linguist) is to formulate the principles that set a limit to admissible hypotheses. I have made detailed suggestions in this regard elsewhere, and will not repeat them here. Roughly, I think it reasonable to postulate that the principles of general linguistics regarding the nature of rules, their organization, the principles by which they function, the kinds of representations to which they apply and which they form, all constitute part of the innate condition that "puts a limit on admissible hypotheses." If this suggestion is correct, then there is no more point asking how these principles are learned than there is in asking how a child learns to breathe, or, for that matter, to have two arms. Rather, the theory of learning should try to characterize the particular strategies that a child uses to determine that the language he is facing is one, rather than another, of the "admissible languages." When the principles just alluded to are made precise, they constitute an empirical assumption about the innate basis for the acquisition of knowledge, an assumption that can be tested in a variety of ways. In particular, we can ask whether it falls between the bounds described earlier: that is, does it ascribe a rich enough innate structure to account for the acquisition of knowledge, but a structure not so rich as to be falsified by the diversity of languages? We might also ask many other questions, for example, how the schema that is proposed as a basis for acquisition of knowledge of language relates to the principles that "give a rule to abduction" in other domains of human (or animal) intelligence.

What I am suggesting is that if we wish to determine the relevance of linguistics to philosophy, we must investigate the conclusions that can be established concerning the nature of language, the ways in which language is used and understood, the basis for its acquisition. I think that these conclusions have interesting consequences for psychological theory – in particular, that they strongly support an account of mental processes that is, in part, familiar, from rationalist speculation about these matters. They support the conclusion that the role of intrinsic organization is very great in perception, and that a highly restrictive initial schema determines what counts as "linguistic experience" and what knowledge arises on the basis of this experience. I also think, and have argued elsewhere, that the empiricist doctrines that have been prevalent in linguistics, philosophy, and psychology in recent years, if formulated in a fairly precise way, can be refuted by careful study of language. If philosophy is what philosophers do, then these conclusions are relevant to philosophy, both in its classical and modern varieties.

At this point, I would like to turn to some of the critical analysis of this point of view that has appeared in the recent philosophical literature, specifically, to the items referred to in note 2.

Goodman's treatment of these questions seems to me to suffer, first, from a historical misunderstanding; second, from a failure to formulate correctly the exact nature of the problem of acquisition of knowledge and third, from a lack of familiarity with the work that has led to the conclusions that he criticizes, those that are outlined above.

His historical misunderstanding has to do with the issue between Locke and whoever it was that Locke thought he was criticizing in his discussion of innate ideas. Goodman believes that "Locke made . . . acutely clear" that the doctrine of innate ideas is "false or meaningless." I will not dwell on this matter, since it is a commonplace of historical scholarship that Locke's critique of the doctrine of innate ideas "assails it in its crudest form, in which it is countenanced by no eminent advocate."[4] Even Lord Herbert makes it clear that the common notions "remain latent" in the absence of appropriate stimulation, that they are the "principles without which we should have no experience at all" but that they will obviously not be constantly in consciousness, even to "normal men," and certainly not to those who are "headstrong, foolish, weak-minded and imprudent," to "madmen, drunkards, and infants," and so on. And as these ideas are elaborated by Descartes and others, it is repeatedly emphasized that while innate ideas and principles determine the nature of experience and the knowledge that can arise from it, they will ordinarily not be in consciousness. Since Locke's arguments fail to come to grips with the "dispositional" nature of innate structure that is insistently maintained by the leading proponents of rationalist doctrine, they also invariably miss the mark; it seems that he must

---

[4] A. C. Fraser (ed.), in his edition of Locke's *Essay Concerning Human Understanding*, 1894 (reprinted by Dover, 1959), p. 38 of the Dover edition.

have mistaken the actual views of Herbert, Descartes, the minor Cartesians, Cudworth, and others.

It is surprising that Goodman accuses those who "identify the innate ideas with capacities" of "sophistry." Goodman is free, if he wishes, to use the terms "idea" and "innate idea" in accordance with Locke's misunderstanding of rationalist doctrine, but hardly to accuse others of "sophistry" when they examine and develop this doctrine in the form in which it was actually presented. It is particularly surprising to hear Goodman speak of the necessity of applying the term "idea," in "its normal use." One would hardly expect Goodman to propose this sort of "ordinary language argument" against the use of a technical term. Furthermore, as Thomas Reid pointed out, if we use "idea" in the nontechnical way, then not only the position of Descartes, but also that of Locke and Hume reduces to absurdity – an observation that is correct, but that shows nothing more than the absurdity of insisting that a technical term must be understood in "the normal use" of the homonymous nontechnical term of ordinary discourse.

Let me turn, however, to the substantive problem of acquisition of knowledge, as Goodman formulates it in the specific case of language acquisition. Quite properly, he distinguishes two cases: initial language, and second-language acquisition. But his analysis of the two cases leaves much to be desired.

Consider first the problem of second-language acquisition. In what I understand to be Goodman's view,[5] second-language acquisition poses no problem, since "once one language is available and can be used for giving explanation and instruction, the limitations [determined by an innate schematism] are transcended." This way of putting the matter misconstrues the situation in two basic respects. First, it is misleading to speak of the innate schematism that has been proposed as merely providing "limitations" for acquisition of language. Rather, what has been proposed is that this schematism *makes possible* the acquisition of a rich and highly specific system on the basis of limited data. To take one example, the problem is to explain how the data available to a language learner (first or second) suffices to establish that the phonological rules (the rules that assign phonetic representations to surface structures) apply cyclically, first to innermost phrases of the surface structure, then to larger phrases, etc., until the maximal domain of phonological processes – in simple cases, the full sentence – is reached. There is in fact good evidence that the rules do apply cyclically, but this evidence is not of a sort that can be used as the basis for induction from phonetic data to the principle of cyclic application, by any procedure of induction that has general validity. In particular, much of this evidence is derived from an analysis of percepts, that is, from investigation of the way in which someone

[5] Cf. his article in the symposium in *Synthese*, Vol. 17, No. 1, March 1967, p. 24. Given the dialogue form of his article, it is difficult to be certain that one is not misrepresenting his position. However, I see no other way to interpret these remarks.

who has already mastered the language interprets speech signals. It seems that this interpretation imposes a certain structure that is not indicated directly in the speech signal, for example, in the determination of stress contours.[6] Obviously the child cannot acquire the knowledge that phonological rules apply cyclically from data that are available to him only after he knows and makes use of this principle. This is an extreme example, but it nevertheless illustrates quite well the basic problem: to explain how a rich and highly specific grammar is developed on the basis of limited data that is consistent with a vast number of other conflicting grammars. An innate schematism is proposed, correctly or incorrectly, as an empirical hypothesis to explain the uniformity, specificity, and richness of detail and structure of the grammars that are, in fact, constructed and used by the person who has mastered the language. Therefore the word "limitation" in Goodman's formulation is quite inappropriate.

More serious, it must be recognized that one does not learn the grammatical structure of a second language through "explanation and instruction," beyond the most elementary rudiments, for the simple reason that no one has enough explicit knowledge about this structure to provide explanation and instruction. For example, consider the property of nominalization in English noted earlier, namely, that a certain class of nominal expressions corresponds only to deep and not surface structures. The person who has learned English as a second language well enough to make the judgments illustrated by examples 1–10 has not acquired this knowledge through "explanation and instruction." Until quite recently, no one, to my knowledge, was aware of this phenomenon; the second-language learner, like the first-language learner, has somehow established the facts for himself, without explanation or instruction. Again, the example is quite typical. Only a trivial part of the knowledge that the second-language learner acquires is presented to him by direct instruction. Even the most cursory attention to the facts of second-language acquisition is sufficient to establish this. Hence, although second-language acquisition is, indeed, to be distinguished from first-language acquisition, the distinction is not of the sort that Goodman suggests. While it may be true that "once some language is available, acquisition of others is relatively easy," it nevertheless remains a very serious problem – not significantly different from the problem of explaining first-language acquisition – to account for this fact.

Consider now the more important matter of first-language acquisition, the problem to which the empirical hypotheses regarding innate schematism have

---

[6] For some discussion, see my paper "Explanatory Models in Linguistics," in E. Nagel, P. Suppes, and A. Tarski, eds., *Logic, Methodology, and Philosophy of Science* (Stanford, Calif.: Stanford University Press, 1962). For some recent and much more extensive discussion, see N. Chomsky and M. Halle, *Sound Patterns of English* (New York: Harper & Row, 1968), and the references cited there, and my paper "Some General Properties of Phonological Rules," *Language*, Vol. 43, March 1967, pp. 102–28.

been directed. Goodman argues that there is no problem in explaining first-language acquisition, because "acquisition of an initial language is acquisition of a secondary symbolic system": the fundamental step has already been taken, and details can be elaborated within an already existing framework. This argument might have some force if it were possible to show that some of the specific properties of grammar – say the distinction of deep and surface structure, the specific properties of grammatical transformations and phonological rules, the principles of rule ordering, and so on – were present in these already acquired prelinguistic "symbolic systems." But there is not the slightest reason to believe that this is so. Goodman's argument is based on a metaphorical use of the term "symbolic system," and collapses as soon as we try to give this term a precise meaning. If it were possible to show that "prelinguistic symbolic systems" share certain significant properties with natural language, we could then argue that these properties of natural language are somehow acquired by "analogy," though we would now face the problem of explaining how the "prelinguistic symbolic systems" developed these properties and how the analogies are established. But the issue is academic, since, for the moment, there is no reason to suppose the assumption to be true. Goodman's argument is a bit like a "demonstration" that there is no problem in accounting for the development of complex organs, because everyone knows that mitosis takes place. This seems to me to be obscurantism, which can be maintained only so long as one fails to come to grips with the actual facts.

There is, furthermore, a non sequitur in Goodman's discussion of first- and second-language acquisition. Recall that he explains the presumed ease of second-language acquisition on the grounds that it is possible to use the first language for explanation and instruction. He then goes on to argue that "acquisition of an initial language is acquisition of a secondary symbolic system," and is hence quite on a par with second-language acquisition. The primary symbolic systems he has in mind are "rudimentary prelinguistic symbolic systems in which gestures and sensory and perceptual occurrences of all sorts function as signs." But evidently these systems, whatever they may be, cannot "be used for giving explanation and instruction" *in the way in which a first language can be used in second-language acquisition.* Consequently, even on his own grounds, Goodman's argument is incoherent.

Goodman maintains that "the claim we are discussing cannot be experimentally tested even when we have an acknowledged example of a 'bad' language, and . . . that the claim has not even been formulated to the extent of citation of a single general property of 'bad' languages." The first of these conclusions is correct, in his sense of "experimental test," namely, a test in which we "take an infant at birth, isolate it from all the influences of our language-bound culture, and attempt to inculcate it with one of the 'bad' artificial languages." Obviously, this is not feasible, exactly as comparable experimental tests are not feasible in any other area of human psychology. But there is no reason for dismay at the impracticality of such direct tests as these. There are many other ways – those discussed earlier, and extensively in the literature – in which evidence can be obtained regarding the properties of grammars and in which hypotheses regarding the general properties of such grammars can be put to empirical test. Any such hypothesis immediately specifies, correctly or incorrectly, certain properties of "bad" languages. It therefore makes an empirical claim that can be falsified by finding counterinstances in some human language, or by showing that under the actual conditions of language acquisition, the properties in question do not appear in the system that is developed by the language learner. In linguistics, as in any other field, it is only in such indirect ways as these that one can hope to find evidence bearing on nontrivial hypotheses. Direct experimental tests of the sort that Goodman, for some reason, regards as necessary, are rarely feasible, a fact that may be unfortunate but that is nevertheless characteristic of most research.

Goodman's further claim, that not "a single general property of 'bad' languages has been formulated," is quite unfair. There are dozens of books and papers concerned with formulating properties of universal grammar and examining their empirical consequences, and each such property specifies "bad" languages, as just noted. One is free to argue that these attempts are misguided, inadequate, unconvincing, refuted by facts, etc., but not to deny blandly that they exist. I do not see how to avoid the conclusion that when Goodman speaks of "the unimpressive evidence adduced with respect to languages," he simply speaks out of ignorance, rather than from a considered analysis of the work that has been done in the field.

In discussing properties of "bad" languages, Goodman refers only to one case, namely, the case of the concocted language *Gruebleen*, which "differs from ordinary English only in that it contains the predicates 'grue' (for "examined before t and green or not so examined and blue") and 'bleen' (for "examined before t and blue or not so examined and green") in place of the predicates 'green' and 'blue.'" He argues that even in this case, one must be "painfully aware of the difficulties of answering" the question of what in general is "the difference between Gruebleen-like and English-like languages." I think that this is a rather marginal issue, since much more deep-seated properties of "English-like languages" have been formulated and investigated, but, since he brings up this example, it is well to point out that the difficulties to which he alludes are in large measure a consequence of the vagueness of the question he asks. Thus there is no difficulty in finding some property of Gruebleen that is not a property of "English-like languages," even a property of some generality. For example, consider the predicate "match" understood as in Goodman's *Structure of Appearance*, but applying now to objects rather than qualia. Thus two objects match "if and only if they are not noticeably different on direct comparison."[7] Gruebleen has the curious property that if an object A is examined before t and an object B is examined after t, and both are found to be grue (or both bleen), then we know that they will not match. But there is no t such that given two objects, one examined before t and one after t, and both found to be green (or blue), we can predict that they will not match. They may not match, but then they also may match, if both are green (or blue). In fact, it is undoubtedly a general property of natural languages that they are "English-like" rather than "Gruebleen-like," in this sense, in the domain of color terms. Thus there is no difficulty in establishing a fairly general distinction between Gruebleen-like and English-like languages, in this specific respect. Of course, this would not satisfy Goodman's requirements, for his special purposes, because one can construct other problems of the gruebleen type that are not taken account of by this property. As long as Goodman's vague notions "English-like" and "Gruebleen-like" are left unspecified, there is of course no way to meet his demand that a *general* property be stated distinguishing the two kinds of language, and any specific distinction that is proposed will always give rise to new riddles of induction. This is an interesting comment about the limitations of inductive methods, but has no more relevance to the problem of specifying the characteristics of universal grammar than to any other enterprise of science, say, the problem of specifying the genetic conditions that determine that a human embyro will develop legs rather than wings, under a given range of conditions.

I am not, incidentally, proposing that the property just cited serves to explain why every language-learner (in fact, every mouse, chimpanzee, etc.) uses green rather than grue as the basis for generalization. No doubt this is a simple consequence of certain properties of the sensory system, a conclusion that is quite uninteresting from Goodman's point of view, but not, for that reason, incorrect.

Returning to the main point, it is interesting that at one stage of his argument Goodman remarks, quite correctly, that even if "for certain remarkable facts I have no alternative explanation," "that alone does not dictate acceptance of . . . an intrinsically repugnant and incomprehensible theory." But now let us consider the theory of innate ideas that arouses Goodman's indignation, and ask whether it is "incomprehensible" and "repugnant."

Consider first the matter of comprehensibility. It does not seem to me incomprehensible that some aspect of the "final state"of an organism or automaton should also be an aspect of its "initial state," prior to any interaction with the environment, just as it is not incomprehensible that this aspect of the final state should have developed through internal processes, perhaps set in motion

---

[7] N. Goodman, *Structure of Appearance*, 2nd edn. (Indianapolis: Bobbs-Merrill, 1966), p. 272. The distinction between Gruebleen and English that I am now discussing is not to be confused with a pseudodistinction, correctly rejected by J. Ullian on the basis of a different usage of the notion "match." See *Philosophical Review*, July 1961.

by organism–environment interaction of some sort. But consider the actual doctrines developed in the speculative psychology of rationalism, rather than Locke's caricature. Descartes, for example, argued that the idea of a triangle is innate in that "the idea of a true triangle . . . can be more easily conceived by our mind than the more complex figure of the triangle drawn on paper," so that when a child first sees the more complex figure, he will "apprehend not it itself, but rather the authentic triangle." As Cudworth elaborates this view, "every irregular and imperfect triangle [is] as perfectly that which it is, as the most perfect triangle," but we interpret sensory images in terms of a notion of "regular figure" that has its source in the "rule, pattern and exemplar" generated by the mind as an "anticipation," just as we interpret all sensory data in terms of certain concepts of object and relations among objects, certain notions of cause and effect, gestalt properties, functions in a "space" of possible human actions, and so on. Neither this view, nor its elaboration in modern psychology, is incomprehensible, though it may of course be misguided or incorrect. Similarly, there is no difficulty in comprehending the proposal that there are certain innate conditions on the form of grammar that determine what constitutes linguistic experience and what knowledge will arise on the basis of this experience. Again, one can easily design an automaton that will function in this manner, so that although the proposal may be wrong, it is not incomprehensible.

Whatever Goodman's attitudes might be to these formulations, it is interesting that he appears quite willing, at least in this paper, to accept the view that in some sense the mature mind contains ideas; it is obviously not incomprehensible, then, that some of these ideas are "implanted in the mind as original equipment," to use his terminology. His argument is directed not against the notion that "ideas are in the mind," but rather against the assumption that they are "in the mind" prior to experience, and surely if one assumption is comprehensible, then the other is as well (though neither, as noted, does justice to the classical rationalist view or to its modern variants). On the other hand, this approach to the problem of acquisition of knowledge will, no doubt, be "repugnant" to one who considers empiricist doctrine immune to doubt or challenge. But this is to treat empiricist doctrines as articles of religious faith. Surely it is not reasonable to be so bound to a tradition as to refuse to examine conflicting views about acquisition of knowledge on their merits.

Let me turn next to Hilary Putnam's contribution to the same symposium. Although his paper deals more directly with the points that are actually at issue, still it seems to me that his arguments are inconclusive, primarily because of certain erroneous assumptions about the nature of the acquired grammars. Specifically, he enormously underestimates, and in part misdescribes, the richness of structure, the particular and detailed properties of grammatical form and organization that must be accounted for by a "language acquisition model," that

are acquired by the normal speaker–hearer and that appear to be uniform among speakers and also across languages.

To begin with, Putnam assumes that at the level of sound structure, the only property that can be proposed in universal grammar is that a language has "a short list of phonemes." This uniformity among languages, he argues, requires no elaborate explanatory hypothesis. It can be explained simply in terms of "such parameters as memory span and memory capacity," and no "rank Behaviorists" would have denied that these are innate properties. In fact, however, very strong empirical hypotheses have been proposed regarding the choice of universal distinctive features, the form of phonological rules, the ordering and organization of these rules, the relation of syntactic structure to phonetic representation, none of which can conceivably be accounted for on grounds of memory limitations. Putnam bases his account largely on my "Explanatory Models in Linguistics" (see note 6), which examines in some detail the principle of cyclic application of phonological rules, a principle that, if correct, raises some rather serious problems. We must ask how the child acquires knowledge of this principle, a feat that is particularly remarkable since, as already noted, much of the evidence that leads the linguist to posit this principle is drawn from the study of percepts and is thus not even available to the child. Similar questions arise with respect to many other aspects of universal phonology. In any event, if the proposals that have been elaborated regarding sound structure are correct or near correct, then the similarities among languages at this level, and the richness of the knowledge acquired by the child, are indeed remarkable facts, and demand an explanation.

Above the level of sound structure, Putnam assumes that the only significant properties of language are that they have proper names, that the grammar contains a phrase-structure component, and that there are rules "abbreviating" sentences generated by the phrase-structure component. He argues that the specific character of the phrase-structure component is determined by the existence of proper names; that the existence of a phrase-structure component is explained by the fact that "all the natural measures of complexity of an algorithm . . . lead to the . . . result" that phrase-structure systems provide the "algorithms which are 'simplest' for virtually any computing system," hence also "for naturally evolved 'computing systems'"; that there is nothing surprising in the fact that languages contain rules of abbreviations. Hence, he concludes, the only innate conditions that must be postulated are those that apply to all reasonable "computing systems," and no Behaviorist should feel any surprise at this.

Each of the three conclusions, however, is vitiated by a false assumption. First, it is obvious that there are many different phrase-structure grammars consistent with the assumption that one of the categories is that of proper names. In fact, there is much dispute at the moment about the general properties of the underlying base system for natural languages; the dispute is not in the least resolved by the existence of proper names as a primitive category in many languages.[8]

As to the second point, it is simply untrue that all measures of complexity and speed of computation lead to phrase-structure rules as the "simplest possible algorithm." The only existing results that have even an indirect relevance to this matter are those dealing with context-free phrase-structure grammars and their automata-theoretic interpretation. Context-free grammars are a reasonable model for the rules generating deep structures, when we exclude the lexical items and the distributional conditions they meet. But even apart from this fundamental discrepancy, the only existing results relate context-free grammars to a class of automata called "nondeterministic pushdown storage automata," and these have no particularly striking properties insofar as speed or complexity of computation are concerned, and are certainly not "natural" from this point of view. In terms of time and space conditions on computation, the somewhat similar but not formally related concept of real-time deterministic automaton would seem to be far more natural. In short, there are no results demonstrating that phrase-structure grammars are optimal in any computational sense (nor, certainly, are there any results dealing with the much more complex notion of base structure with a context-free phrase-structure grammar and a lexicon, with much richer properties, as components).

But there is no point in pursuing this matter, since what is at stake, in any event, is not the "simplicity" of phrase-structure grammars but rather of transformational grammars that contain a phrase-structure component, the latter playing a role in the generation of deep structures. And there is absolutely no mathematical concept of "ease of computation" or "simplicity of algorithm" that even suggests that such systems have some advantage over the various kinds of automata that have been investigated from this point of view. In fact, these systems have never really been considered in a strictly mathematical context, though there are interesting initial attempts to study some of their formal properties.[9] The source of the confusion is a misconception on Putnam's part as to the nature of grammatical transformations. These are not, as he supposes, rules that "abbreviate" sentences generated by phrase-structure rules. Rather, they are operations that form surface structures from underlying deep structures, which are generated, in part, by phrase-structure rules. Although there has been considerable evolution of theory since the notions of transformational

---

[8] Not, incidentally, in all. Although this is hardly important here, it seems that many languages do not have proper names as a primitive category, but rather form proper names by recursive processes of an elaborate sort. See, for example, G. H. Matthews, *Hidatsa Syntax* (The Hague: Mouton, 1965), pp. 191 f.

[9] See, for example, S. Peters and R. Ritchie, "On the Generative Capacity of Transformational Grammars," *Information Sciences* (to be published); and J. P. Kimball, "Predicates Definable over Transformational Derivations by Intersection with Regular Languages," *Information and Control*, Vol. 2, 1967, pp. 177–95.

generative grammar were first proposed, one assumption that has remained constant is that the phrase-structure rules generate only abstract structures, which are then mapped into surface structures by grammatical transformations – the latter being structure-dependent operations of a peculiar sort that have never been studied outside of linguistics, in particular, nor in any branch of mathematics with which I am familiar. To show that transformational grammars are the "simplest possible" one would have to demonstrate that an optimal computing system would take a string of symbols as input and determine its surface structure, the underlying deep structure, and the sequence of transformational operations that relate these two labeled bracketings. Nothing known about ease or simplicity of computation gives any reason to suppose that this is true; in fact, the question has never been raised. One can think of certain kinds of organization of memory that might be well adapted to transformational grammars, but this is a different matter entirely.[10] I would, naturally, assume that there is some more general basis in human mental structure for the fact (if it is a fact) that languages have transformational grammars; one of the primary scientific reasons for studying language is that this study may provide some insight into general properties of mind. Given those specific properties, we may then be able to show that transformational grammars are "natural." This would constitute real progress, since it would now enable us to raise the problem of innate conditions on acquisition of knowledge and belief in a more general framework. But it must be emphasized that, contrary to what Putnam asserts, there is no basis for assuming that "reasonable computing systems" will naturally be organized in the specific manner suggested by transformational grammar.

I believe that this disposes of Putnam's main argument, namely, that there is "nothing surprising," even to a Behaviorist, in the linguistic universals that are now being proposed and investigated. Let me then turn to his second argument, that even if there were surprising linguistic universals, they could be accounted for by a simpler hypothesis than that of an innate universal grammar, namely, the hypothesis of common origin of languages. This proposal misrepresents the problem at issue. As noted earlier, the empirical problem we face is to devise a hypothesis about initial structure rich enough to account for the fact that a specific grammar is acquired, under given conditions of access to data. To this problem, the matter of common origin of language is quite irrelevant. The grammar has to be discovered by the child on the basis of the data available to him, through the use of the innate capacities with which he is endowed. To be concrete, consider again the two examples discussed above: the association of nominal phrases to base structures and the cyclic application of phonological

---

[10] For some speculations on this matter, see G. A. Miller and N. Chomsky, "Finitary Models of Language Users," Part II, in R. D. Luce, R. Bush, and E. Galanter, eds., *Handbook of Mathematical Psychology* (New York: Wiley, 1963), Vol. II.

rules. The child masters these principles (if we are correct in our conclusions about grammar) on the basis of certain linguistic data; he knows nothing about the origin of language and could not make use of such information if he had it. Questions of common origin are relevant to the empirical problems we are discussing only in that the existing languages might not be a "fair sample" of the "possible languages," in which case we might be led mistakenly to propose too narrow a schema for universal grammar. This possibility must be kept in mind, of course, but it seems to me a rather remote consideration, given the problem that is actually at hand, namely, the problem of finding a schema rich enough to account for the development of the grammars that seem empirically justified. The discovery of such a schema may provide an explanation for the empirically determined universal properties of language. The existence of these properties, however, does not explain how a specific grammar is acquired by the child.

Putnam's discussion of the ease of language-learning seems to me beside the point. The question whether there is a critical period for language-learning is interesting,[11] but it has little relevance to the problem under discussion. Suppose that Putnam were correct in believing that "certainly . . . 600 hours [of direct method instruction] will enable any adult to speak and read a foreign language with ease." We would then face the problem of explaining how, on the basis of this restricted data, the learner has succeeded in acquiring the specific and detailed knowledge that enables him to use the language with ease, and to produce and understand a range of structures of which the data presented to him constitute a minute sample.

Finally, consider the alternative approach that Putnam suggests to the problem of language acquisition. He argues that instead of postulating an innate schematism one should attempt to account for this achievement in terms of "general multipurpose learning strategies." It is these that must be innate, not general conditions on the form of the knowledge that is acquired. Evidently, this is an empirical issue. It would be sheer dogmatism to assert of either of these proposals (or of some particular combination of them) that it *must* be correct. Putnam is convinced, on what grounds he does not say, that the innate basis for the acquisition of language must be identical with that for acquiring any other form of knowledge, that there is nothing "special" about the acquisition of language. A nondogmatic approach to this problem can be pursued, through the investigation of specific areas of human competence, such as language, followed by the attempt to devise a hypothesis that will account for the development of such competence. If we discover that the same "learning strategies" are involved in a variety of cases, and that these suffice to account

[11] See E. H. Lenneberg, *Biological Foundations of Language* (New York: Wiley, 1967), for evidence bearing on this issue.

for the acquired competence, then we will have good reason to believe that Putnam's empirical hypothesis is correct. If, on the other hand, we discover that different innate systems (whether involving schemata or heuristics) have to be postulated, then we will have good reason to believe that an adequate theory of mind will incorporate separate "faculties," each with unique or partially unique properties. I cannot see how one can resolutely insist on one or the other conclusion in the light of the evidence now available to us. But one thing is quite clear: Putnam has no justification for his final conclusion, that "invoking 'Innateness' only postpones the problem of learning; it does not solve it."[12] Invoking an innate representation of universal grammar does solve the problem of learning (at least partially), in this case, if in fact it is true that this is the basis (or part of the basis) for language acquisition, as it well may be. If, on the other hand, there exist general learning strategies that account for the acquisition of grammatical knowledge, then postulation of an innate representation of universal grammar will not "postpone" the problem of learning, but will rather offer an incorrect solution to this problem. The issue is an empirical one of truth or falsity, not a methodological one of stages of investigation. At the moment, the only concrete proposal that is at all plausible, in my opinion, is the one sketched above. When some "general learning strategy" is suggested, we can look into the relative adequacy of these alternatives, on empirical grounds.

Henry Hiż's review article deals mainly with the distinction between competence and performance. One can attempt to explain technical concepts such as these in two different ways. At a presystematic level, one can try to indicate,

---

[12] Or for his assumption that the "weighting functions" proposed in universal grammar constitute the "sort of fact . . . [that] . . . learning theory tries to account for; *not* the explanation being sought." No one would say that the genetic basis for the development of arms rather than wings in a human embryo is "the kind of fact that learning theory tries to account for," rather than the basis for explanation of other facts about human behavior. The question whether the weighting function is learned, or whether it is the basis for learning, is an empirical one. There is not the slightest reason to assume, a priori, that it is to be accounted for by learning rather than genetic endowment, or some combination of the two.

There are other minor points in Putnam's discussion that call for some comment. For example, he asserts that since certain ambiguities "require coaching to detect," it follows that "the claim that grammar 'explains the ability to recognize ambiguities' . . . lacks the impressiveness that Chomsky believes it to have." But he misconstrues the claim, which relates to competence, not performance. What the grammar explains is why "the shooting of the hunters" (the example he cites) can be understood with hunters as subject or object but that in "the growth of corn" we can understand "corn" only as subject (the explanation, in this case, turns on the relation of nominalizations to deep structures, noted earlier). The matter of coaching is beside the point. What is at issue is the inherent sound–meaning correlation that is involved in performance, but only as one of many factors. Putnam also misstates the argument for assuming the active–passive relation to be transformational. It is not merely that the speaker knows them to be related. Obviously that would be absurd; the speaker also knows that "John will leave tomorrow" and "John will leave three days after the day before yesterday" are related, but this does not imply that there is a transformational relation between the two. Syntactic arguments are given in many places in the literature. See, for example, my *Syntactic Structures* (The Hague: Mouton, 1957); *Aspects of the Theory of Syntax.*

necessarily in a loose and somewhat vague and only suggestive way, just what role the concept is intended to play in a more general framework, and why it seems to be a useful idea to try to develop. Discussion at this level is entirely legitimate, but there will generally be much room for misunderstanding. At a second level, one can develop the concept in as precise a way as the state of the field permits, with no consideration for motivation or general implications. At this level, the problem is to determine not what the concept in question is, but why there is any point in developing it.

At the presystematic level, I have tried to explain what I mean by "linguistic competence" in terms of models of use and acquisition of language, in the manner outlined earlier. At the systematic level, competence is expressed by a generative grammar that recursively enumerates structural descriptions of sentences, each with its phonetic, syntactic, and semantic aspects. It is hardly necessary to emphasize that any such grammar that we can actually present today is incomplete, not only because our knowledge of particular languages is deficient, but also because our understanding of phonetic and semantic representation and the kinds of structures and rules that mediate between them is limited and unsatisfactory in many respects.

Turning to Hiż's paper, there is, not surprisingly, a certain degree of misunderstanding between us at the presystematic level. Hiż suggests that my use of the notion "competence" "is to be understood as saying that introspection is a source of linguistic knowledge." I do agree that introspection is an excellent source of data for the study of language, but this conclusion does not follow from the decision to study linguistic competence. One might (irrationally, in my opinion) refuse to use such evidence, and still try to discover the generative grammar that represents "what is learned" and that plays a fundamental role in language use. This decision would be pointless, rather on a par with an astronomer's refusal, at one stage of the science, to use what he sees through a telescope as data, but the decision has nothing to do with the distinction between competence and performance. I have no doubt that it would be possible to devise operational and experimental procedures that could replace the reliance on introspection with little loss, but it seems to me that in the present state of the field, this would simply be a waste of time and energy. Obviously, any such procedure would first have to be tested against the introspective evidence. If one were to propose a test for, say, grammaticalness, that fails to make the distinctions noted earlier in the proper way, one would have little faith in the procedure as a test for grammaticalness. To me it seems that current research is not hampered significantly by lack of accurate data, but rather by our inability to explain in a satisfactory way data that are hardly in question. One who feels differently can support his point of view by demonstrating the gains in insight and understanding that can be achieved by refinements in techniques of data collection and analysis, say, by operational techniques for establishing grammaticalness, techniques that have been judged by the prior test of intuition and shown to be sufficiently sound so that one can rely on them in difficult or obscure cases. In any event, the whole matter has nothing to do with the decision to study linguistic competence.

Hiż regards it as "paradoxical" to assert, as I have, that linguistics "attempts to specify what the speaker actually knows, not what he may report about his knowledge." This he regards as "a peculiar sense of 'knowledge.'" To me it seems a rather ordinary sense, and a nonparadoxical usage. A person who knows English may give all sorts of incorrect reports about the knowledge that he actually possesses and makes use of constantly, without awareness. As noted earlier, when we study competence – the speaker–hearer's knowledge of his language – we may make use of his reports and his behavior as evidence, but we must be careful not to confuse "evidence" with the abstract constructs that we develop on the basis of evidence and try to justify in terms of evidence. Thus I would definitely reject three of the five conditions that, Hiż suggests, rules must satisfy if they are to constitute an account of competence in my sense, namely, that the native speaker feels that the sentences generated by the rules are in his language, that they have the assigned structures, and that what the speaker feels is true. Since performance – in particular, judgments about sentences – obviously involves many factors apart from competence, one cannot accept as an absolute principle that the speaker's judgments will give an accurate account of his knowledge. I am surprised that Hiż should offer this interpretation of my views immediately after having quoted my statement that the speaker's reports about his competence may be in error.

At least for the purposes of discussion, Hiż is willing to accept the view that a generative grammar, a system of rules assigning structures to sentences, can serve to characterize competence. He then points out, correctly, that the linguist is guided in his choice of a grammar by certain "general principles about language as such," and that this general theory – universal grammar – will have explanatory value if it selects particular grammars correctly. He then attributes to me, incorrectly, the view that universal grammar is to be identified with "a theory of language acquisition." My view, rather, is that universal grammar is one element of such a theory, much as competence is one element of a theory of performance. There are surely many other factors involved in language acquisition beyond the schematism and weighting function that – if my suggestion is correct – play a part in determining the nature of the acquired competence. This misinterpretation of my proposal regarding the relation of universal grammar to language acquisition parallels the misinterpretation of my proposal regarding the relation of competence to performance; in both cases, what is omitted is the reference to other factors that must be involved. In the case of language acquisition, furthermore, it must be emphasized that the model I am suggesting can at best only be regarded as a first approximation to a theory of learning, since it is an instantaneous model and does not try to capture the interplay between tentative hypotheses that the child may construct, new data interpreted in terms of these hypotheses, new hypotheses based on these interpretations, and so on, until some relatively fixed system of competence is established. I think that an instantaneous model is a reasonable first approximation, but this, as any other aspect of research strategy, must ultimately be evaluated in terms of its success in providing explanations and insight.

Hiż regards the reference to classical formulations of problems of language and mind as "confusing and misleading historical baggage." I disagree with this judgment, but have nothing to add here beyond what I have written elsewhere.[13] My feeling is that the contributions of rationalist psychology and linguistics are interesting in themselves, and are quite relevant to present concerns, more so, in fact, than much of the work of the past century. One who finds these forays into intellectual history "confusing and misleading" can perfectly well disregard them. I see no issue here.

Before leaving this matter, I should mention that Hiż is inaccurate in stating that Herbert of Cherbury restricted himself to "religious knowledge." Nor can Thomas Reid be described as one of those concerned to develop a doctrine of innate universals. Furthermore, it is surely misleading to say that I "call upon" Descartes and others "to support" my "stand on innate universals." Their advocacy of a similar position does not constitute "support." Rather, I am suggesting that their contributions have been inadequately appreciated, and that we can still learn a good deal from a careful study of them.

Hiż objects to the fact that my proposals concerning universal grammar are based on detailed examination of a few languages rather than "examination of many cases." I certainly agree that one should study as many languages as possible. Still, a *caveat* should be entered. It would be quite easy to present enormous masses of data from varied languages that are compatible with all conceptions of universal grammar that have so far been formulated. There is no point in doing so. If one is concerned with the principles of universal grammar, he will try to discover those properties of particular grammars that bear on these principles, putting aside large amounts of material that, so far as he can determine, do not. It is only through intensive studies of particular languages that one can hope to find crucial evidence for the study of universal grammar. One study such as that of Matthews on Hidatsa (see note 8) is worth one thousand superficial studies of varied languages from this point of view. If someone feels that the base of data is too narrow, what he should do is show that some of the material omitted refutes the principles that have been formulated. Otherwise, his criticism has no more force than a criticism of modern genetics for basing its theoretical formulations on the detailed investigation of only a few organisms.

[13] In my *Current Issues in Linguistic Theory* (The Hague: Mouton, 1964), Section 1; *Aspects of the Theory of Syntax*, Chapter 1, Section 8; *Cartesian Linguistics* (New York: Harper & Row, 1966).

Hiż also argues that the principles of universal grammar, even if true, may indicate only "the common historical origin of languages." I have already pointed out why this hypothesis is without explanatory force.

Hiż maintains that decisions about particular parts of grammar (by the linguist) are "determined not by a general theory but by internal usefulness within the particular grammar," and objects that I do not make this clear. Since I have no idea what is meant by "internal usefulness," I have nothing to say about this point. The issue is confused by his misinterpretation of my use of the notion "simplicity." When I speak of "simplicity of grammar," I am referring to a "weighting function," empirically determined, that selects a grammar of the form permitted by the universal schematism over others that are also of the proper form and are compatible with the empirical data. I am not using the term "simplicity" to refer to that poorly understood property of theories that leads the scientist to select one rather than another. The evaluation measure that defines "simplicity of grammars" is part of linguistic theory. We must try to discover this measure on empirical grounds, by considering the actual relations between input data and acquired grammars. Thus the notion "simplicity of grammar" plays a role analogous to that of a physical constant; we must establish it on empirical grounds, and there is no a priori insight on which we can rely. The problems of defining "simplicity of theories" in a general context of epistemology and philosophy of science are entirely irrelevant to the issue of determining, on empirical grounds, the properties of grammars that lead to the selection of one rather than another in language acquisition. This aspect has been emphasized repeatedly. See, for example, *Aspects*, Chapter 1, Section 7.

One final comment. Hiż suggests that "it should be easier to explain why we assign such-and-such a structure to a sentence by pointing out how this sentence changes the readings of neighboring sentences than by referring to innate universal ideas and mental reality." Here he is confusing two entirely different kinds of explanations. If I want to explain why, yesterday afternoon at three o'clock, John Smith understood "the shooting of the hunters" as referring to the act of shooting the hunters, rather than the hunters' act of shooting, I will of course bring into consideration the situational context (not limiting myself to the "readings of neighboring sentences"). If I am interested in explaining why this phrase is susceptible to these two interpretations, but the phrase "the growth of corn" is susceptible to only one (namely, the corn's growing and not the act or process of growing corn), then I will appeal first to the particular grammar of English, and more deeply, to the linguistic universals that led to the construction of this grammar by a child exposed to certain data. Since entirely different things are being explained, it is senseless to claim that one manner of explanation is "easier" than the other.

Harman's critique is also concerned with the matter of competence and performance. He begins by ascribing to me a view that I have never held, and have explicitly rejected on numerous occasions, namely, that "competence [is] the knowledge that the language is described by the rules of the grammar," and that a grammar describes this "competence." Obviously, it is absurd to suppose that the speaker of the language knows the rules in the sense of being able to state them. Having attributed to me this absurd view, Harman goes on to struggle with all sorts of purported confusions and difficulties of interpretation. But he cites nothing that could possibly be regarded as a basis for attributing to me this view, though he does quote remarks in which I explicitly reject it. Therefore, I will not discuss this part of his argument at all.

In Harman's framework, there are two kinds of knowledge: knowing that and knowing how. Obviously knowledge of a language is not a matter of "knowing that." Therefore, for him, it must be a matter of "knowing how." A typical speaker "knows how to understand other speakers"; his competence is his ability "to speak and understand the language described by [the] grammar" that describes the language. I do not know what Harman means by the locution "knows how to understand," but clearly he is using the term "competence" in a different way from what I proposed in the work he is reviewing. In my sense of "competence," the ability to speak and understand the language involves not only "competence" (that is, mastery of the generative grammar of the language, tacit knowledge of the language), but also many other factors. In my usage, the grammar is a formal representation of what I have called "competence." I have no objection to Harman's using the term in a different way, but when he insists on supposing that his usage is mine, naturally, only confusion will result. Again, I see no point in tracing in detail the various difficulties into which this misinterpretation leads him.

According to Harman, the "competence to speak and understand the language" is a skill, analogous to the skill of a bicycle rider. Given his insistence that knowledge of language is a matter of "knowing how" (since it is obviously not "knowing that"), this is not an unexpected conclusion. But he suggests no respect in which ability to use a language (let alone the competence, in my sense, that constitutes an element of this ability) is like the ability to ride a bicycle, nor do I see any. The proper conclusion, then, would be that there is no reason to suppose that knowledge of language can be characterized in terms of "knowing how." I therefore see no point in the analogy that he suggests. Knowledge of language is not a skill, a set of habits, or anything of the sort. I see nothing surprising in the conclusion that knowledge of language cannot be discussed in any useful or informative way in this impoverished framework. In general, it does not seem to me true that the concepts "knowing how" and "knowing that" constitute exhaustive categories for the analysis of knowledge. Nor is it surprising that Harman finds it difficult to understand my remarks, or those of anyone else who is concerned with knowledge of language, given that he insists on restricting himself to this framework.

Harman tries to show that there is a fundamental incoherence in my proposal that in acquiring or using knowledge of a language (in developing "an internal representation of a generative system" or making use of it in speaking or understanding speech), the child makes use of an innate schematism that restricts the choice of grammars (in the case of acquisition) or an internalized grammar (in the case of language use). His argument seems to me unclear. As I understand it, it seems to proceed as follows. He argues that this internalized system must be presented in "another more basic language," which the child must come to understand before he can make use of this schematism to learn this language, or before he can make use of the grammar to understand speech. But this, he argues, leads to a vicious circle or an infinite regress. Thus if we were to say that the child knows the "more basic language" directly, without learning, then why not say also that he knows "directly the language he speaks," without learning; a vicious circle. Or, if we say that he must learn the more basic language, then this raises the question how the more basic language is learned, and leads to an infinite regress. This argument is totally invalid. Consider the case of acquisition of language. Even if we assume that the innate schematism must be represented in an "innate language," neither conclusion follows. The child must know this "innate language," in Harman's terms, but it does not follow that he must "speak and understand it" (whatever this might mean) or that he must learn it. All that we need assume is that he can make use of this schematism when he approaches the task of language learning. So much for the infinite regress. As to the vicious circle, there is a very simple reason why we cannot assume that the child knows the language he speaks directly, without learning, namely, that the assumption is false. We cannot claim that every child is born with a perfect knowledge of English. On the other hand, there is no reason why we should not suppose that the child is born with a perfect knowledge of universal grammar, that is, with a fixed schematism that he uses, in the ways described earlier, in acquiring language. This assumption may be false, but it is quite intelligible. If one insists on describing this knowledge as "direct knowledge of a more basic language," I see no reason to object, so long as we are clear about what we mean, but would merely point out that there is no reason at all to doubt that the child has this direct knowledge. Hence there is no vicious circle, and no infinite regress. Similarly, if we consider the case of language use, there is neither incoherence nor implausibility. There is surely no infinite regress and no vicious circle in the assumption that in language use (speaking or understanding) the user employs an internally represented grammar. We can easily construct a model (say, a computer program) that functions in this way. I therefore fail to see any basis for Harman's belief that there is an infinite regress or vicious circle inherent in, or even suggested by this formulation.

In the second part of his paper, Harman turns to my argument that current work in linguistics supports a view of language and mind that has a distinctly rationalist flavor, and is in conflict with the empiricist views that have dominated the study of language and mind in recent years. He asserts that to infer a grammar from data, a model of language learning must already have detailed information about the theory of performance. This is an interesting proposal, and it deserves to be developed. But I cannot go along with his rather dogmatic claim, hardly argued in the paper, that this approach must necessarily be correct, and that any other approach must fail to provide any insight into the problem of acquisition of knowledge. I think that the work of the past few years on universal grammar does, in fact, suggest and in part support an interesting, rather classical approach to the problem of how knowledge is acquired. In the absence of any argument as to why this approach must fail to be illuminating, I see no reason not to continue with the investigation of how principles of universal grammar might select a particular grammar on the basis of the data available.

Let us turn now to the issue of rationalist and empiricist approaches to problems of language and mind. As Harman points out, if we describe an innate schematism biased toward (or restricted to) a specific form of grammar as part of the "principles of induction used," and define "resourceful empiricism" as a doctrine that makes use of such "principles of induction" as this, then surely "resourceful empiricism" cannot be refuted, "no matter what the facts about language [or anything else] turned out to be." Of course, this new doctrine of "resourceful empiricism" would now incorporate "principles of induction" that are, so it seems, quite specific to the task of language acquisition and of no general validity.

The concept "resourceful empiricism" so defined seems to me of little interest. The issue that concerns me is whether there are "ideas and principles of various kinds that determine the form of the acquired knowledge in what may be a rather restricted and highly organized way," or alternatively, whether "the structure of the acquisition device is limited to certain elementary peripheral processing mechanisms . . . and certain analytical data-processing mechanisms or inductive principles" (*Aspects*, pp. 47 f). I have argued that "it is historically accurate as well as heuristically valuable to distinguish these two very different approaches to the problem of acquisition of knowledge," even though they of course "cannot always be sharply distinguished" in the work of a particular person (*ibid.*, p. 52). In particular, I have tried to show that it is possible to formulate these approaches so that the former incorporates the leading ideas of classical rationalism as well as the modern variant I have been describing, and that the latter includes classical empiricist doctrine as well as the theories of acquisition of knowledge (or belief, or habit) developed in a wide range of modern work (Quine's notions of quality space and formation of knowledge by association and conditioning; Hull's approach in terms of primitive unconditioned reflexes, conditioning, and habit structures; taxonomic linguistics, with its analytic procedures of segmentation and classification and its conception of language as a "habit system," and so on).[14] Needless to say, there is no necessity to view the various attempts to study language acquisition within this framework; I can only say that I think it is both useful and accurate. These alternatives can be made fairly precise and investigated in terms of their empirical consequences. Harman's proposal to define "resourceful empiricism" in such a way as to include both approaches, and to be, as he notes, immune to any factual discovery, is merely a pointless terminological suggestion and cannot obscure the difference between the approaches mentioned or the importance of pursuing and evaluating them.[15]

To summarize, I doubt that linguistics can provide "a new technique" for analytic philosophy that will be of much significance, at least in its present state of development. Nevertheless, it seems to me that the study of language can clarify and in part substantiate certain conclusions about human knowledge that relate directly to classical issues in the philosophy of mind. It is in this domain, I suspect, that one can look forward to a really fruitful collaboration between linguistics and philosophy in coming years.

[14] Harman observes correctly that I ignore the "enormous philosophical literature on induction," and limit myself solely to an investigation of the procedures of taxonomic linguistics as "the only proposals that are explicit enough to support serious study." He does not, however, show how anything in the literature on induction bears on the problems I am considering. The reason is that there is nothing. The literature on induction is quite interesting, but it happens to deal with entirely different questions. It does not even hint at procedures of analysis or acquisition of belief or confirmation that would overcome the problems that I have been discussing. There is, for example, nothing in the literature on induction that gives any insight into how the principles cited above as examples (the cycle of phonological rules or the rule of nominalization) might be reached "by induction" from the data available. But it is such questions as these that must be faced in the study of language acquisition.

[15] Two minor points in this connection. Harman sees only a "tenuous historical connection" between procedures of segmentation and classification and phrase-structure grammar. The connection is actually much closer. Zellig Harris, in his *Methods in Structural Linguistics* (Chicago: University of Chicago Press, 1951), tried to show how a systematic use of such procedures, amplified by a simple inductive step, would lead to a set of rules that might be regarded as generating an infinite set of sentences. A set of Harris' "morpheme to utterance" formulas, though not quite the same as phrase-structure grammar, is quite similar. The concept of "phrase-structure grammar" was explicitly designed to express the richest system that could reasonably be expected to result from the application of Harris-type procedures to a corpus. Harris, and other methodologists of the 1940s, were developing an approach to linguistic analysis that one can trace at least to Saussure.

Secondly, Harman is quite correct in pointing out that in my reference to "the only [empiricist] proposals that are explicit enough to support serious study," I omitted mention of Harris' and Hiż's method of studying co-occurrence relationships. He feels that this method is "similar in spirit to the taxonomic procedures." I don't see the point in arguing this, one way or another. In any event, I know of no reason to suppose that such procedures can lead to or can even provide evidence for or against the postulation of a generative grammar.

7   Biolinguistics and the human capacity

I would like to say a few words about what has come to be called "the biolinguistic perspective," which began to take shape half a century ago in discussions among a few graduate students who were much influenced by developments in biology and mathematics in the early postwar years, including work in ethology that was just coming to be known in the United States. One of them was Eric Lenneberg, whose seminal 1967 study *Biological Foundations of Language* remains a basic document of the field. By then considerable interchange was proceeding, including interdisciplinary seminars and international conferences. The most far-reaching one, in 1974, was called, for the first time, "Biolinguistics." Many of the leading questions discussed there remain very much alive today.

One of these questions, repeatedly brought up as "one of the basic questions to be asked from the biological point of view," is the extent to which apparent principles of language, including some that had only recently come to light, are unique to this cognitive system. An even more basic question from the biological point of view is how much of language can be given a principled explanation, whether or not homologous elements can be found in other domains or organisms. The effort to sharpen these questions and to investigate them for language has come to be called "the minimalist program" in recent years, but the questions arise for any biological system, and are independent of theoretical persuasion, in linguistics and other domains. Answers to these questions are not only fundamental to understanding the nature and functioning of organisms and their subsystems, but also to investigation of their growth and evolution.

The biolinguistic perspective views a person's language in all its aspects – sound, meaning, structure – as a state of some component of the mind, understanding "mind" in the sense of eighteenth-century scientists who recognized that after Newton's demolition of the "mechanical philosophy," based on the intuitive concept of a material world, no coherent mind–body problem remains, and we can only regard aspects of the world "termed mental," as the result of "such an organical structure as that of the brain," as chemist–philosopher Joseph Priestley observed. Thought is a "little agitation of the brain," David Hume remarked; and, as Darwin commented a century later, there is no reason why "thought, being a secretion of the brain," should be considered "more wonderful than gravity, a property of matter." By then, the more tempered view of the goals of science that Newton introduced had become scientific common sense: Newton's reluctant conclusion that we must be satisfied with the fact that universal gravity exists, even if we cannot explain it in terms of the self-evident "mechanical philosophy." As many commentators have observed, this intellectual move "set forth a new view of science" in which the goal is "not to seek ultimate explanations" but to find the best theoretical account we can of the phenomena of experience and experiment (I. Bernard Cohen).

The central issues in the domain of study of mind still arise, in much the same form. They were raised prominently at the end of the "Decade of the Brain," which brought the last millennium to a close. The American Academy of Arts and Sciences published a volume to mark the occasion, summarizing the current state of the art. The guiding theme was formulated by neuroscientist Vernon Mountcastle in his introduction to the volume: it is the thesis that "Things mental, indeed minds, are emergent properties of brains, [though] these emergences are not regarded as irreducible but are produced by principles . . . we do not yet understand." The same thesis, which closely paraphrases Priestley, has been put forth in recent years as an "astonishing hypothesis" of the new biology, a "radically new idea" in the philosophy of mind, "the bold assertion that mental phenomena are entirely natural and caused by the neurophysiological activities of the brain," and so on. But this is a misunderstanding. The thesis follows from the collapse of any coherent concept of "body" or "material" in the seventeenth century, as was soon recognized. Terminology aside, the fundamental thesis remains what has been called "Locke's suggestion": that God might have chosen to "superadd to matter a faculty of thinking" just as he "annexed effects to motion, which we can in no way conceive motion able to produce."

Mountcastle's reference to reductive principles that we "do not yet understand" also begs some interesting questions, as a look at the history of science illustrates, even quite recent science. It is reminiscent of Bertrand Russell's observation in 1929, also reflecting standard beliefs, that "chemical laws cannot at present be reduced to physical laws." The phrase "at present," like Mountcastle's word "yet," expresses the expectation that the reduction should take place in the normal course of scientific progress, perhaps soon. In the case of physics and chemistry, it never did: what happened was unification of a virtually unchanged chemistry with a radically revised physics. It's hardly necessary to add that the state of understanding and achievement in those areas eighty years ago was far beyond anything that can be claimed for the brain and cognitive sciences today. Hence confidence in "reduction" to the little that is understood is not necessarily appropriate.

From the array of phenomena that one might loosely consider language-related, the biolinguistic approach focuses attention on a component of human biology that enters into the use and acquisition of language, however one interprets the term "language." Call it the "faculty of language," adapting a traditional term to a new usage. This component is more or less on a par with the system of mammalian vision, insect navigation, or others. In many of these cases, the best available explanatory theories attribute to the organism computational systems and what is called "rule-following" in informal usage – for example, when a recent text on vision presents the so-called "rigidity principle" as it was formulated fifty years ago: "if possible, and other rules permit, interpret image motions as projections of rigid motions in three dimensions." In this case, later work provided substantial insight into the mental computations that seem to be involved when the visual system follows these rules, but even for very simple organisms, that is typically no slight task, and relating mental computations to analysis at the cellular level is commonly a distant goal. Some philosophers have objected to the notion "rule-following" – for language, rarely vision. But I think that is another misunderstanding, one of many in my opinion. It is of some interest to compare qualms expressed today about theories of language, and aspects of the world "termed mental" more generally, with debates among leading scientists well into the 1920s as to whether chemistry was a mere calculating device predicting the results of experiments, or whether it merits the honorific status of an account of "physical reality," debates later understood to be completely pointless. The similarities, which I have discussed elsewhere, are striking and I think instructive.

Putting these interesting topics aside, if we adopt the biolinguistic perspective, a language is a state of the faculty of language – an I-language in technical usage, where "I" underscores the fact that the conception is internalist, individual, and intensional (with an "s," not a "t") – that is, the actual formulation of the generative principles, not the set it enumerates; the latter we can think of as a more abstract property of the I-language, rather as we can think of the set of possible trajectories of a comet through the solar system as an abstract property of that system.

The decision to study language as part of the world in this sense was regarded as highly controversial at the time, and still is, by many linguists as well. It seems to me that the arguments advanced against the legitimacy of the approach have little force – a weak thesis; and that its basic assumptions are tacitly adopted even by those who strenuously reject them – a much stronger thesis. I will not enter into this chapter of contemporary intellectual history here, but will simply assume that crucial aspects of language can be studied as part of the natural world in the sense of the biolinguistic approach that took shape half a century ago, and has been intensively pursued since, along various different paths.

The language faculty is one component of what the co-founder of modern evolutionary theory, Alfred Russel Wallace, called "man's intellectual and moral nature" : the human capacities for creative imagination, language and other modes of symbolism, mathematics, interpretation and recording of natural phenomena, intricate social practices and the like, a complex of capacities that seem to have crystallized fairly recently, perhaps a little over 50,000 years ago, among a small breeding group of which we are all descendants – a complex that sets humans apart rather sharply from other animals, including other hominids, judging by the archaeological record. The nature of the "human capacity," as some researchers now call it, remains a considerable mystery. It was one element of a famous disagreement between the two founders of the theory of evolution, with Wallace holding, contrary to Darwin, that evolution of these faculties cannot be accounted for in terms of variation and natural selection alone, but requires "some other influence, law, or agency," some principle of nature alongside gravitation, cohesion, and other forces without which the material universe could not exist. Although the issues are differently framed today, they have not disappeared.

It is commonly assumed that whatever the human intellectual capacity is, the faculty of language is essential to it. Many scientists agree with paleoanthropologist Ian Tattersall, who writes that he is "almost sure that it was the invention of language" that was the "sudden and emergent" event that was the "releasing stimulus" for the appearance of the human capacity in the evolutionary record – the "great leap forward" as Jared Diamond called it, the result of some genetic event that rewired the brain, allowing for the origin of human language with the rich syntax that provides a multitude of modes of expression of thought, a prerequisite for social development and the sharp changes of behavior that are revealed in the archaeological record, also generally assumed to be the trigger for the rapid trek from Africa, where otherwise modern humans had apparently been present for hundreds of thousands of years. The view is similar to that of the Cartesians, but stronger: they regarded normal use of language as the clearest empirical evidence that another creature has a mind like ours, but not the criterial evidence for mind and the origin of the human capacity.

If this general picture has some validity, then the evolution of language may be a very brief affair, even though it is a very recent product of evolution. Of course, there are innumerable precursors, and they doubtless had a long evolutionary history. For example, the bones of the middle ear are a marvellous sound-amplifying system, wonderfully designed for interpreting speech, but they appear to have migrated from the reptilian jaw as a mechanical effect of growth of the neocortex in mammals that began 160 million years ago, so it is reported. We know far too little about conceptual systems to say much, but it's reasonable to suppose that they too had a long history after the separation of hominids, yielding results with no close similarity elsewhere. But the question of evolution of language itself has to do with how these various precursors were organized into the faculty of language, perhaps through some slight genetic event that brought a crucial innovation. If that is so, then the evolution of language itself is brief, speculations that have some bearing on the kind of inquiry into language that is likely to be productive.

Tattersall takes language to be "virtually synonymous with symbolic thought." Elaborating, one of the initiators of the 1974 symposium, Nobel Laureate François Jacob, observed that "the role of language as a communication system between individuals would have come about only secondarily," perhaps referring to discussions at the 1974 conference, where his fellow Nobel Laureate Salvador Luria was one of the more forceful advocates of the view that communicative needs would not have provided "any great selective pressure to produce a system such as language," with its crucial relation to "development of abstract or productive thinking." "The quality of language that makes it unique does not seem to be so much its role in communicating directives for action" or other common features of animal communication, Jacob continues, but rather "its role in symbolizing, in evoking cognitive images," in "molding" our notion of reality and yielding our capacity for thought and planning, through its unique property of allowing "infinite combinations of symbols" and therefore "mental creation of possible worlds," ideas that trace back to the seventeeth-century cognitive revolution.

Jacob also stressed the common understanding that answers to questions about evolution "in most instances . . . can hardly be more than more or less reasonable guesses." And in most cases, hardly even that. An example that is perhaps of interest here is the study of evolution of the bee communication system, unusual in that in principle it permits transmission of information over an infinite (continuous) range. There are hundreds of species of honey and stingless bees, some having variants of communication systems, some not, though they all seem to survive well enough. So there is plenty of opportunity for comparative work. Bees are incomparably easier to study than humans, along every dimension. But little is understood. Even the literature is sparse. The most recent extensive review I have seen, by entomologist Fred Dyer, notes that even the basic computational problems of coding spatial information to motor commands, and the reverse for follower bees, remains "puzzling," and "What sorts of neural events might underlie these various mapping processes is unknown," while evolutionary origins scarcely go beyond speculation. There is nothing like the huge literature and confident pronouncements about the evolution of human language – something that one might also find a bit "puzzling."

We can add another insight of seventeeth-and eighteenth-century philosophy, with roots as far back as Aristotle's analysis of what were later interpreted as mental entities: that even the most elementary concepts of human language do not relate to mind-independent objects by means of some reference-like relation between symbols and identifiable physical features of the external world, as seems to be universal in animal communication systems. Rather, they are creations of the "cognoscitive powers" that provide us with rich means to refer to the outside world from certain perspectives, but are individuated by mental operations that cannot be reduced to a "peculiar nature belonging" to the thing we are talking about, as Hume summarized a century of inquiry. Julius Moravcsik's "aitiational theory of semantics" is a recent development of some of these ideas, from their Aristotelian origins and with rich implications for natural language semantics.

These are critical observations about the elementary semantics of natural language, suggesting that its most primitive elements are related to the mind-independent world much as the internal elements of phonology are, not by a reference-like relation but as part of a considerably more intricate species of conception and action. I cannot try to elaborate here, but I think such considerations, if seriously pursued, reveal that it is idle to try to base the semantics of natural language on any kind of "word–object" relation, however intricate the constructed notion of "object," just as it would be idle to base the phonetics of natural language on a "symbol–sound" relation, where sounds are taken to be constructed physical events – perhaps indescribable four-dimensional constructs based on motions of molecules, with further questions dispatched to the physics department, or if one wants to make the problem still more hopeless, to the sociology department as well. It is universally agreed that these moves are the wrong ones for the study of the sound side of language, and I think the conclusions are just as reasonable on the meaning side. For each utterance, there is a physical event, but that does not imply that we have to seek some mythical relation between such an internal object as the syllable [ta] and an identifiable mind-independent event; and for each act of referring there is some complex aspect of the experienced or imagined world on which attention is focused by that act, but that is not to say that a relation of reference exists for natural language. I think it does not, even at the most primitive level.

If this much is generally on the right track, then, at least two basic problems arise when we consider the origins of the faculty of language and its role in the sudden emergence of the human intellectual capacity: first, the core semantics of minimal meaning-bearing elements, including the simplest of them; and second, the principles that allow unbounded combinations of symbols, hierarchically organized, which provide the means for use of language in its many aspects. By the same token, the core theory of language – universal grammar, UG – must provide, first, a structured inventory of possible lexical items that are related to or perhaps identical with the concepts that are the elements of the "cognoscitive powers" and second, means to construct from these lexical items the infinite variety of internal structures that enter into thought, interpretation, planning, and other human mental acts, and are sometimes externalized, a secondary process if the speculations just reviewed turn out to be correct. On the first problem, the apparently human-specific conceptual–lexical apparatus, there is insightful work on relational notions linked to syntactic structures and on the partially mind-internal objects that appear to play a critical role (events, propositions, etc.). But there is little beyond descriptive remarks on the core referential apparatus that is used to talk about the world. The second problem has been central to linguistic research for a half-century, with a long history before in different terms.

The biolinguistic approach adopted from the outset the point of view that cognitive neuroscientist R. G. Gallistel calls "the norm in neuroscience" today, the "modular view of learning": the conclusion that in all animals, learning is based on specialized mechanisms, "instincts to learn" in specific ways. He suggests that we think of these mechanisms as "organs within the brain," achieving states in which they perform specific kinds of computation. Apart from "extremely hostile environments," they change states under the triggering and shaping effect of external factors, more or less reflexively, and in accordance with internal design. That is the "process of learning," though "growth" might be a more appropriate term, avoiding misleading connotations of the term "learning." One might relate these ideas to Gallistel's encyclopedic work on organization of motion, based on "structural constraints" that set "limits on the kinds of solutions an animal will come up with in a learning situation."

The modular view of learning of course does not entail that the components of the module are unique to it: at some level, everyone assumes that they are not – the cell, for example. The question of the level of organization at which unique properties emerge remains a basic question from a biological point of view, as it was at the 1974 conference. Gallistel's observations recall the concept of "canalization" introduced into evolutionary and developmental biology by C. H. Waddington sixty years ago, referring to processes "adjusted so as to bring about one definite end result regardless of minor variations in conditions during the course of the reaction," thus ensuring "the production of the normal, that is optimal type in the face of the unavoidable hazards of existence." That seems to be a fair description of the growth of language in the individual. A core problem of the study of the faculty of language is to discover the mechanisms that limit outcomes to "optimal types."

It has been recognized since the origins of modern biology that organism-external developmental constraints and architectural-structural principles enter not only into the growth of organisms but also their evolution. In a classic contemporary paper, Maynard Smith and associates trace the post-Darwinian version back to Thomas Huxley, who was struck by the fact that there appear to be "predetermined lines of modification" that lead natural selection to "produce varieties of a limited number and kind" for every species. They review a variety of such constraints in the organic world and describe how "limitations on phenotypic variability" are "caused by the structure, character, composition, or dynamics of the developmental system." They also point out that such "developmental constraints undoubtedly play a significant role in evolution" though there is yet "little agreement on their importance as compared with selection, drift, and other such factors in shaping evolutionary history." At about the same time, Jacob wrote that "the rules controlling embryonic development," almost entirely unknown, interact with other physical factors to "restrict possible changes of structures and functions" in evolutionary development, providing "architectural constraints" that "limit adaptive scope and channel evolutionary patterns," to quote a recent review. The best-known of the figures who devoted much of their work to these topics are D'Arcy Thompson and Alan Turing, who took a very strong view on the central role of such factors in biology. In recent years, such considerations have been adduced for a wide range of problems of development and evolution, from cell division in bacteria to optimization of structure and function of cortical networks, even to proposals that organisms have "the best of all possible brains," as argued by computational neuroscientist Chris Cherniak. The problems are the border of inquiry, but their significance is not controversial.

Assuming that the faculty of language has the general properties of other biological systems, we should, therefore, be seeking three factors that enter into the growth of language in the individual:

(1) Genetic factors, apparently near uniform for the species, the topic of UG. The genetic endowment interprets part of the environment as linguistic experience, a nontrivial task that the infant carries out reflexively, and determines the general course of the development of the language faculty to the languages attained.

(2) Experience, which leads to variation, within a fairly narrow range, as in the case of other subsystems of the human capacity and the organism generally.

(3) Principles not specific to the faculty of language.

The third factor includes principles of structural architecture that restrict outcomes, including principles of efficient computation, which would be expected to be of particular significance for computational systems such as language, determining the general character of attainable languages.

One can trace interest in this third factor back to the Galilean intuition that "nature is perfect," from the tides to the flight of birds, and that it is the task of the scientist to discover in just what sense this is true. Newton's confidence that Nature must be "very simple" reflects the same intuition. However obscure it may be, that intuition about what Ernst Haeckel called nature's "drive for the beautiful" ("Sinn fuer das Schoene") has been a guiding theme of modern science ever since its modern origins.

Biologists have tended to think differently about the objects of their inquiry, adopting Jacob's image of nature as a tinkerer, which does the best it can with materials at hand – often a pretty poor job, as human intelligence seems to be intent on demonstrating about itself. British geneticist Gabriel Dover captures the prevailing view when he concludes that "biology is a strange and messy business and 'perfection' is the last word one would use to describe how organisms work, particularly for anything produced by natural selection" – though produced only in part by natural selection, as he emphasizes, and as every biologist knows, and to an extent that cannot be quantified by available tools. These expectations make good sense for systems with a long and complex evolutionary history, with plenty of accidents, lingering effects of evolutionary history that lead to nonoptimal solutions of problems, and so on. But the logic does not apply to relatively sudden emergence, which might very well lead to systems that are unlike the complex outcomes of millions of years of Jacobian "bricolage," perhaps more like snowflakes, or phyllotaxis, or cell division into spheres rather than cubes, or polyhedra as construction materials, or much else that is found in the natural world. The minimalist program is motivated by the suspicion that something like that may indeed be true for human language, and I think recent work has given some reason to believe that language is in many respects an optimal solution to conditions it must satisfy, far more so than could have been anticipated a few years ago.

Returning to the early days, within the structuralist/behaviorist frameworks of the 1950s, the closest analogues to UG were the procedural approaches developed by Trubetzkoy, Harris, and others, devised to determine linguistic units and their patterns from a corpus of linguistic data. At best, these cannot reach very far, no matter how vast the corpus and futuristic the computational devices used. Even the elementary formal and meaning-bearing elements, morphemes, do not have the "beads on a string" character that is required for procedural approaches, but relate much more indirectly to phonetic form. Their nature and properties are fixed within the more abstract computational system that determines the unbounded range of expressions. The earliest approaches to generative grammar therefore assumed that the genetic endowment provides a format for rule systems and a method for selecting the optimal instantiation of it, given data of experience. Specific proposals were made then and in the years that followed. In principle, they provided a possible solution to the problem of language acquisition, but involved astronomical calculation, and therefore did not seriously address the issues.

The main concerns in those years were quite different, as they still are. It may be hard to believe today, but it was commonly assumed fifty years ago that the basic technology of linguistic description was available, and that language variation was so free that nothing of much generality was likely to be discovered. As soon as efforts were made to provide fairly explicit accounts of the properties of languages, it immediately became obvious how little was known, in any domain. Every specific proposal yielded a treasure trove of counter-evidence, requiring complex and varied rule systems even to achieve a very limited approximation to descriptive adequacy. That was highly stimulating for inquiry into language, but also left a serious quandary, since the most elementary considerations led to the conclusion that UG must impose narrow constraints on possible outcomes in order to account for the acquisition of language, the task of achieving "explanatory adequacy," so called. Sometimes these are called "poverty of stimulus" problems in the study of language, though the term is misleading because this is just a special case of basic issues that arise universally for organic growth, including cognitive growth, a variant of problems recognized as far back as Plato.

A number of paths were pursued to try to resolve the tension. The most successful turned out to be efforts to formulate general principles, attributed to UG – that is, the genetic endowment – leaving a somewhat reduced residue of phenomena that would result, somehow, from experience. These approaches had some success, but the basic tensions remained unresolved at the time of the 1974 conference.

Within a few years, the landscape changed considerably. In part this was the result of a vast array of new materials from studies of much greater depth than previously, in part from opening new topics to investigation. About twenty-five years ago, much of this work crystallized in a radically different approach to UG, the "Principles and Parameters" (P&P) framework, which for the first time offered the hope of overcoming the tension between descriptive and explanatory adequacy. This approach sought to eliminate the format framework entirely, and with it, the traditional conception of rules and constructions that had been pretty much taken over into generative grammar. In these respects, it was a much more radical departure from the rich tradition of 2,500 years than early generative grammar. The new P&P framework led to an explosion of inquiry into languages of the most varied typology, leading to new problems previously not envisioned, sometimes answers, and the reinvigoration of neighboring disciplines concerned with acquisition and processing, their guiding questions now reframed in terms of parameter-setting within a fixed system of principles of UG. No one familiar with the field has any illusion today that the horizons of inquiry are even visible, let alone at hand.

Abandonment of the format framework also had a significant impact on the biolinguistic program. If, as had been assumed, acquisition is a matter of selection among options made available by the format provided by UG, then the format must be rich and highly articulated, allowing relatively few options; otherwise, explanatory adequacy is out of reach. The best theory of language must be a very unsatisfactory one from other points of view, with a complex array of conditions specific to human language, restricting possible instantiations. The fundamental biological issue of principled explanation could barely be contemplated, and correspondingly, the prospects for some serious inquiry into evolution of language were dim; evidently, the more varied and intricate the conditions specific to language, the less hope there is for a reasonable account of the evolutionary origins of UG. These are among the questions that were raised at the 1974 symposium and others of the period, but they were left as apparently irresoluble problems.

The P&P framework offered prospects for resolution of these tensions as well. Insofar as this framework proves valid, acquisition is a matter of parameter setting, and is therefore divorced entirely from the remaining format for grammar: the principles of UG. There is no longer a conceptual barrier to the hope that the UG might be reduced to a much simpler form, and that basic properties of the computational systems of language might have a principled explanation instead of being stipulated in terms of a highly restrictive language-specific format for grammars. Returning to the three factors of language design, adoption of a P&P framework overcomes a difficult conceptual barrier to shifting the burden of explanation from factor (1), the genetic endowment, to factor (3), language-independent principles of structural architecture and computational efficiency, thereby providing some answers to the fundamental questions of biology of language, its nature and use, and perhaps its evolution.

With the conceptual barriers imposed by the format framework overcome, we can try more realistically to sharpen the question of what constitutes a principled explanation for properties of language, and turn to one of the most fundamental questions of the biology of language: to what extent does language approximate an optimal solution to conditions that it must satisfy to be usable at all, given extra-linguistic structural architecture? These conditions take us back to the traditional characterization of language since Aristotle as a system that links sound and meaning. In our terms, the expressions generated by a language must satisfy two interface conditions: those imposed by the sensorimotor system and by the conceptual–intentional system that enters into the human intellectual capacity and the variety of speech acts.

We can regard an explanation of properties of language as *principled* insofar as it can be reduced to properties of the interface systems and general considerations of computational efficiency and the like. Independently, the interface systems can be studied on their own, including comparative study that has been productively underway. And the same is true of principles of efficient computation, applied to language in recent work by many investigators with important results, and perhaps also amenable to comparative inquiry. In a variety of ways, then, it is possible both to clarify and to address some of the basic problems of the biology of language.

At this point we have to move on to more technical discussion than is possible here, but a few informal remarks may help sketch the general landscape, at least.

An elementary fact about the language faculty is that it is a system of discrete infinity, rare in the organic world. Any such system is based on a primitive operation that takes objects already constructed, and constructs from them a new object: in the simplest case, the set containing them. Call that operation Merge. Either Merge or some equivalent is a minimal requirement. With Merge available, we instantly have an unbounded system of hierarchically structured expressions. The simplest account of the "Great Leap Forward" in the evolution of humans would be that the brain was rewired, perhaps by some slight mutation, to provide the operation Merge, at once laying a core part of the basis for what is found at that dramatic moment of human evolution: at least in principle; to connect the dots is far from a trivial problem. There are speculations about the evolution of language that postulate a far more complex process: first some mutation that permits two-unit expressions, perhaps yielding selectional advantage by reducing memory load for lexical items; then further mutations to permit larger ones; and finally the Great Leap that yields Merge. Perhaps the earlier steps really took place, though there is no empirical or serious conceptual argument for the belief. A more parsimonious speculation is that they did not, and that the Great Leap was effectively instantaneous, in a single individual, who was instantly endowed with intellectual capacities far superior to those of others, transmitted to offspring and coming to predominate. At best a reasonable guess, as are all speculations about such matters, but about the simplest one imaginable, and not inconsistent with anything known or plausibly surmised. It is hard to see what account of human evolution would not assume at least this much, in one or another form.

Similar questions arise about growth of language in the individual. It is commonly assumed that there is a two-word stage, a three-word stage, and so on, with an ultimate Great Leap Forward to unbounded generation. That is observed in performance, but it is also observed that at the early stage the child understands much more complex expressions, and that random modification of longer ones – even such simple changes as placement of function words in a manner inconsistent with UG or the adult language – leads to confusion and misinterpretation. It could be that unbounded Merge, and whatever else is involved in UG, is present at once, but only manifested in limited ways for extraneous reasons, memory and attention limitation and the like; matters discussed at the 1974 symposium, and now possible to investigate much more systematically and productively.

The most restrictive case of Merge applies to a single object, forming a singleton set. Restriction to this case yields the successor function, from which the rest of the theory of natural numbers can be developed in familiar ways. That suggests a possible answer to a problem that troubled Wallace in the late nineteenth century: in his words, that the "gigantic development of the mathematical capacity is wholly unexplained by the theory of natural selection, and must be due to some altogether distinct cause," if only because it remained unused. One possibility is that the natural numbers result from a simple constraint on the language faculty, hence not given by God, in accord with Kronecker's famous aphorism, though the rest is created by man, as he continued. Speculations about the origin of the mathematical capacity as an abstraction from linguistic

operations are not unfamiliar. There are apparent problems, including disso-
ciation with lesions and diversity of localization, but the significance of such
phenomena is unclear for many reasons (including the issue of possession vs.
use of the capacity). There may be something to these speculations, perhaps
along the lines just indicated.

Elementary considerations of computational efficiency impose other conditions on the optimal solution to the task of linking sound and meaning. There
is by now extensive literature exploring problems of this kind, and I think it is
fair to say that there has been considerable progress in moving towards principled explanation. It is even more clear that these efforts have met one primary
requirement for a sensible research program: stimulating inquiry that has been
able to overcome some old problems while even more rapidly bringing to light
new ones, previously unrecognized and scarcely even formulable, and enriching
greatly the empirical challenges of descriptive and explanatory adequacy that
have to be faced; and for the first time, opening a realistic prospect of moving
significantly beyond explanatory adequacy to principled explanation along the
lines indicated.

The quest for principled explanation faces daunting tasks. We can formulate
the goals with reasonable clarity. We cannot, of course, know in advance how
well they can be attained – that is, to what extent the states of the language
faculty are attributable to general principles, possibly even holding for organisms generally. With each step toward this goal, we gain a clearer grasp of the
core properties that are specific to the language faculty, still leaving quite unresolved problems that have been raised for hundreds of years. Among these are
the question how properties "termed mental" relate to "the organical structure
of the brain," problems far from resolution even for insects, and with unique
and deeply mysterious aspects when we consider the human capacity and its
evolutionary origins.

Index

A-over-A principle 45–48, 49, 50
abduction xvi–xvii, 80, 81, 84, 152
active and passive transformations 136
Akmajian, Adrian 96
Alsop, Joseph 84
ambiguity 28–32, 134
American Academy of Arts and Sciences 174
animal communication 9–10, 60, 61, 72, 177
  and human language 10, 59–60, 88–91
Ardrey, Robert 84
Aristotle 177, 183
Austin, J. L. 143
automata 3, 4, 5, 161

Barlow, H.B. 83
behavioral sciences x, 57
  behavioralist approaches to the study of
    language 22, 181
  and linguistics vii, 146, 162
  psychology and 21, 63
belief 150
Bever, T. G. 82–83
biolinguistics 173–85
Bloomfield, Leonard 2, 13
Bower, Thomas 83

canalization 179
Cartesian philosophers 5–6, 22
  animal behavior 11
  contribution of 6
  mind, problems of 7, 11–12, 176
categorial features of universal grammar 114,
    124, 125–27, 128, 131, 137, 138
  phonetic 114
  syntactic 124, 125–27, 128, 130, 131, 137,
    138
Cherniak, Chris 180
cognitive sciences xiv–xvi, xvii, 149
Cohen, I. Bernard 174
communication
  animal 9–10, 59–60, 61, 72, 177
  mathematical theory of 3, 4

confirmation, problem of 79
conservation (of volume) 82–83
Cordemoy, Géraud de 5–6
creative aspect of language use 6, 8, 9, 87,
    88–91, 175
  Descartes on 10, 89
  mechanisms enabling 90
Cudworth, Ralph 159
culture 69
cyclic application, principle of 39–42, 49, 66,
    116–19, 141, 154, 160

Darwin, Charles xv, 173, 176
deep structure x, 15, 25, 93, 94, 97, 140
  base phrase-markers and 131
  character of 32
  functions of 26
  and labeled bracketing 122
  and meaning 94, 97, 146
  and pronominalization 97
  relation to surface structure 15, 27, 62, 135,
    137, 138, 144
  rules generating 124
  and semantic interpretation 111, 120, 123,
    131, 145
  and syntax 123
  theory of 15–16, 17
  and transformations 134, 135, 137, 138,
    144, 145
  and universal syntax 137
  variation from language to language
    66–67, 140
Delbrük, Berthold 18
deletion transformations 31, 49, 50–52
derivations 127, 128, 129
Descartes, Rene 7
  innate ideas 71, 73–74, 153, 154, 159, 167
  language xv, 9–12, 89
  mind 5, 6
Diamond, Jared 176
dispositions 31, 33
Dougherty, Ray 96

mathematics 176, 184, 185
Matthews, G. H. 161, 167
meaning 88–01, 133, 143
see also semantic interpretation
and deep structure 94, 97
and surface structure 96, 97
Mehler, J. 82–83
mental processes xv, 21, 153, 173, 177, 185
Merge operation 183, 184
Miller, G. A. 55, 81, 105, 162
mind 5, 85, 90, 164, 174
evolution of 86
linguistic contributions to the study of
1–20, 21–56, 57–87
other minds 9
philosophy of 172
problems of 25, 57, 167
rationalist theory of 99, 171–72
Minsky, M. 82
Moracvsik, Julius 178
Mountcastle, Vernon 174

Nelson, R. J. 75
Newton, Isaac 7, 174, 180
nominalization 93, 94, 155
numbers, natural 184

other minds, problem of 9

Papert, S. 82
Peirce, Charles Sanders xvi–xvii, 79–82, 84,
85, 152
perception, role of belief in 150
perceptual model 103–04, 106, 118, 119,
149–50
performance 102, 139, 151, 166, 171
Perlmutter, David 51
Peters, S. 161
philosophical grammar 13, 14, 16, 18, 19, 57,
66–67
philosophy
analytic 145
Cartesian 5–6, 7, 22
and linguistics 1, 143
of language 57–58
of mind 22
phonetic representation 37, 38, 97, 103
categorial features 114
formatives 113, 114, 115
junctures 113, 114, 115
and surface structure 94, 113, 116
phonetics, universal 107–09
phonological rules 35–38, 65, 66, 114, 115
cyclic application of 40
ordering of 116

phrase-markers 130, 137, 139
base phrase-markers 127, 131, 137
phrase structure 14, 74, 75, 115, 125, 160
rules 75, 127, 161, 162
physics 7
Piaget, J. 82
poetry 90
Polignac, Melchior de 10
Popper, Karl 59
Port-Royal *Grammar and Logic* 13, 14–15,
16, 17
Postal, P. 27, 34, 142
predicate-of relation 122
presupposition 95, 96
Pribram, K. H. 105
Priestley, Joseph 173, 174
Principles and Parameters approach to
linguistics xviii, 182, 183
pronominalization 96, 97
proper names 160
psychic distance 23, 55, 69
psychology 6, 14, 21, 63, 68, 79, 104
and intelligence 98
and linguistics 1, 64, 67, 78, 82, 100
rationalist 25, 167
stimulus–response 2, 3, 4
Putnam, Hilary 70, 74–77, 149, 159–64

Quine, W. V. O. xiii, 63, 171

Racine, Louis 10
reductive principles 174
redundancy rules 125
refernential opacity 145, 146
Reid, Thomas 154, 167
rigidty principle 175
Ritchie, R. 161
romanticism 9, 67, 99
Rosenbaum, Peter S. 27, 41, 50–51, 53, 142
Rosenfield, Leonora Cohen 10
Ross, John 29, 30, 43, 49
Rousseau, J.-J. 67
rule-following 175
Russell, Bertrand 2, 174
Ryle, Gilbert 12

Salzinger, K. 81
Sanctius 16, 17, 18
Saussure, Ferdinand de 17–18, 20
Schlegel, A. W. 90
Schützenberger, M. P. 86
science, seventeenth century developments in
5, 7, 8, 14, 71, 177
semantic interpretation 97, 111, 123, 137,
145, 178